The Denial and Its Cost
Reflections on the Nanking Massacre 70 years ago and beyond

Best Essays
from Iris Chang Memorial Essay Contest 2007

Iris Chang Memorial Fund
Global Alliance for Preserving the History of WW II in Asia

𝒢 Cozy House Publisher
New York 2008

Front Cover: Photo of Iris Chang, Courtesy of AsianWeek

PUBLISHED BY COZY HOUSE
www.cozygraphics.com

ISBN 978-1-59343-080-1 $12.00

CONTENTS

The Denial and Its Cost
Reflections on the Nanking Massacre
70 years ago and beyond

Receipients of Iris Chang Youth Award
(High-school-age Writers of Essays of Honor)

Essays of Honor

Essays of Distinction

Reflections on the Nanking Massacre After 70 Years of Denial
In Memory of Our Daughter, Iris Chang

Introduction

The year of 2007 marks the 70th anniversary of the Rape of Nanking. The Nanking Massacre, as it is also known, was one of the most atrocious war crimes that Imperial Japan committed against China during its aggression in WWII. It was in 1997, on the 60th anniversary of the massacre, when Iris Chang published her book *"The Rape of Nanking, the Forgotten Holocaust of WWII"* which broke the silence and shocked the Western world with details of this horrific historical tragedy. Ten years after the book's publication, the Japanese government still has not made a formal apology to the victims of the Nanking Massacre. Japan continues to evade responsibility for its heinous war crimes committed in China and other Asian countries during WWII to this day. Worse yet, Japanese nationalist groups deny the Rape of Nanking ever occurred and claim it is a fabrication. In light of this and in commemoration of the 70th anniversary of the Rape of Nanking, the Essay Contest Committee decided the topic of the 2007 Iris Chang Memorial Essay Contest as **"The Denial and Its Cost, Reflections on the Nanking Massacre 70 years ago and beyond"** to raise the conscience of Japanese people as well as that of the world.

The Essay Contest Committee asked the contestants to reflect on the Rape of Nanking in the following directions: How has Japan been able to escape responsibility for its horrific war crimes committed against its Asian neighbors for so long? How can Japan regain the trust and respect of its neighbors who were brutally victimized during World War II? What can one do to heighten awareness for the Japanese atrocities committed in Asia during the Pacific War? How has the world learned from man's inhumanity against man and how has it been affected by the aggressor's post-war denial? And what can one

1

do to help bring this tragic chapter of history to a proper closure?

This year, we received a total of 270 essays, of which over half (56%) were from the United States. The rest came from around the globe, such as Australia, Canada, China, India, Japan, South Korea, Pakistan, the Philippines, Singapore, Sweden and the United Kingdom.

Among the 270 contestants, 77% were students at the graduate, undergraduate, high school and middle school level. Other participants came from diverse fields including education, business, engineering, homemaking, law, medicine and news media. The age range of the contestants was also extremely wide; spanning the early teens to 87. Many of the essays were of exceptional quality. Indeed, it was a rather challenging process to select the top winners as there were a large number of unique and distinguished writings.

This year we were very fortunate to have a judging panel of seventeen scholars to review the essays through three rounds. To ensure fairness in the selection process, each essay was read independently by at least two reviewers. In the first round, a total of 51 essays were selected. In the second round, 21 essays were selected from the previous pool of 51. In the last round, the top three essays were selected from the previous 21. This year, we also selected four top essays written by high school students and designated them for the Iris Chang Youth Award. The remaining 14 essays from the top 21 were designated as essays of honor, and the remaining 30 from the 51 essays were the essays of distinction. The names of the authors of the top 51 essays are printed on page 231, and are also posted on our website: www.irischangmemorialfund.net.

We felt these top essays were outstanding in answering the questions given in this year's topic. We hope that, by compiling and publishing these top essays, the message for education of this tragic chapter of history can be spread. Remembering history is the first step to preventing such tragedies from ever being repeated. This is the goal of the Iris Chang Memorial Fund: to raise the awareness of the painful history of World War II in Asia and to support the education and research of younger generations in the U.S. with regard to Asian history. But, due to the limitation of space, we could only publish 21 top essays plus 8 of essays of distinction in this volume.

At the end of this book, we also printed several photos showing the many activities we were involved in the past two years. We, together with Global Alliance for Preserving the History of WWII in Asia, helped to publicize two films, the documentary *"Nanking"* and the docu-drama *"Iris Chang—The Rape of Nanking."* We were also invited to participate in several panel discussions organized by university students on the occasion of the 70th anniversary of the Nanking Massacre. The Iris Chang Memorial Fund has also been supporting high school teachers for the annual China Study Tour as well as a campaign to pass House Resolution 121 in U.S. House of Representatives. Indeed, the past few years have been full of activities aimed at raising public awareness for the Rape of Nanking.

Here we would like to express our thanks to all who served on the judging panel for their devotion and scholarly evaluation throughout the entire essay selection process. Their generosity and sacrifice among their busy lives are highly appreciated. They are: Kuei-Sheng Chang, Steven Clemons, Richard Chu, Ignatius Y. Ding, Werner Gruhl, George Koo, Michael Lee, Peter Li, Thekla Lit, Jiu-Fong Lo, Jack Meng, John Price, Rodger Scott, Peter Stanek, Jane Wu Tcheng, Ping Tcheng and Kaimay Yuen Terry.

We would like to thank the Essay Contest Committee members Cindy Chan, Cinian Zheng-Durbin, Jane Wu Tcheng and Ping Tcheng. Without their passion and dedication, the essay contest and the publication of this volume would not be possible. Special thanks to Cinian Zheng-Durbin for her continuous support and maintenance of our website and the artistic design of this volume's cover. Thanks also go to C. C. Chang for the design of the flower of iris. We also like to thank Victor Fic, Rodger Scott, Susan Hsieh and Amy Hsieh for their carefully edited some of the essays published in this volume and for their valuable suggestions in improving our essay contest.

We would also like to give special thanks to the following organizations for their kind support and assistance in publicizing the contest: AsianWeek, Asian American Journalist Association, BayareaDragon.com, California Center for the Book, Chinese Southern Weekend Magazine Newspaper, Douwei News Net, Johns Hopkins University Public Communication Department, KTSF Channel 26, New America Media, Rape of Nanking Redress Coalition, U. S. Holocaust Memorial Museum, University of Illinois Laboratory High School, University of Minnesota Center of Holocaust Studies and Human Rights, Washington State Holocaust Education Resource Center, World Journal Chinese Newspaper, and Yale University Library.

Finally, we like to thank Bihua Zeng and the Cozy House Publisher for their careful planning in publishing this book.

Ying-Ying & Shau-Jin Chang
Co-managers of Iris Chang Memorial Fund
www.irischangmemorialfund.net

Preface

From the 60th Anniversary
to
the 70th Anniversary

We are honored to be invited to write the Preface for this book.

In the past 10 years, the Canada Association for Learning and Preserving the History of WWII in Asia (Canada ALPHA) has been working hard in two Canadian provinces, British Colombia (BC) and Ontario (BC ALPHA and Toronto ALPHA), to promote education and awareness of the World War II history in Asia .

It was also 10 years ago, the year of the 60th anniversary of the Nanking Massacre, that Iris Chang's book *"The Rape of Nanking, the Forgotten Holocaust of World War II,"* brought new hope to AL-PHA.

Being the first book written in English on the subject, with extensive research materials and many historical details about the Nanking Massacre, Iris' book shocked the West's conscience and generated a ripple effect in arousing the interest in and awareness of this vastly unknown atrocity, which is one of the darkest chapters of human history.

We are very proud to be the first organization in the world to recognize the value of Iris' work and to promote the book immediately after it was published in November 1997. The memories are still so vivid that it seems like yesterday when Iris presented her book at the book launching events in Vancouver and Toronto Dec. 8-14, 1997, during the 60th Anniversary of the Rape of Nanking. She shared her feelings about the process of writing the book. Her courage to seek the truth and her conviction to seek justice touched and inspired every one of us. We had a strong feeling: How could the world, particularly 1.3 billion Chinese people, put all the burden on her shoulders to uncover and tell the story of the Massacre on our behalf? Iris' book and her spirit brought us not only hope, but also confidence and encouragement that one day the truth about Nanking would be known the world over.

Inspired by Iris, and through many years of hard work and persistence, Canada ALPHA succeeded in gaining the recognition of the Ministries of Education of British Columbia and Ontario and convincing them to incorporate the Asian holocaust into the high school curriculum. These two provinces became the first Western jurisdictions to introduce this neglected part of world history to high school students.

Iris Chang's book also became a major reference to the teachers' guide on *Human Rights in the Asia Pacific 1931-1945: Social responsibility and Global Citizenship*, jointly published by the BC Ministry of Education and BC ALPHA in 2001, and the Ontario teaching resource guide published by Toronto ALPHA in 2005. The former is the first of its kind in the world featuring human rights violations during WW II in Asia for high school students.

There are close to 100 educators from BC and Ontario who have participated in the "Peace and Reconciliation Study Tours" organized and financed by Canada ALPHA since 2004. Iris' book, "*The Rape of Nanking*," is a must read for their pre-tour preparation to facilitate a better understanding of and deeper reflection on the lessons learned from this chapter of history. After returning to Canada, these teachers have shared their knowledge and testimonies with their colleagues and students. Many of them initiated projects and programs, with or without support from ALPHA, keeping the promises to the victims, bringing their stories and pain to people in other parts of the world.

In addition to participants from B.C. and Ontario, educators from Alberta and Australia are joining the 2008 Study Tour. The tour will also take educators to Seoul, Korea for an in-depth study of the horrific "Comfort Women" sexual slavery system perpetrated by the Japanese Military during WWII. Our educational initiative inspired our counterpart in the U.S. to start their own study tours for teachers in 2007.

Apart from promoting Asian holocaust education in the school system, Canada ALPHA also holds academic seminars and conferences to increase the awareness of Canadians about the forgotten Asian holocaust. One seminar that was held in 2003 at University of British Colombia (UBC), titled "Preventing Crimes Against Humanity: Lessons from the Asia Pacific War (1931-1945)," was jointly organized by Canada ALPHA, the Human Rights Committee of the Japanese-Canadian Citizens' Association, Canadian Asian Pacific Resource Network, and three departments of UBC. As our keynote speaker, Iris made a presentation on "Racism and the Rape of Nanking." Her vivid discussion and in-depth analysis enabled the participants of different ethnic backgrounds to have a better understanding of the lessons learned from this dark chapter of history.

Many commemorative events in Toronto and Vancouver in December, 2007 marked the 70th Anniversary of the Nanking Massacre. The writings of Iris Chang and the efforts of Canada ALPHA and its sister organizations all over the world have contributed to the redress movement of the Asian holocaust victims. Nowadays, the Nanking Massacre and Japan's military sexual slavery system (the so-called "Comfort Women") are no longer totally ignored by the international media. The denial of historical facts and the evasion of responsibility for war crimes by the Japanese right-wingers will no longer be tolerated. The world can't continue to disregard the cry for justice from these survivors.

The year 2007 was an important milestone for Canada ALPHA and the worldwide movement to preserve the truth of Asian WWII history. The unanimous passage of H. R. 121 in the American Congress, urging Japan to "acknowledge the facts and accept responsibility of the sex slavery system and apologize formally in a clear and unequivocal manner" is a tremendous breakthrough the world has been waiting for since the end of the war over 60 years ago. Canada ALPHA, working together with the Korean and Filipino communities in Canada, has been able to get over 50,000 Canadians to sign a petition asking our Parliament to pass Motion 291, similar to H. R. 121 passed in the U.S. House of Representatives. With four "Comfort Women" victims coming from Korea, China, the Philippines and Holland, Canadians and their Members of Parliament have had the opportunity to learn about this horrific sexual slavery system devised by the Japanese Military during WWII. On November 28, 2007, the Parliament of Canada unanimously passed a motion, joining the U.S. and Holland in a collective voice for justice demanding that Japan acknowledge the facts of history and make a formal apology to the victims. Two weeks after the passage of the Canadian motion, on the precise date of the 70th Anniversary of the Rape of Nanking, the European Union Parliament also passed a strongly-worded motion to the same effect.

The completion of the docudrama film "*Iris Chang--The Rape of Nanking*" in November 2007, conceived and funded by Toronto ALPHA, caps dramatically that very successful year. The two stories of the film, one of Iris Chang's courage and conviction to reveal the historical truth, and the other of exposing the massive horrors of the Nanking Massacre, interweave together so well that we believe it will have a great impact in promoting public awareness worldwide of the Nanking Massacre. It is our fervent hope that hundreds of millions of people the world over will see the film. The legacy of Iris will live forever.

Joseph Wong and Thekla Lit
Co-founders and Co-chairs
of Canada ALPHA
(Association for Learning & Preserving the History of WWII in Asia)

Rev. Yoshikuni Kaneda, D. Min.
Retired Minister
United Church of Christ
Bonita, California, USA

Misplaced Loyalty With Racism The Denial and Its Cost of the Nanking Massacre

Humans are killers not because of any biological imperative, but because of our capacity for misplaced loyalty. We have and will commit crimes to serve a wider allegiance which we would shun as individuals. Our massive, organized killings (which distinguish us from all other animals) are often done in "good faith." We kill others because we are loyal to our gods. We have been obedient for so long to our tribal gods that we have made them our idols.

Meeting with Iris Chang

I was one among fifty or so people listening to a lecture by Iris Chang in the community hall of a downtown bookstore in Austin, Texas, on February 8th, 1998. That was when Chang had distinguished herself with her best seller, *The Rape of Nanking: The Forgotten Holocaust of World War II*. I was deeply concerned about the massive atrocious genocide committed by the Imperial Japanese Army in December 1937, although I was not fully aware of the far-reaching scope of war crimes in Nanking.

She started the lecture with her own life experience of hearing and learning of the war crimes in Nanking, and proceeded to how she collected the data by conducting numerous interviews with the victims and their descendants in writing her book. As she heard the witnesses and looked at the numerous detailed pictures of an orgy of violence

First Prize

9

that included looting, burning, raping, torturing and murdering, she spent many sleepless nights and lost considerable weight. I was deeply moved by her capacity to suffer with the victims and her passion for justice.

Chang was invited to be a keynote speaker at the fifth Biennial Conference of the Global Alliance for Preserving the History of WW II in Asia (GA) which took place in San Diego in November of 2002. Then I met Chang for the second time. Participating in that conference was an eye-opening experience for me and I decided to join the local chapter of GA. The officers and members of The Association for Preserving the Historical Accuracy of Foreign Invasion in China, APHAFIC, have welcomed me and I too have shared in the pains, frustrations and passions for justice with the group as the sole native Japanese member. Through the activities of this group I was able to meet Chang for the third time face to face. I was privileged to give a speech at Chang's Memorial Dinner Party sponsored by APHAFIC.

Emperor Worship

"Banzai! Banzai! Banzai!" Whenever a young man was recruited by the military authority, all the neighbors gathered in front of his house and shouted these cheers with great pride. "I will fight for the emperor to the ultimate limit of my capacity and will not regret to die for the honor of him if necessary," the young recruit would respond in oath. I witnessed many "sending off" parties in Osaka during the World War II. Even my father, who was a Christian minister and was engaged in social work in the poor district there, was cheered three times as he recited the routine oath to get ready to go to the front near the end of the W.W. II.

We all were brainwashed to believe that to die for the emperor was the highest honor we could get when recruited and sent to the front. The Japanese soldiers were proud of being the "emperor's soldiers." We had been told time and time again that all soldiers who died on the front line shouted, "Tenno Heika (The Heavenly Emperor) Banzai!" The status of the emperor was raised up to that of a divinity. He was literally worshiped as a god. I can recall during my elementary school days when we were indoctrinated to worship the emperor. At every morning assembly the principal of our school led us to turn to the east and to bow down deeply to show our respect and devotion to the emperor. Oh, such was the power of education!

My father taught his children to honor both the emperor and the Christian God. The main reason that we honored the emperor was to avoid our neighbors' suspicious eyes and ears towards our Christianity, then considered an enemy's religion. We sang two songs out loud before meals. One was a Christian song that says, "Praised be the gracious God who gives us daily food. Amen," and the other was a popular military song which meant, "When we proceed to the sea, there are a lot of corpses in the water. When we walk on the mountains, we see many corpses rotten in the grass. We will, however, never regret of our death, for we die for the honor of the emperor." During the War, one's ultimate proof of loyalty meant to die for the emperor, the divine being.

The military government tightly monopolized all the media in Japan under its authority. This, in effect, was to brainwash and to have total thought control over its citizens. I recall some of the wartime posters raised on electricity poles, street corners and bathhouse bulletin boards. "Devilish Animals = Americans and Britons." "Attack and Destroy the Enemies Without Ceasing." "Don't Spread any Demagoguery." "100 Millions Shall Die for Honor." The Emperor Hirohito's voice was only heard for the first time on the radio by the most Japanese when he announced the unconditional surrender of Japan to the United States on August 15th, 1945. During his short radio broadcast, men and women knelt and cried and cried bitterly. Why? They blamed themselves for shaming the emperor with unbearable defeat. "We failed to be loyal to your majesty till our death."

Although he completely renounced his "divinity" after W.W. II, recent right-wing loyalists and conservative politicians have tried to revive the emperor's divine status whenever possible. The modern media has assisted in this trend by calling the emperor's family members, even a newborn baby boy, with the title of honor, "sama". My friend in Tokyo, a professor emeritus, just recently remarked, "We can no longer talk about the emperor system freely as we used to. It has become a taboo." Being awarded an order by the emperor means receiving the highest honor for one's achievement. Those who are awarded this honor are the leaders of society. The emperor has now taken to calling them, "My Subjects." Ominously it seems, emperor worship has gradually come back to Japan.

Japanese Racism

In his book "Rising Sun," Michael Crichton makes a sweeping statement: "The Japanese are the most racist people on earth." (1) Partly, it is true. At least 4 percent of the total population consists of oppressed minorities who suffered much the same fate that Blacks and other minorities suffered in the United States and Europe. These minorities are Burakumin, Koreans, Ainu, Okinawans, Amerasians and foreigners.

Japan's racism is solely based upon the belief in the myth of the emperor system. The people of the "pure" blooded Yamato tribe (the "original" Japanese) are believed to be all descendants of emperors. The prewar government claimed it and people in general wanted to believe it as their proud ancestral heritage. The origin of the Emperor System goes back to a system that was brought over by the conquering immigrants from Korea. Yet, the Imperial Household Agency in Japan has stubbornly rejected to endorse this point of view. The 10th emperor, Sujin, was actually a Korean chief from the Kaya Kingdom in Korea. Yet, the right-wing loyalists and conservative politicians cannot stomach the fact that the Yamato tribe is the direct descendants of Koreans. The people in general want to believe that they are homogeneous, although they are in fact the mixed blood race of Mongolians, Chinese, Koreans, Southeast Asians and South Pacific Islanders. This blind belief in homogeneity has long been nurtured in the people's psyche as part of the superiority complex toward foreigners.

I must confess that I too had been one of the vicious racists while in Japan and, worse, I didn't even know it. I was made aware of the humiliating and embarrassing effects of racism as my family and I experienced and suffered racism, mostly subtle and institutional, here in the United States.

This racism stemming from the fictitious superiority complex is still alive and strong in today's Japan. It devours many victims who happen to be considered the "outsiders" in Japanese society.

The Denial and Its Cost

In Japan's national anthem Kimigayo, the people plea for the eternal reign of the emperor. It has a powerful unifying effect when sung at award ceremonies of sporting events, the entrance and graduation ceremonies at public schools and other special events. The song can evoke a strong national pride in the Japanese people. The national flag of Hinomaru (The Rising Sun) has been proudly displayed at these occasions to remind people of their unique ancestry as the pure descendants of the Yamato tribe. In the past decades, the conservative ruling party has succeeded in enforcing their policy to increase and to restore this long dormant national pride among its citizens.

Recent remarks by Prime Minister Shinzo Abe regarding "the comfort women" revealed his real intention for the denial of war crimes committed by the imperial military forces during World War II. His campaign slogan last year was "Beautiful Japan," which reflects the right-wing loyalists' hope to restore "national self-identity and self-esteem." Because the Japanese take great pride in their recent past history of practicing more than 60 years of pacifism and becoming the world's second largest economy, they feel a sense of arrogance in their shallow and showy nationalism. By the same token, the international community cannot ignore this peculiar Japanese nationalism. It has led to international furor when the Japanese government's intentional denial of the historical facts of its brutal and massive war crimes grabs the world's attention. CBS News Correspondent Barry Petersen states, "The anger revolves around recently approved school textbooks, which whitewash Japan's history of the first half of the 20th Century: its decades long occupation of Korea, its invasion of China, its brutal 1937 massacre in Nanjing that, by most accounts, took 300,000 lives."(2)   300,000 victims? Although the numbers are in dispute among historians, the obvious fact that brutal and massive killings took place under the Japanese military forces in Nanking should not be whitewashed in any textbook be it Japanese or otherwise.

Conscientious Japanese lawyers, historians and citizen activists have vigorously supported the more than two dozen lawsuits filed by Chinese victims of biological warfare, abandoned chemical weapons, the Nanking massacre, indiscriminate aerial bombing, military sexual slavery, and forced labor in Japan. Nearly all the lawsuits have, however, failed on the ground that the Joint Communiqué signed by China and Japan in 1972 waived the right of Chinese individuals to seek redress from the Japanese government or its corporations. This stance has become the Japanese government's unbending position. However, the Joint Communiqué waived only the Chinese government's reparations claims against the Japanese government, while leaving the claim rights of private Chinese citizens intact.(3) Morally speaking, the Supreme Court has missed many great opportunities to rule in favor of the Chinese plaintiffs who deserved to have their day in court. Their painful stories should have been heard and they should have been compensated for their losses. Instead, the Supreme Court upheld the government position denying the plaintiffs a just and humane ruling.

John Rabe, who helped save hundreds of thousands of Chinese during the Rape of Nanking as the dedicated and efficient leader of the International Safety Zone, found himself destitute and leading a miserable life on his return to his native Germany. Madame Chiang Kai-shek and the Chinese officials offered him an apartment and a pension if he resettled in China. "All he had to do was to be a witness for the prosecution at the Tokyo war crimes tribunal. However, John Rabe declined. In a message he left for his grandchildren, he explained: 'I didn't want to see any Japanese hang, although they deserve it. . . There must be some atonement, some just punishment; but in my view the judgment should be spoken only by their own na-

tion." (4)

14

The denial of Japan's war crimes by the ruling conservative party and the right-wing loyalists will never instill national self identity and pride among the majority of conscientious people in Japan. Intentional amnesia would not raise up any patriotism, either. One simply cannot rewrite history as one pleases.

The denial of wartime atrocities costs too much. It has jeopardized international trust and respect for Japan. It has greatly damaged Japan's relations with its neighbors. The international community again calls for Japan's sincere acknowledgment and apology for its wartime atrocities and just compensation for the victims.

Human beings are killers because of our capacity for misplaced loyalty which can lead to disastrous consequences. Loyalty to any emperor is nothing but idolatry.

It is up to the emperor himself, as the most powerful symbol and the living idol of Japan, to lead the whole nation in sincere acknowledgment and apology for the past brutal war crimes. He must encourage Japan to own all of the past history. He must demand just and fair compensation for all the victims.

What Can I Do?

I welcome opportunities to give speeches and lectures on this subject at schools, churches and other organizations in Japan.

1. Crichton, Michael, "Rising Sun," (New York: Knopf, Random House, 1992), page 219. Also see: page 204, pp. 260ff., pp. 327ff.

2. Petersen, Barry, "Japan's Nonstop Amnesia," Tokyo, April 13th, 2005. cbsnews.com/stories/2005/04/13/listening_post/main687759.shtml

3. Underwood, William and Kang, Jian, "Japan's Top Court Poised to Kill Lawsuits by Chinese War Victims," posted at *Japan Focus*, March 2, 2007.

4. Rabe, John, "The Goodman of Nanking: The Diaries of John Rabe," translated by John Woods, (New York: A.A. Knopf, Random House, 1998), page 256. The footnote of this quote states: "From a small manuscript that Rabe left for his grandchildren and titled *Lest We Forget*."

Kevin Ng
University Graduate
Singapore

The Great Denial

How Japan's policies regarding its actions during WWII are denying both its own people and the world moral betterment, social progress and political integration.

The numerous stygian and saturnine concrete slabs lay row after row, column upon column. Each cubic slab varied in height to convey the reality and truth that the victims consisted of a multitude of personalities and pasts, but whose lives converged on a similar tragic end. Each glossy block had been paid for by the very institutions that profited from the injustices that prevailed during a time of madness. Each block had the names of the Jewish victims that perished during an era of lunacy indelibly carved upon it. The Holocaust memorial in Berlin is a profoundly poignant symbol of a new Germany's acknowledgement of its past mistakes, and its deep desire to seek forgiveness from those who suffered. The alleys that crisscrossed the massive memorial are nevertheless redolent with a dignified air of truthfulness and openness. The central location of the memorial between the German parliament and the Brandenburg Gate further demonstrates the unabashed manner in which Germany has come to terms with the events of the Holocaust. When I strolled ponderously along the pathways within the Holocaust memorial, my own thoughts strayed inevitably to another catastrophe that unfolded during the course of the Second World War, with a certain propinquity to events of the Holocaust. Events that followed that other catastrophe had however taken a very different path. That event was the Asian Holocaust.

In stark contrast to what can be witnessed in Germany today, there are no memorials in Japan to remind the current generation of the lunacy and cruelty man is capable of doing to his fellow brethren. There are no efforts to educate today's youth of the region's turbulent past. And there are definitely no substantial signs of apologies, nor serious signals of atonement for the massive sufferings Japan had inflicted through its aggressions and assailments. There is only an atmosphere of baneful silence, bald ignorance and blatant denial. Instead of honest rapprochement between nations, there is but acerbic and unresolved animosity. A country is to be judged not entirely based on the mistakes it commits, but also on its subsequent efforts to exonerate itself, and alleviate the sufferings and injustices it might have unduly caused.

I cannot think of any more relevant and yet contrasting example to Japan's handling of the Nanking massacre legacy than Germany's grappling with its own Nazi past. I remember visiting the Wannsee Villa outside of Berlin, where senior Nazi officials met in 1942 to plan and coordinate the mass extermination of the Jews. Young school children were given a brutally frank and honest lecture on their country's past atrocities, and a very objective outline of why and how such events occurred. I was deeply impressed by the way school children were being taught this history, and more importantly the lessons it can and should provide. Germans today are perhaps amongst the most culturally sensitive and active participants in human rights issues, and I believe that stems largely from the manner in which they have come to terms with their history. If so, then the events of the Holocaust were in some sense an impetus for a greater moral progress and awareness, and the lessons of the past are indeed remembered through both memory and action.

It is plausible that the reason why I was so thoroughly impressed by the scene I encountered in the Wannsee Villa is because of my own experiences. My own grandparents in Singapore were tortured during the Japanese occupation in the Second World War. I learned about Japanese atrocities and brutality both from academic schooling and from my grandparents' anecdotal accounts. Their experiences are still vivid and upsetting till this very day. I once met a Japanese student studying the Chinese language in the USA. Our conversation turned unexpectedly to the war on one occasion, and I mentioned the Japanese invasion and occupation of Singapore. I halted in the middle of my speech when I noticed an exasperated and distraught expression on her face. Apparently she had absolutely no idea that Japan had even invaded and occupied a vast tract of Southeast Asian countries. I myself had heard that Japan's youth tended to be ignorant of the events of the Second World War. I had however never expected that this ignorance would extend to even the lack of the most basic and rudimentary knowledge of the war. Subsequently, I informed this Japanese young lady of the events that occurred. I sensed a genuine urge from her to learn this history; and yet there was a sense of fear and incredulousness. I would not have been surprised if she had cried at that instance.

It is perhaps inconceivable to find in Germany anyone who is ignorant of the Holocaust perpetrated by the Nazis. In this context and comparison, the outrageous and preposterous notion that there are Japanese nationals ignorant of Imperial Japan's invasion of its Asian neighbors is a disconcerting reality. This flagrant and relentless refusal to admit and accept the responsibility for the heinous crimes committed is the paramount source of the rancorous animosity that persists between Japan and other Asian countries. In fact, Japan's arrant celebration and commemoration of its soldiers buried at the Yasukuni Shrine continue to aggravate existing animosities, if not serving to remind the entire world of its conspicuous efforts to obfuscate history. Former Japanese Prime Minister Junichiro Koizumi's annual visits to the shrine can be juxtaposed with former West German Chancellor's visit to the monument of the victims of Warsaw Ghetto Uprising in Poland, where he famously knelt to the victims in a moving gesture of apology. Great strides have been made in European reconciliation and subsequent cooperation due to this spirit of sincerity.

Japan's obstinate refusal to budge on the issue of atonement for its mistakes during the Second World War would plausibly hinder and obstruct the greater potential cooperation amongst itself and other

Asian nations. The moral character and spiritual content of a country would be judged and evaluated based on how it manages the great moral and spiritual issues it faces. The systematic denial of information to a new generation of Japanese youth has deprived them of an opportunity to strengthen their generation's bonds with other Asian countries, and also of the chance to morally rejuvenate their country. The failure of Japan to recognize and take responsibility for its war crimes perhaps exposes a much larger flaw in humanity. Japan's shunning of its responsibility reflects a certain disregard for morality and humanity itself. Perhaps Japan's actions can be explained by its disregard and disdain for human lives and suffering, or as a product of national pride and ego.

Another country that has perpetually refused to admit to a genocide it has committed is Turkey. Turkey's genocide of the Armenians during the First World War is well documented and is widely accepted, but Turkey still refuses to concede and atone for the genocide. National pride might be one of the crucial reasons for Turkey's intractable stance. A Turk who mentions the mere notion of admitting to the genocide is immediately deemed unpatriotic and a traitor. This stance has been further reinforced by the Western world's gradual and sure acceptance of Turkey as a civilized counterpart in the economic, cultural and military spheres. This behavior can be explained through the diaphanous prism of self interests. For example, it is plausible to consider that the world's apparent oblivion to the massacres that occurred during the course of the First World War is because of Turkey's role in the war. Europe chose largely to ignore the issue of justice for the Armenians after the Second World War, and even admitted Turkey into NATO since geopolitical necessities made it crucial to possess Turkish territories for staging NATO missiles aimed at the Soviet Union. Armenia's crusade for justice has thus been repeatedly betrayed due to the continuing and changing interests in the world. The quests of many Asian nations to seek justice and compensation from Japan have similarly been repeatedly hijacked and deluded perhaps by those who prioritize other items above that of human justice and morality. These items could range from political gains to business profits. This is a sad reflection on the human tendency to focus on short term profits and personal interests, to ignore the lessons and imperatives learned from history, along with the greater interests of society and solidarity with humanity.

Japan's actions are a stain on humanity and a snag on human progress. The world's similar disregard and silence regarding Japan's actions and failure to take responsibility for its crimes signify a tacit approval and even encouragement. Sadly, it appears that the movement of time, coupled with the business and political imperatives of the contemporary world make it easy to ignore and forget the injustices suffered and the crimes committed against the older generation. The glossing over of the unresolved injustices of a previous generation, of a generation that is still alive and from which our world today is directly descended from, is then a betrayal of our own human heritage and the moral obligations all mankind should have towards humanity. If and when Japan feels the burdens and costs for its denials, perhaps it might seriously begin to consider a change of its policies. If international interactions and correspondences with Japan begin to include a moral component, then that would be a strong incentive for reform. There are many areas that in fact deserve reforms and sometimes outright remodeling. These would include education for the children, foreign policy toward its neighbours, compensation for the living victims, and commemoration of events to ensure history does not ever repeat itself again.

It is feasible that the continued and enforced ignorance in Japan itself will manifest itself in the situation we face today. I have faith in the moral character of a modern society of Japan that should the majority of its people become fully aware of its wartime role, there would indeed be substantial pressures for change. It is lamentable that such a technologically advanced nation in the information age would still be fettered with historical censorship and revisionism. It is perhaps natural to contemplate and compare how censorship on Japan's history is tantamount to discarding a portion of its morality. In a progressive society, would it not be better for the younger generation to have full access to the facts of history, and decide for themselves? Is

21

not the current denial of information to the youth in Japan a denial for the entirety of humanity to progress forward? Propaganda is not simply the addition and distortion of selected information, but also the omission of vital information. The minority of the conservatives, bureaucrats and business leaders are then holding hostage the entire Japanese nation's conscience by withholding from them the vital information they need to understand the world they live in, and the history from which their heritage derives. I cannot help but wonder sometimes, if every single Japanese who travels out of Japan is confronted by someone somewhere about his or her country's past, would that gradual seeping of information into Japan create an impetus for reform?

The principal and foremost hindrance towards recognition and reconciliation is perhaps the education of the Japanese people on those issues so tender and stirring for so many of its Asian neighbors. When the abundant contradictions between official Japanese versions of events and the world's version become evident and lucid, the inherent pressures in such a revelation would then spur the beginning of change that just might result in a new generation of more conscious Japanese eager to follow the German example. Still it is not enough just for those directly inflicted in the massacres to cry for justice, but the duty of the entire world and humanity to enforce their collective moral might. The situation of ignorance and denial in Japan continues in part due to the indifference and inattention of the larger world. For now, the first step towards a larger reform is for the average Japanese person to learn that the Second World War for Japan did not begin and end with the dropping of the atomic bomb on Hiroshima and Nagasaki, but with the many atrocities committed by Japanese military on the shores of its Asian neighbours many years before Hiroshima and Nagasaki.

The lack of historical consciousness is one of the primary causes of reinforcements and aggravations of conflicts today. People tend to forget or overlook the injustices their nations have inflicted on other nations, and thus fail to empathize or react appropriately to events. Consider when Stalin deported the entire Chechen populace to Siberia and Kazakhstan during the Second World War. It was an unprecedented catastrophe for the Chechen nation and culture. Chechnya as a national and cultural entity was obliterated, and thousands upon thousands of Chechens died as a result of the deportations and forced relocations. They were allowed to return to their homeland only during the period of de-Stalinization under Khruschev. Stalin's actions as far as Chechens are concerned are synonymous to those of Russia's today. It is therefore arguable that Chechens have indeed a valid grievance when they fight for independence from Russia. It is also understandable why then they want their independence from a larger entity in which they consider themselves to be neglected, abused or simply downtrodden. The majority of Russians however do not recall those tragic events so pivotal in shaping the current Chechen mentality and resolve. They do not place the so-called terrorist attacks of the Chechens in the larger historical context; and thus, to them, the Chechens are simply cold blooded murderers. The victims have somehow become the aggressors in this distorted and narrow view of history. The subsequent Russian oppression of Chechnya under President Putin could be compared to the moral equivalent of a modern day Germany invading Poland yet again. Of course, the latter is considered impossible in Europe due to the widespread and high levels of historical appreciation.

Most violent conflicts have their intensity and ferocity linked to certain historical events that tend to be unperceived and unrecognized by opposing factions. Most Americans do not remember how the US-led sanctions had caused such sufferings before America invaded Iraq in 2003. Whenever there is violence caused by a Palestinian, many people do not consider how Israeli tactics have caused such alienation and suffering for the Palestinian people, but view it in a terrorist context. Instances when Israel inflicts suffering on the Palestinians are omitted in the American media, but Palestinian attacks on Israelis would in contrast be focused upon and generously covered in the media. In this light, it is not surprising that the majority of Americans would be pro-Israel. The examples of such instances are ample throughout history. The lack of information, whether deliberate or accidental, has resulted in or prolonged the intensity and duration of so many human conflicts. Perhaps the best way to mitigate future conflicts, and even to prevent them, is through education. Educate the Japanese youth about the Rape of Nanking, the Great East Asian Co-prosperity Sphere, the Marco Polo Bridge Incident, and the dropping of the atomic bombs. Educate the youth on all that history has to offer, from the shameful to the glorious, and from the disgraceful to the honorable, so that the full spectrum of wisdom that history can offer will be bestowed upon them. Educate them so that not just they might benefit, but that all those around them, and humanity as a whole will be bettered, bringing an assuasive, if not an entirely satisfactory and responsible conclusion to a tragic chapter of history.

Philip Dorsey Iglauer
Editor, ICD
Communications Officer, ICAO
International Economic Cooperation Department
The National Agricultural Cooperative Federation
Republic of Korea

Nanjing's 70-year-old ghost story

Memories stay with people. Bad memories can haunt you like a ghost. History works like this as well, like an Asian horror movie. The history of the Pacific War torments China and Japan – indeed, all of Asia and the Pacific. But like a Japanese *onryo*, or vengeful spirit, the ghosts of Nanjing indiscriminately torment the innocent and the guilty. Karl Marx's observation that "The history of past generations weighs like a nightmare on the minds of the living" is as true for 21st century East Asia as it was for 19th century Europe. The only problem is, the ghosts of Nanjing are for real, so how do we exorcise them? How can China and Japan rid themselves of the nightmare of the Nanjing Massacre and finally put the past behind them?

In East Asia, historical wounds are still festering. Seventy years on, and the memories of Nanjing continue to haunt the Japanese, as well as the Chinese. The ghosts of Nanjing feed an increasingly bitter competition of nationalisms. But Japan's leaders only hurt their country with jingoism, as a perception of Japan's former aggression is revived and overshadows the country's many accomplishments.

The bitterness of the war years is frequently summoned to the present by Chinese feelings of injustice and a Japanese sense of being unfairly singled out for wrongs committed decades ago. When the re-certification of a history textbook in Japan can spark weeks of riots across China in April 2005, sending crowds thousands strong vandalizing Japanese businesses and consulates, it is clear the value of history in East Asia is palpable.

The waves of anger were touched off by Tokyo imbuing credibility into claims made in the New History Textbook, published by a right-wing Japanese group. In one demonstration, some 10,000 angry protesters surrounded Jusco supermarket run by Japanese firm Aeon in the bustling port city Shenzhen, a hub of foreign investment in South China. Many saw the government as sanctioning a whitewashing of the history of Imperial Army atrocities in Nanjing during Japan's 1937 invasion of China.

The riots vividly illustrate how the memories of Japan's former aggression, seared into minds of present-day Chinese as feelings of injustice, are unwittingly resurrected as expressions of patriotism. China sees a Japan that is boorish and unapologetic. In fact, hardly any of Japan's junior high schools have actually adopted the text - just 18 out of more than 11,000, according to one news report. But to the Chinese, it's enough that the government even extended its seal of approval to such a book.

Now, the ghosts of Nanjing will be channeled into a number of new films. In December, as the world observes the 70th anniversary of the "Rape of Nanjing," at least three films are starting or are already in production this year (by directors Yim Ho, Stanley Tong and Lu Chuan), in addition to the American production Nanking, which screened at Sundance in January, and focuses on the point-of-view of Westerners in Nanjing when the city succumbed to the Imperial Army's onslaught. With that, 10 years after the publication of Iris Chang's incisive work, the Nanjing Massacre has become a cinema sensation.

Unfortunately, extremists in Japan have a film of their own: The Truth About Nanjing. Its theme is predictable, as will be the reactions. Japan's ruling Liberal Democratic Party (LDP), too, exacerbates bitter feelings, inflaming painful memories with peremptory remarks that deny Japan's responsibility for atrocities committed by the country's Imperial Army in the 1930s and '40s.

But ironically, the caustic remarks of mainstream Japanese leaders hurt themselves most. Japan has the most to pay for its recalcitrance, not China. The more these LDP politicians run their mouths the more they drag Japan's national image through the mud, soiling what would otherwise be an inspiring record of peace, prosperity and freedom.

By denying the past today, Japan will be condemned to forever re-live the shame of what it did in the 1930s and '40s. Thoughtless behavior and insensitive quips overshadow Japan's accomplishments and re-cast the nation in its image of two generations ago. Who will be able to identify with an image of a Japan calloused by a shameful history?

Expressions of Japanese nationalism, even now, make headlines and incite emotional demonstrations. This is because the images that it invokes in the minds of Chinese – and in the minds of people all over Asia - are invariably informed by haunting recollections of the country's wartime atrocities, such as the images summoned from Tokyo's incursions into China. The rape and massacre of civilians in Nanjing upon the city's collapse in December 1937 – including women, children and the elderly – are quintessential examples of the Japanese army's brutality.

These images provoke anxiety over the safety of loved ones and a visceral desire to protect the vulnerable. And these same images prevent the Japanese from demonstrating old-fashioned patriotism. What's more, Chinese nationalism gets a boost.

In 1972, Asia's greatest cinematic hero became the champion of everyone who recognizes right from wrong and yearns to defend the downtrodden. That was the year Bruce Lee's breakthrough film, "Fist of Fury," titled "The Chinese Connection" in the U.S., screened for the first time in San Francisco.

Who was not outraged by the Japanese man mocking Lee's character, Chen Zhen, at a park entrance, as he pointed to a sign reading "No Chinese or Dogs Allowed?" And who was not stirred when Chen – inspired by a real-life patriotic insurgent – broke the sign in half with a jump-spinning dropkick? Or when he destroyed a framed calligraphy penned by Japanese imperialists declaring China the "Sick Man of Asia?"

The actor Bruce Lee and the symbols he destroys in the film are vital to Chinese nationalism. Indeed, every country's nationalism is about piecing together images that the people can be proud of and rally around. These images inculcate patriotic feelings; in patriotism, symbolism is everything.

In a way, Chinese nationalism became more compelling than Japanese nationalism because it appeals to universal sentiments. Anyone can identify with defending the downtrodden against unprovoked aggression.

Japan's denial of the past retards the country's ability to recover from the war just as it stunts the country's relations with China and Korea. Japan's denial of the atrocities it committed in Nanjing inflames an infection the Imperial Army left more than 70 years ago. Leaving historical wounds to fester makes demonstrating Japanese patriotism impossible.

In one incident between December 1937 and March 1938, some 350,000 Chinese civilians and prisoners of war were slaughtered by the invading Japanese troops, according to mainstream historians. Tens of thousands of victims were beheaded, burned, bayoneted, buried alive or disemboweled.

Worse than that, an estimated 80,000 women and girls were raped. Many were then mutilated and tortured before being murdered. It is in recognition of them that we call this inhumanity the "Rape of Nanjing." The gruesome details are rendered compellingly in Iris Chang's 1997 book, likely the first written in English. Even sworn Nazi John Rabe was so horrified by Japanese sadism, he urged Adolf Hilter to intervene.

To this day the Japanese government has refused to apologize for these and other World War II atrocities. But unlike Holocaust deniers, the revisionism of the Rape of Nanjing has been largely successful in Japan, where a large swath of Japanese society believes they never happened. This has had consequences for Japan, even while it continues the charade.

In fact, soon after the war 28 men went on trial in an international criminal court in Tokyo for the Nanjing Massacre and other crimes. And during the trial, it became clear that Tokyo had known about the atrocities but ignored them. Of the 28, 25 were found guilty on one or more of the charges. All were sentenced in 1948 either to death by hanging or life imprisonment, but by 1956 every one of them had been paroled.

Decades after the massacre, Japan began to deny and distort the history of Nanjing. In books and columns in Japan, a revisionist perspective of the incident began to emerge, including outright denials that it had ever taken place. Ikuhiko Hata's "Nanjing Incident" is considered by the Japanese Ministry of Education to be the definitive historical text on the subject. This book puts the official death count at between 38,000 and 42,000.

In the 1990s, some top Japanese government officials claimed that the massacre was fabricated. Shocked by this, conscientious professors and parliamentarian ministers tried to set the record straight, but they were thwarted at every turn. Official apologies or compensation have, as a result, not been forthcoming.

In 1997, Japan's former Prime Minister Tomiichi Murayama apologized to the victims of Japan's unprovoked aggression. His apology a decade ago, as well as Prime Minister Junichiro Koizumi's in Indonesia in 2005, should be welcome. However, their apologies are personal ones, not government recognitions of atrocities.

The majority of Murayama's colleagues in the Japanese government did not share his feelings. And he failed to make a formal and official apology in the so-called "No War Resolution." Only 26 percent of the members of Japan's Diet supported the resolution. Shockingly, 47 percent voiced opposition. Furthermore, Seisuke Okuno, the former education minister, managed to organize a national campaign collecting 4.5 million signatures against the resolution.

The gaff prone Tokyo Governor Shintaro Ishihara said in a 1990 interview: "People say that the Japanese made a holocaust but that is not true. It is a story made up by the Chinese. It has tarnished the image of Japan, but it is a lie." He has been the top political leader of Japan's most important city since 1999 and has a realistic chance of becoming Japan's next prime minister.

In the battle of competing Japanese and Chinese nationalism, the struggle over the re-construction of Japan's national identity, and whether it will incorporate its past into that re-construction, will determine whether a "normal" Japan can be accepted by its Asian neighbors. It behooves Japanese people everywhere to join in the re-construction by acknowledging what really happened 70 years ago. Otherwise, the country will remain stuck in the past, preventing itself from taking the leadership role it deserves.

Japan pays dearly in denying this history, a fact poignantly illustrated by Japanese Prime Minister Shinzo Abe's visit to the United States in April. He reacted defensively to a salvo of questions on "comfort women" and Japan's wartime responsibility. Contrast that with former Chancellor Gerhard Schroeder joining with his French, American and British counterparts in D-Day ceremonies in France in June three years ago. These two pictures starkly show how far Japan is behind Germany in coming to terms with its past – and how far Asia is from exorcising the ghosts of Nanjing as compared to Europe's exorcism of the memories of Auschwitz.

Japan also pays with its international reputation. Japan's denials cost it permanent membership on the U.N. Security Council. China's Premier Wen Jiabao specifically said in April 2005 that Beijing would wield its veto power to block Japan's U.N. aspirations until Tokyo "respects history, takes responsibility for history and wins over the trust of peoples in Asia." If strained relations with its neighbors have such real political costs for Tokyo, then why do Japanese leaders cling to their delusions?

One possible reason is that they hinge pride in their country on the sacrifices their fathers and grandfathers made fighting in Japan's Pacific War. Many Japanese have falsely conflated Japanese slogans of "support the troops" with supporting the country's past militarism. For them, to apologize for Japan's wars of aggression in Asia, and indeed, to acknowledge war crimes the Imperial Army committed during its invasion of China in 1937, would be tantamount to believing the lives of millions of their countrymen were sacrificed in vain, and that the lives of those enshrined at Yasukuni were wasted.

The vast majority of the interred at the Yasukuni Shrine were fighters in the Pacific War, or what many on the right in Japan continue to call the "Greater East Asia War" – a term banned by the American General Headquarters during its post-war occupation due to the name's association with Japan's wartime policies, namely the notion of a Greater East Asia Co-prosperity Sphere.

Suspicions about the role of Yasukuni in Japanese nationalism are due in part to Shrine priests secretly adding 1,068 convicted war criminals to the "Book of Souls," Yasukuni's official registry. If Japan's leaders honestly acknowledge the past, the ghosts of Nanjing would be finally laid to rest.

Since the Tiananmen Square massacre in 1989, the United States has done a lot to support intellectuals and artists suppressed in China or forced to escape their country. And Japan? The oldest democracy in East Asia, and perhaps its freest society, has been conspicuously silent on free speech in China. This is not just a matter of Tokyo prioritizing economic relations over political rights. Do Japanese perhaps feel they have no right to criticize China because of some historical guilt?

Japan's national image depends on its people's pride and sense of self. Japan, without building a base of credibility through acknowledging its wartime aggression, has failed to effect true reconciliation with its neighbors. The efforts of Japanese volunteer doctors, engineers and students from NGOs and charities working in many countries in Asia are undermined by the denials their country harbors. Their moral dedication is misdirected by Tokyo's denial of the past and the value of their work is cheapened. Without that credibility, Japan cannot take on the international role its people can be proud of, a role commensurate with the country's greatness.

Japanese denials and distortions of history hurt Japan itself. Moreover, those distortions of history make it easier to identify with nationalist Chinese protests, and harder for Japan to join the world in remembering a shameful chapter in its history as Germany does in remembering World War II and the Holocaust.

In May 2005, I attended a public dialogue in Seoul in which Nobel prize-winning novelist Kenzaburo Oe spoke on the importance of

Japan acknowledging its historic wrong doings. He said for Japan to be a full and proper member of the community of East Asian nations, it must properly face its former militarism. Oe observed that true national pride cannot be founded on misrepresenting the past and encouraging collective amnesia about war responsibility.

Until the ghosts of Nanjing are exorcised, Japan cannot achieve its national goal of "normalcy;" it won't be free from the nightmare of its wartime guilt, until it faces Nanjing's ghosts. In Asian horror movies, *onryo* are borne out of a brutal murder. The haunted protagonists in these films free themselves from these maligned spirits only after first acknowledging the crime that made these bitter ghosts. Upon a foundation of honesty and contrition, Japan, too, can free itself, build a solid relationship with its neighbors and take its rightful place as a beacon of freedom in the region.

Jenny Chen
High School Student
North Potomac, Maryland
USA

Whitewashing History:
The Japanese Denial of its World War II Crimes

Even in awful acts such as war, there are rules. The Hague Conventions of 1899 dictated the humane treatment of prisoners of war (POW), the Geneva Gas Protocol of 1925 prohibited the "use of poison gas and practice of bacteriological warfare"[1], the four Geneva Conventions of 1949 extended protections to civilians. Diplomats from Japan were present at all these conventions and signed every law. No one would dream that Japan would be guilty of violating these laws in a horrible massacre later known as The Rape of Nanking. Almost 70 years later, the Japanese government still refuses to acknowledge its war crimes. This denial threatens pan-Asian relations, betrays the Japanese people, and ultimately obstructs the progress of humanity as a whole.

In December 1937, the Japanese army began its ruthless takeover of China with capturing the capital (Nanking) as the ultimate goal. The Japanese Imperial Army launched an orgy of senseless bloodshed. In six weeks, an estimated 260,000–300,000 Chinese people were killed through the most horrific means. Men would be used for bayonet practices and suffered many wounds before dying. People would be forced to undergo "water treatment" in which water and kerosene was pumped into their noses and mouths until their bowels burst. Victims would be buried waist deep before the Japanese unleashed German shepherds and watched as the dogs tore the bodies up. The Japanese nailed prisoners to boards and ran over them with army tanks. Soldiers would entertain themselves by drenching groups of Chinese people and lighting them on fire, watching as the group burst into flames and were slowly reduced to ashes. Witnesses saw soldiers stripping a victim before ordering a German shepard to bite several parts of the body. The dog not only "ripped open his belly but jerked out his intestines along the ground for a distance"[2]. Japanese soldiers ate the hearts and livers of victims. Soldiers cut the penises off of dead men and sold them to "Japanese customers who believed that eating them would increase virility"[2].

While violent raiding was taking place, a more secret operation was being manned by Major General Ishii. On April 18, 1939, Ishii established Unit 1644, a biological warfare operation in Nanking in addition to his already sprawling network of germ research throughout China. Hiroshi Matsumoto, a former Japanese soldier confessed in a 1997 interview that prisoners were completely dehumanized and "were all naked and kept in cages that looked like cages for animals... in the size of 1.2 meters to 1.3 meters in height, side, and width. [Prisoners] had to always have their legs crossed...after [Japanese scientists] injected live germs into prisoners [the scientists] would wait until the germs spread in the blood"[3]. The Japanese soldiers often infected whole villages with cholera, typhoid, and dysentry. Bacteria assuming the identity of vaccines were administered to children and poisoned foods were given to hungry villagers.

There was also a literal rape of more than 80,000 Chinese women after Nanking succumbed to the Japanese forces. No female on the streets – whether eight or eighty years old – was spared. Japanese soldiers also crammed various assortments of objects into the women's vaginas – bamboo sticks, knives, nails, and even firecrackers. Once a firecracker was lit, the victim would be blown up amidst jeers from Japanese soldiers. In some cases, the Japanese sliced open the vaginas of preteen girls in order to "ravish them more effectively"[2]. Each raped woman was killed "because dead bodies don't talk"[2], says Azuma Shiro, a former Japanese World War II soldier.

But there was a figurative rape as well. The Japanese government has denied its painful history for many decades, stripping its Asian victims of dignity and self-worth. It has taken Japan 68 years to issue a formal, albeit vague, apology for "wartime aggression",[4] but one must question the sincerity of this apology. It came after Japan had submitted a formal bid for a permanent seat on the UN Security Council and Japanese history textbooks still decidedly ignore Japan's war crimes during World War II. The government defends its censorship of textbooks by saying that there is a need to "teach our children a history of Japan that they can be proud of"[5]. As writer Paul Gordon Shalow says, "According to this way of thinking, a shameful past is not something to be acknowledged, reflected upon, and overcome, but to be ignored or whitewashed, and forgotten"[5].

Immediately following the massacre, imperial authorities "imposed a blackout in Japan of all mass media info related to the matter. Few Japanese nationals on the home front or elsewhere had any idea of the horrors their military had perpetrated. Since then and right up to this day, Japanese [revisionists], right wing publishers have salted the deep wounds with double talk, justifications, and bald-faced denial"[6]. Japanese writers such as Katsuichi Honda who have written and researched extensively about the Rape of Nanking and other Japanese war crimes are reviled and ostracized by the Japanese public. Honda receives death-threats from high officials and is so criticized that he must wear a bulletproof vest, and a disguise whenever he speaks in public for fear of his life. Former, conscience-ridden soldiers such as Shiro Azuma who kept a diary documenting the atrocities in Nanking and published it after the war have been attacked by many right-wing politicians for being involved in a conspiracy with the Chinese. Jun Kamei, a former Shukan Shincho newsmagazine writer and assistant editor, recognizes that "Magazines such as Shukan Shincho and Shukan Bunshun clearly embody the tendency to beat to the drum of nationalism"[6]. Although Japan claims to be a democratic country, its government still possesses eerily nationalistic overtones. In what truly democratic country would writers of the truth such as Honda be forced to walk outside in public in disguise and be bombarded with death threats that are not investigated by the police? In what truly democratic country would the government issue a "blackout" of all information relating to its war crimes and the media be used for propaganda and claim that all those who affirm the truth of the Japanese atrocities to be involved in an "anti-Japanese" conspiracy?

The Japanese people have been denied a true and accurate story of their history and have been led to believe lies. They have been bombarded with such news titles as "A Strange Japanese Who Makes Up Stories of the Mobilization of Comfort Women" (Shukan Shincho, January 5, 1995)[5]. The public is being groomed for a similar mindset that was present shortly before World War II – that Japanese people are superior and incapable of making mistakes and that they are victim of a worldwide vendetta that seeks to control them. Should Japan enter another war with this mindset, its people will blindly fight for a false cause. In the end however, it will be the betrayed Japanese people who will suffer enormous consequences–deaths of beloved ones, and perhaps defeat once again.

It is crucial for other nations to remember and publicize this dark period of history. If Japan enters another war because of its militaristic and nationalistic undertones, the whole world will suffer because methods of warfare have evolved to be more deadly than ever. The public investigation of Japanese war crimes would alert other nations to the other atrocities that humans are capable of doing and advise them to take appropriate precautions. Imagine if we did not know that the Holocaust had happened. The Geneva Conventions that protect civilians would not have been held and the UN would not be created. Because of our knowledge of humans' potential for cruelty, the world has reacted quickly to crises like Darfur and 9/11. Finally, there is a moral issue to acknowledging and compensating victims for their suffering. There are hundreds of victims and former soldiers who are plagued with nightmares of the past. There are also the souls of so many people who have died as a result of Japanese crimes whose deaths are denied. It is the responsibility of the human population to right these wrongs and to help bring out the truths to honor the deaths of our fellow human beings. These people are being imprisoned – not in a concentration camp, nor a biological camp – but by the shackles of lies and deception.

But why has the Japanese government been able to get away with denial for such a long time? The war ridden Asian governments at that time were too weak to petition for justice. Once "China became Communist and the United States had solidified its cooperative arrangements with Japan, the United States lost virtually all interest in exposing war crimes"[6]. The pressure that was placed on Germany for its war crimes was not placed on Japan. Sadly, some United States decision makers were also willing to compromise justice in order to gain much coveted information that was documented from the Japanese cruel biological experimentation programs. Although an investigation had been made immediately after the surrender of the Japanese by the Soviet Union during the Khabarovsk proceedings in which twelve Japanese bio-war complicit officials were convicted, General MacArthur had struck a deal with General Ishii that granted Ishii full immunity in exchange for information. Thus, during the Tokyo War Crimes Trial, the whole issue of a bio-war program was avoided and general Ishii and several of his subordinates were never convicted. The cover-ups and the lack of pressure resulted in a trial where much evidence was not brought out into the public. As a result, only 25 Japanese generals were found guilty. Only six were sentenced to death, the rest were convicted with a few decades or life imprisonment. 15 of the 25 convicted were paroled within 10 years. Many of those paroled ended up occupying the highest positions in the government and universities and have set up the nationalistic government that exists today.

It is clear that more needs to be done to bring out the Japanese crimes to the general public. The Western world should shoulder the responsibility of being the most advanced nations of the world and start teaching more about the Japanese Imperial Army's purge of Asia, with the same weight that they give the Holocaust. Indeed, the purge of Asia killed more than 22 million non-Japanese Asians – most of them civilians – which is more than double the amount of people killed during the Holocaust. This is not to belittle the importance of the Nazi's Holocaust but to point out that the Japanese campaign to eradicate all non-Japanese Asians merits an equal examination by today's scholars and students. The Rape of Nanking receives less than a couple of sentences in American textbooks whereas entire units in elementary school, middle school, and high school are devoted to the Holocaust.

There needs to be a cohesive group started in the United States filled with full-time staff who are dedicated to bringing out the truth of World War II in Asia. This group must establish itself quickly, fundraise and educate the American community. But most importantly, this group must lobby the United States Congress for more attention to this forgotten history and to place more political pressure on Japan. Secondly, this organization should lobby the United Nations to have this issue placed on the international agenda of items to discuss. There must be more pressure from the international community. There needs to be an unbiased investigation that brings forth testimony, pictures, and documentation. There is also a lack of scholarly research and written material on this topic such as Iris Chang's *The Rape of Nanking,* and *The Good Man of Nanking* by John Rabe[7]. Young students and seasoned researchers should be encouraged to bring the truth out into print. Finally, money should be raised to build a museum or a memorial, similar to the Holocaust Museum, commemorating the deaths of so many innocent people in Asia, Once such a memorial has been erected, there can be no denying that such an event happened. The victimized Asians cannot achieve recognition alone; they need the support of the international community and other prominent officials. Only when the international community pressures Japan will the Japanese government realize that its wartime crimes are not taken lightly by other nations. It will finally be forced to face their history.

No amount of compensation can even begin to adequately offset the damages created by the Japanese Imperial Army in the wake of World War II. However, compensation must be made to prove the sincerity of Japanese apologies and will alleviate some of the pain that their victims have endured. Furthermore, compensation will prove to the international community that Japan is serious about not committing such a crime again. Of the 6 million Jews that were killed during the Nazi regime, Germany has paid compensation of more than $10.8 billion. The Japanese government has paid nothing. In addition, the Japanese government must fully acknowledge their past by ending their persecution of those who have spoken out about the Rape of Nanking and educating their youth on the war crimes by revising their textbooks and starting a unit that teaches children about the horrors of the war that was fought years ago. This issue cannot be glossed over again. In addition, the war criminals that are enshrined as martyrs at the Yasukuni Shrine who ordered the deaths of many innocent civilians should be removed from the shrine. While worshipping ancestors is part of a religion that is steeped in tradition, there is no religion in the world that advocates the worship of men who were cold-blooded mass murderers.

Perhaps the most chilling truth of the war is that the soldiers who fought and committed these crimes were ordinary people. How were they mobilized to commit such heinous crimes against fellow human beings? The answer lies in Japanese propaganda before the war. As is common knowledge, Japanese propaganda painted Japan as a country that is superior to all other countries and was being threatened by those who felt resentful of Japan's superiority. Emperor Hirohito was known as a living god. Prior to Japan's defeat, no ordinary Japanese citizen had even seen the Emperor. The Japanese people were led blindly into the war, believing that they were defending Japan – with its holy Emperor – against the inferior countries of the world. This mindset is eerily similar to the propaganda that is spewed through Japan's media today – that no crimes had ever happened, that the Japanese government is above such evil mistakes, and that everyone who says otherwise is part of an anti-Japanese conspiracy. Given the killing of the truth in Japan today, committing the same crimes as they did in the past is a very real possibility for the Japanese people. As Sherwood Eddy and Kirby Page wrote in *The Abolition of War* (1924), "The first casualty of war is truth".

1. Trombley, Maria. "A Brief History of the Laws of War." *Society of Professional Journalists*. 2003. 27 June 2007 <http://spj.org/ gc-history.asp>.

2. Chang, Iris. *The Rape of Nanking: The Forgotten Holocaust of World War II.* New York: BasicBooks, 1997.

3. Barenblatt, Daniel. *A Plague Against Humanity: The Hidden History of Japan's Biological Warfare Program* . New York: Harper Collins, 2004

4. "Japan's Koizumi apologises for wartime aggression amid China row" AFP News, April 22, 2005

5. "Japan's War Responsibilty and the Pan-Asian Movement for Redress and Compensation: An Overview East Asia by: Paul Gordon Schalow

6. Gamble, Adam, and Takesato Watanabe. *A Public Betrayed: An Inside Look at Japanese Medi Atrocities and Their Warnings to the West*. Washington D.C: Regnery, 2004.

7. Rebe, John. *The Good Man of Nanking*. New York: Alfred A. Knopf. 1998

Glenn McLaurin
High School Student
Garner, North Carolina
USA

Closure and Unity

What we can touch, we experiment with; what we understand, we seek to control: we are human. We organize to increase productivity; we establish complex societies on mores of kinship and justice; we rule them with logic and reason. But even as we seek order in the world, and strive to secure and balance our lives, we struggle against the darker side of mankind, the flaws that undermine the stability we struggle to preserve.

Despite all that we create, humans have an uncanny ability to destroy. We are not perfect; we indulge in sin and commit crimes that cannot be justified. Jealousy, anger, greed: these are the driving forces behind much of the pain and suffering in the world. We try our hardest to contain these emotions and motivations, but when we fail, we are left only with a burden, the knowledge of the crime we have committed. When Cain slew Abel in cold blood, he was cursed to spend his days as a restless wanderer, condemned to a harsh, meaningless existence as persecution for committing the first murder. In society today, murderers carry a similar burden – their actions, regardless of their impetus, haunt them for the entirety of their lives.

But what of men and women who are mere pawns in a larger game? Soldiers, who kill and are killed, minor players in the politicking between nations? Bloodshed is a consequence of war, occurring with frightening regularity as violence always seems to be the choice manner in which conflicts are resolved. War, fought for land, love, luxury, is entrenched in the history of mankind, entangled in our oldest stories and the source of our greatest innovations and expansions. Rules, however, govern modern warfare: in the world of today, precautions are taken to minimize civilian casualties; leaders are scrutinized

41

for hints of corruption; the lives of many innocents are preserved.

Murderers have no place in society; they are barred from living amongst the innocent, and are forever branded for their action. Nations guilty of heinous crimes against humanity carry a similar burden, for they become known for barbaric brutality, as less civilized, primitive.

No apology or memorial will ever return a life once it is taken. Nevertheless, they serve as a public display of regret, and provide solace to family, friends, and the affected community. To commemorate the innocents affected by great crimes is to profess guilt; a physical manifestation of shame is a monument to the stolen lives, a solemn promise that such tragedy will never occur again. It may be largely symbolic, but it ensures the lives lost are not forgotten.

Therefore, it is distressing that, seventy years after the genocide, Japan refuses to take responsibility for the Massacre of Nanking.

The present-day indifference that is so widespread in the Land of the Rising Sun will never resolve the long-standing Sino-Japanese tensions. Prince Asaka, the highest ranking officer at the time of the tragedy, walked away from the Nanking Tribunal a free man, and since 1946, Japan has continued to deny involvement in the massacre. For over sixty years, and with the passing of two generations, the stories that Asaka told in order to escape punishment for the crimes of war have slowly been established as fact. It is widely held that only Chinese soldiers were involved in the massacre, that the casualties were a result of a rebellion, that only a few hundred killings occurred, spanned over the course of a few months. These accounts are attempts to avoid the facts of the matter, and all fail to reveal the awful truth: beginning in 1937, the civilians of Nanking, China, endured weeks of horrific mutilation, rape, and slaughter. This horrific extermination of human life was somehow hidden and ignored, and for decades, the genocide was almost forgotten.

It is difficult not to look at the Nanking Massacre and associate it with the European Holocaust. Though the genocide in Europe had a far greater number of casualties, spanning religion, ethnicities, and social class, both atrocities involved merciless slaying, and later, the heinous denial of such an event.

It took years of dedicated research and courageous effort to bring the Holocaust to public light, and the survivors fought, and continue to fight, to make certain that such a crime will never be forgotten. Slowly, the Nanking Massacre is receiving similar attention. But as the years pass, more and more of the Massacre will be forgotten, no matter how hard a few select individuals work. To enter the Nanking Massacre into the public conscience will require a mass effort on behalf of the victims, historians, and the offending nation. Before the ordeal can ever be brought to a closure, Japan must make amends for its actions, and become a leader in preserving the lives and stories of the three-hundred thousand innocents who perished seventy years ago.

The Asian continent contains some of the oldest civilizations known to mankind, and the relationships between its nations are ancient and complex. Disputes between a few countries ultimately impact many other communities; as such, easing Sino-Japanese tensions would potentially play a hand in settling the entire region. Japan should encourage research into the events of the Nanking Massacre, amongst its own citizens and members of other Asian communities. Though this heinous crime was limited a particular city, it is not the only instance of violence throughout Asia. Though divided by war, there is still potential for unity, but leaders of the nations must make a commitment to bring closure to the animosity. With a resolution to preserve the memory and prevent other massacres from occurring again, Japan could become a forerunner in an international movement.

On an individual basis, citizens of Japan owe it to themselves and their Asian neighbors to take action. The current policy of denial serves only as fuel for cynics and fringe groups, for it suggests that Japan is unwilling to take responsibility for its actions, and leads others to wonder what else the Land of the Rising Sun is hiding from the public. But an educational campaign would foster a revolution in political beliefs, both in Japan and abroad. The truth, when presented fairly and without prejudice, is insurmountable to lies and falsification. Global awareness, be it started through a grassroots movement or an international organization, will guarantee that the Rape of Nanking is never forgotten, and ensures it will never occur again.

Elie Wiesel, Nobel Laureate and Holocaust survivor, has become the face for preserving the memory of the victims of Germany's inhumane actions. One of his most famous quotes, "Neutrality helps the oppressor, never the victim. Silence encourages the tormentor, never the tormented," is a startlingly accurate portrayal of the means through which tragic massacres occur. In the face of utter inhumanity, mankind cannot afford to back down and ignore rape, slaughter, and genocide.

Too often, however, the path of least resistance – indifference – is chosen. Nations and individuals alike are afraid to involve themselves in conflict, afraid of meddling in matters that they feel they do not belong. In Germany, they first came for the gypsies, and I didn't speak up because I wasn't a gypsy. Then they came for the Bolsheviks, and I didn't speak up because I wasn't a Bolshevik. Then they came for the Jews, and I didn't speak up because I wasn't a Jew. Then they came for the trade unionists and I didn't speak up because I wasn't a trade unionist... Then they came for me, and there was no one left to speak up.

Martin Niemoller, a pastor in Germany, penned this address in response to the Holocaust, as a testimony to the tragic impact of human indifference. The message is simple, yet powerful: we must not only advocate for ourselves, but we are obligated; it is our duty, to speak for those who have no voice.

This is the lesson that must be drawn from the Rape of Nanking, this is the good that can stem from so much of the negativity that flows from the incident. The world still has much to learn about the Nanking Massacre, and Japan still owes much reparation to China and those affected by the slaughter. Nevertheless, as we become more educated about this particular atrocity, we become more sensitive to other heinous crimes being committed around the globe, and we become more apt to speak against such brutalities.

The Nanking Massacre has been shamefully denied, just as the concentration camps of the Holocaust were ignored first by neighboring towns, and later, the world at large. From these tragedies though, we have realized that we cannot sit idle behind the borders of our own countries as evil spreads into another region of the world. The leaders of the genocide in Yugoslavia eventually faced prosecution for their actions. Saddam Hussein was tried and sentenced to death by hanging for his brutal tactics against the Kurds, amongst a myriad of other crimes. Currently, the genocide in Darfur is triggering an international backlash as industrialized nations are readily denouncing the Sudanese government's inability to control warring factions. Citizens across the globe have united under the flags of a variety of organizations to protest the violence, and the message is slowly being heard.

It is this energy, this earnestness, which needs to continue. We are so often prompted to action through tragedy, an apparent knee-jerk response to the current events flickering across the television screen. We cannot just focus on the present, however. We must reach back into our past, and look ahead to the future, and become fully aware of the violence that seeps into darkest corners of our world, flowing like a toxin, propagating death and destruction.

No service or memorial will return life to the hundreds of thousands who perished in those awful weeks of 1937. However, we are capable of doing far more than just mourning their passing; we can celebrate our – and their – humanity by treasuring and protecting life. By becoming more aware of the Nanking Massacre – its causes, the methods in which it was denied, and the most effective means in which to educate others, we can recognize the warning signs of future massacres and genocide, and stop them before they can begin. The influence that each individual has is astounding; every person who becomes informed become empowered to spread the knowledge and stand for change. United, we can demand action, demand a revolution, demand progress.

But before we can bring closure to the Nanking Massacre, Japan must make amends for its actions. It is a different set of leaders now, an entirely different government, than the party that led the Massacre. Times have changed, people have changed, and knowledge has spread. The world is now aware of the Nanking Massacre, and the time is ripe for change. But Japan must lead through example: the issuance of an official apology, an effort to make reparations to those who still suffer as a result of the Massacre.

A simple gesture, the construction of a memorial, would be an appropriate first step for Japan to take. Perhaps a garden, symbolic of future life, rather than the violent past, would signify a shift toward engendering creation instead of encouraging death. A concrete structure would stand for future generations, slowly achieving goals shared by both Japan and China: awareness, education, and preservation of the memory of the Massacre.

By taking responsibility for its actions, Japan will strengthen its relationships abroad, and closure will be reached. On the seventieth anniversary of the tragedy, the aggressor has an important choice to make: continue to deny the rape of Nanking and delay progress for human rights across the globe, or alleviate the burden it has carried for so many decades. Should Japan refuse to make an effort for closure, the status quo will simply be maintained; though the government may not suffer for its decision, millions of people struggling in the face of violence and death will.

In his writings, Elie Wiesel once decreed, "Mankind must remember that peace is not God's gift to his creatures; peace is our gift to each other." This truth has been corroborated by humanity's endless waltz of war, resolution, and revolution: closure does not occur naturally, it is a conscious decision on the behalf of both parties. Mankind is blessed with a sense of innovation, reason, and justice, but also with the ability of choice. We may choose to carry the burden of malevolence and deny the memory of our sins, or we may choose to relieve ourselves of that awful burden, and advocate for peace and unity, struggling not in the face of violence, but down the path to enlightenment. Japan now faces this choice, and we owe it to ourselves, and the nameless victims of countless massacres, to urge the nation to make the right decision.

Works Cited

(1) "Nanking 1937." *Nanking Massacre*. Nanking Massacre 1937. 25 June 2007

<http://prion.bchs.uh.edu/~zzhang/1/Nanking_Massacre/index.html>.

(2) Niemoller, Martin. "First They Came..." 25 June 2007

<http://www.peacethrujustice.org/post911rights.htm>

(3) Wiesel, Elie. Elie Wiesel Quotes. 25 June 2007

<http://thinkexist.com/quotes/elie_wiesel/>

Daniel Joseph Pearlstein
Freshman
University Laboratory High School
Urbana, Illinois, USA

Japanese Denials of Responsibility for War Crimes: Historical Background and Continuing Implications

Largely due to the efforts of Iris Chang, the Rape of Nanking has come to epitomize the brutality of the Japanese Imperial Army during the period 1931-1945. To this day, the Japanese government contin- ues to deny or minimize Japanese responsibility for a vast number of atrocities committed in East Asia. In this essay, I discuss the conse- quences of these atrocities and denials for Japanese relations with its neighbors and the United States.

Anti-Japanese sentiment in China, Korea, the Philippines, and Taiwan continues to be a problem in the relations of these countries to Japan. While in the cases of Korea, China, and Taiwan this anger can be traced to Japanese colonialism that began in the late nineteenth and early twentieth centuries (Nehmer & McCune 1962, p. 483; Latourette & Wilbur, 1962, pp. 526-528), the wartime atrocities of the Japanese Imperial Army during its invasions and occupations over the period 1931-1945 are everywhere at the heart of the issue. Moreover, anti- Japanese sentiments in these countries are reinforced by attempts of Japanese political leaders to deny that certain atrocities and other war crimes occurred, or by denials of responsibility for atrocities whose occurrence cannot be questioned. Combined with obvious efforts to not educate Japanese children about wartime atrocities, these efforts of denial pose a serious obstacle to the establishment of cordial rela- tions between Japan and several of its important neighbors. It is now clear that these issues will continue to fester until Japan makes satis- factory apologies, and possibly payments for its wartime acts.

Beginning in the late nineteenth century, Japan became a colo- nial power in East Asia. Japanese rule first came to what is now Tai- wan in 1895 (Latourette & Wilbur, 1962, pp. 526-528) and to Korea in 1910 (Nehmer & McCune 1962, p. 483). The Japanese did not treat the local people well, and this colonial experience has not been forgotten. Beginning in 1931, the Japanese army invaded and occupied progressively larger portions of China. Beginning in December of 1941, Japan invaded and subsequently occupied Thailand, the American-ruled Philippines, the Dutch-ruled East Indies (now Indonesia), British-ruled Burma, Malaya, and Singapore, and French Indo-China. In each of these places, the Japanese army committed horrible crimes against the local populations and captured Allied military personnel, and in most cases against captured Western civilians. Among the most infamous and best known of these are *the Rape of Nanking*, the Bataan Death March (Shipley, 1962, p. 520), and the construction of the Burma-Thailand railway. Beyond these few well-known atrocities, the Japanese army systematically murdered, mutilated, raped, and degraded millions of Asians and many tens of thousands of Westerners throughout all of the lands that it invaded and occupied.

World War II ended in Asia with what is frequently described as the "unconditional surrender" of Japan. Unlike the truly unconditional surrender of Germany, however, the Japanese surrender was a conditional one, with the Japanese being allowed to retain the imperial system. Also unlike the case of Germany, the occupying power (the United States in the case of Japan) did not undertake to systematically purge the country of all of the attitudes that had contributed to Japanese militarism (Jansen, 1962, p. 932).

The differences between Japan and Germany were apparent in the war-crimes trials which took place after the war. In Germany, these led to a thorough public accounting of the responsibility of the entire German leadership for the crimes committed in the name of the German nation (Levie, 1962, p. 348A). Combined with effective and systematic education of German children and substantial payments to the state of Israel and to individual Jewish (and later, non-Jewish) survivors, the policies of the occupying powers (United States, United Kingdom, Soviet Union, and France) led to a general acceptance of national responsibility among the German people. In Japan, on the other hand, teaching about Japanese atrocities in the public schools has been spotty (Masalski, 2001, pp. 1-2), and there have been no substantial payments to nations or individuals victimized by the Japanese.

An example of the failure to make Japan deal with the atrocities committed was the 1951 Treaty of San Francisco, in which the United States, Japan, and 48 other countries concluded a peace in East Asia with no admission of Japanese responsibility for a vast catalogue of war crimes, with only a token payment of less than $20 million in liquidated Japanese assets to be distributed for the benefit of captured Allied military personnel and their families. This treaty provided for no compensation to Asians or other Westerners brutalized by the Japanese (San Francisco Peace Treaty, 1951). [Full disclosure: my grandfather's uncle, Joseph N. Pearlstein, after whom I was named, was a U.S. marine in Shanghai during the late 1930's and until November 1941, when he was sent to Corregidor, in the Philippines. Following his capture there in 1942, he apparently survived the Bataan Death March. He subsequently died at the hands of the Japanese while performing slave labor in a zinc mine in the mountains of Western Japan (Pittsburgh Jewish Criterion, May 7, 1943; December 21, 1945; February 3, 1950).]

This failure to clearly assign responsibility immediately after World War II has led, over the years, to the development of a "revisionist" movement in Japanese politics, led by right-wing politicians who seek to use denial of Japanese war crimes as an issue to highlight their "nationalist" approach, particularly with respect to relations with other East Asian countries (French, 2006). These denials include recent assertions that the Japanese army played no role in the forcible procurement into sexual slavery of tens or hundreds of thousands of mostly Asian women (Onishi, 2007), as well as claims that few if any civilians were killed by the Japanese army in Nanking in 1937 and 1938 (Shibuichi, 2005, p. 203). Those who deny that these atrocities occurred are not people on the margins of Japanese society, but rather members of Parliament and more recently government ministers, including the prime minister (Onishi, 2007).

More than any other issue, Japanese denial of its wartime atrocities affects Japan's relations with its East Asian neighbors.

In China, the communists used revulsion against Japanese atrocities to their benefit before coming to power in 1949. For many years following the 1949 revolution, the communist government made relatively little effort to encourage public protests against Japan, and largely confined its efforts to the educational sphere. In recent years, however, the Chinese government has openly encouraged public demonstrations and other displays of anger at Japanese denials of responsibility, and many observers think that building popular feeling against Japan has been used to distract the Chinese people from the shortcomings of their own government. Regardless of the underlying purpose of this encouragement, its effect has been to create a broad-based antipathy to Japan (Reilly, 2004).

In Korea, anti-Japanese sentiment goes back to the malevolent occupation that began in 1910, and that went from bad to worse during World War II. A key issue has been the failure of successive Japanese governments to accept Japanese responsibility for the sexual enslavement of large numbers of Korean women during World War II (Onishi, 2007). In the case of South Korea, there is no evidence that the government uses the issue to deliberately inflame the population. However, continued Japanese denials make it impossible for South Korean politicians to ignore the issue.

While it might have been possible in the immediate post-war period to have imposed on Japan the same level of acceptance of responsibility as was imposed on Germany, that was not done, and the conditions now are so different from what they were in the late 1940's that such an approach is no longer feasible. Since the requirements imposed on Germany (clear assignment of responsibility, effective public education, and significant payments to the state of Israel and to surviving individual victims) has worked relatively well, it is important to understand why present conditions in Japan and the countries where Japanese war crimes were committed are so different.

First, West Germany accepted responsibility for its crimes in the late 1940's and early 1950's while it was under the occupation and guidance of the Americans, British, and French. West Germany was led by enlightened politicians who wanted a clear break with the Nazi regime and its crimes, and who saw no political advantage in denying those crimes. Modern Japan, on the other hand, has been free of U.S. military occupation for over 55 years and is led by politicians who, in some cases see considerable political advantage in denying Japanese responsibility for war crimes as part of a broader "nationalist" appeal (Onishi, 2007).

Second, in the early 1950's, Germany was trying to rebuild its economy following devastating damage to its industrial base, infrastructure, and housing. The U.S., as the only major power to have emerged undamaged from World War II, played the major role in this reconstruction, and had considerable influence on the German government beyond the large number of Allied troops stationed there until the collapse of the communist system in 1989-1991. Modern-day Japan, on the other hand, is a prosperous, industrialized country in which U.S. influence is largely limited to providing a nuclear "umbrella."

Finally, Germany accepted responsibility at a time when memories of its atrocities were very fresh, and when hundreds of thousands of surviving victims were young and vigorous. In contrast, the passage of over 60 years has reduced the number of living victims and witnesses of Japanese atrocities to a small fraction of their original number. Descendants of Japanese involved in wartime atrocities are reluctant to label their elderly relatives war criminals (Shibuichi, 2005, p. 200). It is much easier for Japanese to deny the facts in 2007 than it was for the West Germans in 1949.

Since the countries central to these disputes (Japan, China, and Korea) are all independent and relatively prosperous, the German model is not applicable. Rather, it is clear that any settlement of the disputes between Japan and its neighbors regarding Japanese war crimes will have to come from mutual agreements among the parties.

Elements of a settlement might include Japanese apologies for crimes committed during the first half of the twentieth century, passage of laws requiring accurate treatment of Japanese war crimes in Japanese textbooks [without intermittent political interference (Masalski, 2001, pp. 1-2)], payments to survivors of these crimes, and discontinuing symbolic visits to the Yasukuni Shrine which houses the remains of notorious Japanese war criminals (Shibuichi, 2005, p. 198). The idea of limiting direct payments to survivors, while excluding the relatives of victims who perished at the hands of the Japanese or who died later, has precedence in the German model (German Embassy, undated) as well as from the program by which the U.S. government compensated, in the late 1980's, Japanese-Americans interned during World War II (Associated Press, 1988).

Whatever its approach, the Japanese government must act quickly to acknowledge and apologize for Japan's war crimes, educate its people about them, and compensate the victims. To do otherwise would allow this wound to fester indefinitely.

(1) Associated Press, "Measure to Pay War Detainees Goes to Reagan." The New York Times, August 5, 1988.

(2) Burress, Charles. "Wars of Memory." SFGate.com (San Francisco Chronicle online) Sunday, July 26, 1998

(3) French, Howard W. "Letter from China; China Hails a Good Nazi and Makes Japan Take Notice." The New York Times, March 15, 2006.

(4) German Embassy to the United States. "German Compensation for National Socialist Crimes," retrieved from http://www.germany.info/relaunch/info/archives/background/ns_crimes.html

(5) Jansen, Marius B. "Japan: History." Encyclopaedia Britannica, 1962 edition, Vol. 12, pp. 905-936.

(6) Jeans, Roger B. "Victims or Victimizers? Museums, Textbooks, and the War Debate in Contemporary Japan" The Journal of Military History, Vol. 69, pp149-195   (2005)

(7) Latourette, Kenneth S. and Wilbur, C. Martin. "China: History." Encyclopaedia Britannica, 1962 edition, Vol. 5, pp. 518-539.

(8) Levie, Howard S. "War Crimes." Encyclopaedia Britannica, 1962 edition, Vol. 23, pp. 348-348A.

(9) Masalski, Kathleen Woods. "Examining the Japanese History Textbook Controversies." November 2001. Japan Digest. National Clearinghouse for U.S.-Japan Studies. Indiana University. http://www.indiana.edu/~japan/Digests/textbook.html

(10) Nehmer, Stanley and McCune, Shannon. "Korea: History." Encyclopaedia Britannica, 1962 edition, Vol. 13, pp. 482-485.

(11) Onishi, Norimitsu. "The Saturday Profile; In Japan, a Historian Stands by Proof of Wartime Sex Slavery." The New York Times, March 31, 2007.

(12) Prugh, George S. "Prisoners of War." Encyclopaedia Britannica, 1962 edition, Vol. 11, pp. 520-522.

(13) Reilly, James. "China's History Activists and the War of Resistance Against Japan." Asian Survey, Vol. 44, pp. 276-294 (2004).

(14) San Francisco Peace Treaty, September 8, 1951. Retrieved from: http://www.uni-erfurt.de/ostasiatische_geschichte/texte/japan/dokumente/19/19510908_treaty.htm on 4/22/2007.

(15) Shibuichi, Daiki. "The Yasukuni Shrine Dispute and the Politics of Identity in Japan: Why All the Fuss?" Asian Survey, Vol. 45, pp. 197-215 (2005).

Tianshu Zhang
High School Student
Fuzhou, Fujian,
P. R. China

Standing in front of the gate of Nanking Massacre Memorial Hall in a humid summer morning, I felt like crying, but with no tears. There was a huge marble crucifix with two dates carved "1937.12.13~1938.1". Staring at the marble, I saw the scar of one nation bleeding. It seemed that my heart stopped beating.

The Memorial Hall was closed to visitors due to renovation. I could only let my thoughts fly inside, where one of the darkest pages of human history, the atrocity committed by the Japanese Emperor Army to the people of Nanking during WWII, is recorded.

Although Japan launched the war of aggression against China two years prior to Germany's intrusion into Poland, the fact is hardly known to many people, especially Westerners. The horror of Nanking massacre and the suffering of Chinese people are barely covered by any Western writers' work, and became gradually revealed only after the publishing of THE RAPE OF NANKING.

Description of the catastrophe is chilling, and the cruelty was beyond imagination. One cannot help but wonder how fragile humanity may be and how vulnerable the civilization of human kind may be. It seems unreal to have the painstakingly established destroyed in a flash, and the destruction is done by human kind itself.

People may not be willing to believe that such atrocities ever existed, but we must face the truth no matter how painful it may be. The facts having been ignored for such a long time, and the concern is we may not learn the lesson as we should have. Even more alarming is that Japanese right-wingers have been defending the Japanese Emperor Army's invasion of China and other Asian countries. They have also attempted repeatedly to deny Nanking massacre and accused China and other countries of making up the Massacre. But history cannot be distorted.

Iris Chang Youth Award

The tragedy was not just to the Chinese people, it was also one for the Japanese. People are fallible, and so are nations. One will not lose his dignity by admitting his wrongdoings. It is the courage to confront one's own dark side and the willingness to learn from the past that make it worth. We can recall that Willy Brandt, the former premier of the Federal Republic of Germany knelt down in front of Warsaw Jewish Martyrs Monument on December 6th, 1970 for his country's guilt of mistreating the Polish people as well as for waging the war against humanity during WWII. The great courage and strong sense of responsibility he demonstrated shocked the world. It was one of the brightest moment in history. The German government has also committed to compensating war victims for the suffering they had endured, which has won the respect of the world.

As compared with Germany, the attitude of the Japanese government toward its role as war aggressor is disappointing. Lenin said, "Forgetting the past means betrayal." The denial and even twisting of historical facts by certain Japanese right-wingers are insulting and more worrisome. What lies behind is their nationalism. Nationalism is distinctly different from patriotism. Patriotism is the love for one's motherland and his people, but nationalism is about collective egocentrism, strong willpower, and violence. The distinctions have been articulated by Iikolay Aleksaidrovich Berdyaev, "Nation and people are absolutely two different things. To love their own people shows a good feeling; nationalism needs to despise and hate other people. Nationalism is a potential war." Everyone who loves his or her country wants to preserve the dignity of their motherland. But the Japanese right-wingers' words and action lead just to the opposite. Dealing with historical issues with the right attitude is the key to improving the relationship between Japan and those countries who suffered from Japanese invasion. Unfortunately, this denial has become an obstacle in the course.

Stunned by the unspeakable cruelty of war, one shall look beyond the war itself for soul searching. War is only a violent means to obtain benefits. The people who waged wars were all well-educated, and those who kill have their families in their own country. The duty of soldier is to obey the order. Fighting in a battle is their work, and losing life for their country is a great honor. We can accept the fact that death cannot be avoided in war. But what we cannot understand is why they tortured the civilians and even put them to death in such a horrible way. One should ask how the ordinary soldiers turned to beasts, or what may be responsible for such a sudden change in human nature? Was it just an accident or a danger that has been hidden broke out in a sudden?

As far as I know, Japanese have the greatest esteem for bushido - an extreme spirit of devotion. Bushido transformed into militarism step by step during the world's Great Depression period. In order to shake off its economic crisis, the Japanese government chose external expansion. Leaving home, bleeding in nowhere, and uncertainty of future is a difficult text to every soldier. So the policy makers need a more powerful volition to control their army better. With the strong will the soldiers are trained in cold blood. The stronger the body can be, the firmer the mind can be. As I learned more by literature search about the details of Japanese military training, I cannot help sympathizing with those Japanese soldiers who destroyed one of the richest and most beautiful cities of my nation. They were instilled the idea of war. At a tender age, they were controlled tightly and brain-washed. They were under tight control. Through bitter and even inhuman military training, soldiers were forced to suppress their desires and emotion. However, like temporarily dormant volcanoes, stifled hate and anger will break out sooner or later. Unfortunately, war became a way of venting. Killing and committing other war crimes became the only and most gratifying way to serve their animal desire. Their acts are despicable, but they are also the victims of war, physically and emotionally.

We should not only remember the wonderful gift, but also the evil we suffered......forgetting is the abandonment of memory, betrayed memory, is the perfidy of history. In other words, forgetting is to take the risk of war.

—**Elie Wiesel**

Soul searching is not at all easy. People tend to opt to forget for various reasons. For the right-wing Japanese, they may have chosen to forget, to deny, and to twist that particular piece of history for political reasons or out of their nationalism. If I am offended by the Japanese right-wingers' behavior, I am saddened by that of many forgetful Chinese, teenagers in particular. When asked about their view of Japan, most of them will cry for Japan carton, pop stars, and fashionable clothes and hairstyle. Only a few would mention the painful past. Several years ago, a hostess of a popular entertainment program, when asked about the number of the death in Nanking massacre, her first response was, "I don't know." Being told by her co-host the number of victims, she uttered out, "how few!" She may be just ignorant of history, but what she showed may be a reflection of the current mindset of many Chinese teenagers. Maybe looking at the miserable past is too heavy to bear, but we should never forget what our predecessors have gone through to fight for the course of great country. If we do not respect history ourselves, how can we expect an apology from the Japanese government and those who have committed the heinous crime?

As a developing country, China will play a more important role in the world. For Japan, building on its economic strength, enhancing its international reputation is its ambition. The best direction for both China and Japan is to face up the historical issues and to take proper actions to improve bilateral relations. In the recent past, the communication between China and Japan appears to be in a strange situation, the so-called "cold in political and hot in economy". The foot-setting on the wrong side of history by the Japanese right-wingers and the ambiguity of the Japanese government should be responsible. We are not suggesting hatred and revenge that may lead ourselves to nationalism. But it is high time for all parties involved to face up the issues and to prepare us for the future, prosperous and peaceful.

Only not forgetting the past, can we be the masters in the future. Only by remembering the darkness and evil, can we be away from them.

Shayaan Zaraq Bari
Undergraduate Student of Law
University of London
LLB. Programme
Lahore, Pakistan

Denying History

If nations are allowed to commit genocide with impunity, to hide their guilt in a camouflage of lies and denials, there is a real danger that other brutal regimes will be encouraged to attempt genocides.

—**Baroness Caroline Cox**

There's no denying it: Denial inevitably follows genocide. In his Eight Stages of Genocide, Dr. Gregory Stanton lists it as the final stage of a genocidal event.[1] The perpetrators of such acts do their utmost to cover up the evidence. They dig graves and burn bodies, destroy historical records, question the credibility of sources, intimidate witnesses, impede investigations and play down the number of people killed. All of these methods have been used to some extent in rejecting the Massacre of Nanking in 1937-1938, a six-week massacre of the Chinese population by the Imperial Japanese Army.

There are many eye-witness accounts that describe how the Japanese military swept into the city and not only pillaged and burnt Nanking but methodically raped, tormented and murdered its citizens. The Nazi businessman John Rabe, whose diaries were uncovered by Iris Chang in *The Rape of Nanking: The Forgotten Holocaust of World War II*, wrote in his diary entry of December 24th: "I have had to look at so many corpses over the last few weeks...but I wanted to see these atrocities with my own eyes, so that I can speak as an eye-witness later. A man cannot be silent about this kind of cruelty!"[2]

Apart from Rabe's diaries, other accounts of Westerners in the city include the letters of Robert Wilson and John Magee and the documents of Miner Bates, a history professor at the University of Nanking. But perhaps the most damning evidence of the massacre comes from those Japanese sources that Iris Chang documents in *The Rape of Nanking*. In an interview mentioned in her book, the former Japanese soldier Nagatomi Hakudo recounts how a superior officer beheaded a Chinese boy and presented him with the cleanly severed head as a "souvenir." As a test of courage, Hakudo then proceeded to kill other prisoners.[3]

Another former combatant, Azuma Shiro, describes how military personnel took turns raping women and killed them afterward "because dead bodies don't talk."[4] Many Japanese soldiers believed that raping virgins would magically empower them and even wore amulets made from the victims' pubic hair. There are even rough estimations of the number of dead from firsthand sources, e.g. the Japanese military correspondent Imai Masatake describes a "mountain made of dead bodies" at the Hsiakwan wharves and how one Japanese officer at the scene estimated that 20,000 dead.[5]

Even in these scattered accounts, one gets an overwhelming impression that the Japanese army was hard at work hiding these atrocities. So, for instance, Masatake describes how bodies were dragged from a "mountain of corpses" and tossed into the Yangtze River. Rabe was particularly aware of the Japanese attempt to destroy all evidence of these atrocities and in his December 21st diary entry wrote that "there can no longer be any doubt that the Japanese are burning the city, presumably to erase all traces of their looting and thievery."[6] He feared that his diaries would also receive the same treatment, but these passed safely to his granddaughter and later to the Alliance in the Memory of Victims of the Nanking Massacre at the insistence of Iris Chang.

The denial of the Rape of Nanking would only strengthen with time. Certain parts of Nanking were cleared of bodies and opened to Japanese tourists. Every effort was made to convince the Japanese people that nothing was amiss. Over the years, the Japanese government has tried to rewrite history by issuing school textbooks that denied instances of Japanese imperial aggression and the Nanking atrocities.

In 1955, the Japanese Ministry of Education banned one third of the textbooks in use and insisted that textbooks avoid any description of Japan invading China.[7] Thus Japanese school curricula simply failed to acknowledge the Sino-Japanese War or adequately mention the Nanking atrocities and this continued for the next twenty years. The change in position came in the 1970s but so did the advent of the denial movement.

Refusal to believe until proof is given is a rational position; denial of all evidence outside of our own limited experience is absurd.

—Annie Besant

The most outspoken proponent of the denial movement is the ex-soldier Tanaka Masaaki, whose book What Really Happened in Nanking: the Refutation of a Common Myth attempts a rebuttal of the "massacre proposition." However, his arguments are speciously reasoned and thus easily discredited. As pointed out by Hora Tomio in The Proof of the Nanking Massacre, his arguments centre on disputed facts and often distort historical evidence. Sometimes Masaaki even resorts to armchair theorizing which involves making generalizations without offering even a modicum of proof.

Masaaki highlights the fact that he was personally asked by General Matsui to investigate whether Nanking was still peaceful and orderly. He writes: "I explored every inch of Nanking. The population, and the city was safe enough for women to venture out alone at night. I submitted a report to that effect to Gen. Matsui."[8] However, Masaaki undertook the task in July 1938, a full seven months after the fall of Nanking. No significance can be attached to what could only be termed as Masaaki's "limited experience."

Perhaps a more animated debate centres on the number of people massacred at Nanking. Most recently, a controversial month-long study of the massacre by the Japanese ruling party concluded from government archives that some 20,000 people were killed instead of the generally accepted numbers of 150,000 to 200,000 dead.[9] Understandably, Masaaki also contends that very few people were killed.

This is singularly unfortunate because numbers from other historians reach well into the hundreds of thousands. For example, Tomio has asserted that there were as many as 200,000 victims while Chang has cited numbers ranging from 260,000 to 350,000 people killed. Even the self-described "moderate proponent" of the Nanking atrocities Hata Ikuhiko lists an estimate of 38,000 to 42,000.[10] Thus the Japanese government's continued ploy of minimising the number of victims killed signifies yet another aspect of denial.

What is the price we ask for our friendship? Justice, and the comity usually observed between nation and nation.

—**Thomas Jefferson**

The denial of the Nanking Massacre continues to test Sino-Japanese relationships. China blames Japan for failing to repent for its war of aggression and humanitarian crimes. Japanese mistrust of China also runs deep and emanates from the country's right wing and nationalist groups. Ultra right-wingers assert that Japan's militaristic and expansionist aggression in Asia was a war 'liberating Asia from Western colonialism.'

But it is not only Sino-Japanese relations that are affected. The Imperial Japanese Army committed crimes all over South Asia. There is ample evidence to suggest that the Japanese developed and tested chemical and biological weapons against prisoners of war and civilians in Asia. Tens of thousands of Asian women were forced to become "comfort women" or sex slaves for the Japanese army. These incidents not only evoke the wrath of Chinese activists but South Korea and Taiwan as well.

At the heart of each controversy lies a common thread of historical resentment. Only by banishing such resentment can Japan ensure permanent peace with its neighbours. The Japanese government has taken some initiatives to heal war wounds, e.g. it announced the Asian Women's Fund to compensate "comfort women" at the 50th anniversary of the end of World War II. Victims also received a letter of apology signed by the incumbent Japanese Prime Minister. But the fund became the subject of some debate when South Korean and Taiwanese critics pointed out that the letter was a personal rather than an official apology and the compensation came from charity funds instead of state coffers.[11]

Moreover, China declined such a system for Chinese comfort

women. Mr. Haruki Wada, executive director of the fund, explained that "there were lots of different sorts of victims of the war in China, and...it was difficult for the Chinese government just to single out comfort women for help."[12]

The Japanese government also makes a point that it has compensated China through the 1951 San Francisco Peace Treaty and points out that China agreed to forgo demands for war reparations in the 1972 joint communiqué. But an official apology by the Japanese government for its war crimes has not been forthcoming.

Several Japanese Prime Ministers have offered personal regrets over Japan's war policies. For example, former Prime Minister Tomiichi Murayama made a "heartfelt apology" at the 50th anniversary of the end of the Second World War.[13] However, these statements are a weak substitute for an official national apology by the Japanese government. Meanwhile Japanese history books continue to downplay past war crimes. The visits by former Prime Minister Junichiro Koizumi to the Yasukuni shrine, which honours 14 convicted or suspected Imperial Army war criminals, also damaged Japan's relations with its East Asian neighbours.

Most recently, Prime Minister Shinzo Abe roused criticism when he told reporters that Asian comfort women were not forced to become sex slaves by the Imperial Army, since there was "no evidence to prove there was coercion' involved."[14] It seems that conservative Japanese politicians continue to doubt the extent of the country's wartime atrocities. These latest attempts seem a dramatic volte-face from the Japanese government's 1993 acknowledgement that the Imperial Army ran brothels for its troops during the war to the current denial of the "coercion" of sex slaves. Immediately, the US Congress passed a resolution calling on Abe to "formally acknowledge, apologise and accept historical responsibility" for the comfort women.

Who remembers now the destruction of the Armenians?

—**Adolph Hitler**

Hitler is reported to have said this statement during a meeting with his generals in August 1939, in which he justifies the Polish invasion and the creation of a new world order. It seems that he was aware of the Armenian genocide perpetrated by the Young Turk government. It is not improbable that the failure of the world in remembering the destruction of the Armenians led Hitler to believe that his own crimes against humanity would be similarly forgotten. After all, what better immunity for war crimes is there than global amnesia?

We must think carefully about Hitler's proclamation, and how it triggered the tyrannical excesses of an authoritarian government. Mankind has, through the ages, shown itself to be capable of unimaginable horror. We need to be reminded of this inhumanity so that succeeding generations need not suffer needless carnage. We must strive to better ourselves, and it seems that a sure-fire way of doing that is by bolstering the democratic institutions of our countries. As Iris Chang stated in an interview:

"We should see it [the Nanking Massacre] as a story that transcends what the Japanese did to the Chinese and a metaphor of what a human being can do to another human being. We have to be vigilant to understand how these atrocities happened and make sure that power is defused among people in a democratic system, because it seems that only democracy prevents these kinds of things from happening."[15]

It is not a coincidence that the worst atrocities committed by the human race usually occur in a political setup that lacks democratic legitimacy. The very nature of dictatorships is such that a small group of persons wield untrammeled power over a wider community. In such states, power is concentrated in the hands of the few rather than dispersed among the many.

Democracy, however, promotes integration among the general public and ensures that everyone in even the most diverse of countries is suitably represented in state organs and engaged with political issues that affect them all. Only democratic peoples are sensitized to the needs and concerns of their fellow human beings. Ideologies of hate, such as wartime persecution of innocent civilians, do not usually take root in nations that adopt such a system of government.

What is most distressing is that the Nanking Massacre itself was so easily forgotten in the Western world until the issue was taken up by Iris Chang in *The Rape of Nanking*. Throughout her childhood, Chang had thought about the Japanese atrocities that her parents told her about but could find no information about them in libraries. As she informs us: "I learned about the event from my parents. Then in December 1994 I went to a Cupertino conference on the Nanjing Massacre and learned that there was no English-language book on the subject. I wanted to change that situation."[16]

As responsible global citizens, we must follow in Chang's footsteps and bring the Rape of Nanking and other atrocities to the fore in international political discourse. We must make others aware of how denial of massacres such as Nanking amount to a kind of racial abuse that negates the pain of victims and survivors and demeans it as a solely Chinese concern. In fact, Nanking is a proper concern of all humanity.

For these reasons, we must designate a suitable day – perhaps the day Nanking fell to the Japanese on the 13th of December nearly seventy years ago – as a worldwide Memorial Day for the Nanking Massacres. We must commemorate the numerous sufferers of Japanese persecution to make sure that such crimes are not repeated. In this way, we may be able to avoid what Chang has termed the second rape of Nanking, that is, silence about the massacres.

Compared to the Holocaust, the Nanking atrocities still lie in relative obscurity. As a historian, Iris Chang sought to amend this. The utility of the historian underlies the fact that people possess short memories. Part of his or her work is to counteract claims that historic facts can ever be viewed in isolation. Those that do not remember the past, warned George Santayana, are condemned to repeat it. If we accept this proposition, then it becomes clear that history is a cyclic phenomenon rather than a chronologically linear timeline some would have us believe.

Any doctrine averse to this conception of history is not only irksome but ignorant. Thus, the way forward must be to embrace history rather than to deny it. To heal the wounds of war, Japan must offer an adequate apology for the Nanking tragedy, pay compensation to survivors and teach future Japanese generations about its dark past. Only by confronting the ghosts of history can we finally exorcise them.

1. Stanton, Gregory, "The Eight Stages of Genocide," Genocide Watch (1996), available at http://www.genocidewatch.org/8stages1996.htm.

2. "What Westerners Witnessed — A Collection of Diaries, Letters and Other Documents Written by Members of the International Committee for the Nanking Safety Zone" Online Documentary: The Nanking Atrocities, available at http://www.geocities.com/nankingatrocities/Terror/terror_03.htm.

3. Chang, Iris, "*The Rape of Nanking: The Forgotten Holocaust*," Penguin Books: New York (1998) at p. 59.

4. Ibid., at p. 49.

5. Ibid., at p. 47.

6. Chapel, Joseph, "Denying Genocide: The Evolution of the Denial of the Holocaust and the Nanking Massacre," Student Research Paper for UCSB History 133P Proseminar (2004), available at http://www.history.ucsb.edu/faculty/marcuse/classes/133p/133p04papers/JChapelNanjing046.htm.

7. Ibid.

8. Masaaki, Tanaka, In the Introduction to "What Really Happened in Nanking: the Refutation of a Common Myth," available at http://www.ne.jp/asahi/unko/tamezou/nankin/whatreally/index.html#foreword.

9. The Associated Press, "Ruling Party Lawmakers Dispute 'Rape of Nanking' Death Toll" International Herald Tribune (June 19, 2007), available at http://www.iht.com/articles/ap/2007/06/19/asia/AS-GEN-Japan-Rape-of-Nanking.php.

10. Ikuhiko, Hata, "The Nanking Atrocities: Fact and Fable," Japan Echo (August 1998), available at http://www.wellesley.edu/Polisci/wj/China/Nanjing/nanjing2.html.

11. Hogg, Chris, "Japan's divisive 'comfort women' fund" BBC News, Tokyo (10 April 2007), available at http://news.bbc.co.uk/1/hi/world/asia-pacific/6530197.stm.

12. Ibid.

13. Murayama, Tomiichi, "On the occasion of the 50th anniversary of the war's end" (15 August 1995), available at http://www.mofa.go.jp/announce/press/pm/murayama/9508.html.

14. "Abe Questions Sex Slave 'Coercion'", BBC News (Friday, 2 March 2007), available at http://news.bbc.co.uk/1/hi/world/asia-pacific/6530197.stm

15. Yu, Jim, "A CND Interview With Iris Chang" CND (February 24, 1998), available at http://www.cnd.org/CND-Global/CND-Global.98.1st/CND-Global.98-02-23.html.

16. Ibid.

Minjie Chen
Graduate Student
Urbana, Illinois, USA

Stories for the Young

It all started on the morning of a late summer day in year 1942. People in my hometown had barely gotten used to the shriek of air alarms and the routine of dropping everything and seeking safety at the earliest alert, or "escaping the flying machine," ［逃飛機］ a new word in the Yunhe dialect of southwest Zhejiang Province, China, which meant running towards air raid shelters. The bombings on August 26th and the next day were strange. Bombs whooshed down from the sky, punching holes through roofs and into the ground, but they did not explode. Though townsfolk suspected it, they would take decades of time to fully understand the secret connection between the "dummy" bombs released by the Japanese army and the darkest days that befell the place: Soon afterwards, the bubonic plague swept the tiny town and surrounding villages, just as it did in many other cities in China during the Pacific War, cutting lives short and tearing families apart.

After losing his wife and two youngest sons to the deadly disease, my grandfather, then a man in his thirties, married again and found a stepmother for his remaining four children. A baby daughter was born into the new family. Many years later, she would have her own daughter, who was named Minjie and who is telling you this story. Yes, I was brought into the world via a carefully planned genocide. The bacteria of the plague were first cultivated through medical experiments conducted on live human beings, then mass produced, and, finally, deliberately spread to murder Chinese civilians. Unit 731, a Japanese detachment disguised as a water purification unit in northeastern China, was the most notorious killer behind the biological warfare (Harris, 2002).

Until I finished a family history project with my mother as part of my doctoral coursework at the University of Illinois, Urbana-Champaign, however, I was unburdened by any knowledge of the biggest irony about my life. Even after I learnt about the disaster from which dwindling, and elderly, survivors in my hometown were still suffering physically and mentally with absolutely no compensation from the Japanese government, I did not stop asking why the murder had become a secret in the very place it was committed. Growing up in this mountainous town in the 1980s and 1990s, except for some brief mentions of the plague by my parents, I had never read about it in history textbooks, nor heard about it when local history and information was taught in school. I never encountered the topic in children's books that I read as a child. There was no, and still is no, memorial museum or monument to remind residents and visitors of the pain and horror that once haunted here, not that our poor rural town has established a museum of any sort. It was not surprising that daughters of my cousins', both Chinese teenagers at high school, admitted never having heard of the plague in Yunhe and never having expected that Japanese wartime atrocities struck so close to home, although they were well aware of the Nanking Massacre, "comfort women," and medical experiments by Unit 731—currently the three best publicized Japanese war crimes by Chinese media.

I did not feel the urge to break the silence and secrecy until a year ago. I was reading Hiroshima No Pika, a picture book assigned in my doctoral seminar on youth literature. Toshi Maruki, the Japanese author and illustrator[1], used powerful images to tell the traumatic experience of a little girl and her family during the atomic bombing of Hiroshima. Maruki's bold rendering of a horrific topic for a young audience awakened me from nonchalance. I asked myself: I have read many children's books about China and Chinese published in the U.S. How come that not one of them told Chinese experience during World War II? A search in the online catalog of the University of Illinois Library, which held the second largest collection of children's and young adult literature in the United State, found not a single juvenile title focused on Japanese war crimes committed in China. Iris Chang's groundbreaking work, ***The Rape of Nanking: The Forgotten Holocaust of World War II***, is not for the faint heart and hardly an age-appropriate reading for youth under fourteen. Not that atrocities and genocide are taboo topics for young readers. Our library has collected about two hundred titles, dozens of which award-winning books, written on the Jewish Holocaust for youth.

In fact, according to a comprehensive bibliography compiled by Sullivan, 495 titles of English-language Holocaust literature intended for young people from kindergarten to high school had been published through 1999, forming a rich and mature body of literature encompassing diversified age level, genre, perspective, and subject matter. American authors do not shun other grim and ugly topics such as the apartheid system in South Africa, genocides in Armenia and Cambodia, the enslavement of Africans, ethnic cleansing in the former Yugoslavia, the atomic bombing of Hiroshima and Nagasaki, Japanese-American internment, and the Native American experience in the Americas, and have published more than a hundred titles for youth (Sullivan, 1999).

I left the library feeling disappointed and outraged. The American publishing industry of youth literature boasts an output of 5,000 titles each year, yet it could afford little room for stories about what happened during Japan's invasion and colonization of China, a country where one fifth of the world population dwells. Young people may come across this history from other sources — newspapers, television documentaries (one of my friends cited the History Channel as the source from which she learnt about Japan's biological warfare in China), movies, the Internet, and, for older teens, even a handful of books targeting adult readers, but the dearth of information about Chinese experience during World War II in youth literature must be changed.

I was by far not the first person to notice the issue. After hearing about the Rape of Nanking from her parents, a young Iris Chang searched the local public libraries but nothing about the massacre turned up (Chang, 1997, p. 8). American school textbooks are an equally poor source for information about Japan's wartime atrocities in Asia. Chang did a thorough examination of secondary-school history textbooks in the United Sates and found that "only a few even mention the Rape of Nanking" (1997, p. 6). There has not been substantial improvement for the past ten years. In a recent study, Zhao examined eight American and world history textbooks commonly used in middle and high school social studies classrooms, and found no mention of the major war crimes committed by Japanese troops: the Nanking Massacre, "comfort women," and the Japanese biological warfare. Zhao's informal survey of 55 social studies teachers indicated that none of them had ever taught about these war crimes in their history classrooms. Only seven of them knew about the Nanking Massacre, either learnt through Chang's book or heard from friends who had read the book (Zhao and Hoge, 2006).

I shared with my class the story of my family's experience during the plague, a story which was told from my grandfather to my mother and from her to me. I hoped the small audience of ten classmates, who were future faculty in the teaching and research of literature and library services for young people, would pass my story on and gain a new critical perspective in American youth literature.

With my advisor's encouragement and under her guidance, I shifted the focus of my dissertation research to information sources about the Sino-Japanese War (1937-1945) for American and Chinese young people. Too many questions puzzled me since I became aware of the uneven treatment of World War II atrocities in books written for American young readers. Why is there only scanty information in US publications about World War II history in China? What has contributed to this historical amnesia? What is the relationship between a changing political climate — particularly the development of the Cold War and international relationships among U.S., China, and Japan — and the memory curve in this country?

My initial research in novels found thirty titles, considered suitable reading for young people, set during Imperial Japan's invasion of China from 1931 to the end of World War II. Exactly half of them were published from 1940 through 1946. Often written by authors who were familiar with Chinese culture and life, these stories showed the suffering and bravery of Chinese people, particularly children, during war years. Interest in the Chinese experience under Japan's occupation varied, evidenced by the intensity of publications when the American "Flying Tigers" were helping China to fight Japan, but which died down rapidly after the U.S. and Communist China became enemies. Until Iris Chang revived the memory of the Rape of Nanking in the Western world, publications of juvenile novels on the Sino-Japanese War were far between and sparse. Out of the thirty titles, only nine remain in print today, and quite a few of the in-print tend to be books written for adults though readable for high school students.

Quality issues in Chinese publications about the Sino-Japanese War, too, caught my attention. The seemingly ample Chinese-language information about the combat history of the Sino-Japanese War is overwhelmingly about Chinese guerillas fighting against Japan and resistance led by the Chinese Communist Party. Thanks to the Chinese civil war (1946-1949) and Cold War, achievements and sacrifices made by the Chinese Nationalist army and American aid were conspicuously missing in the children's books and school textbooks that I examined in a preliminary survey. Despite increasing publications which disclose Japan's wartime atrocities in China, little has been offered to help Chinese youth understand racism and prejudice—the real danger that can turn men and women into murderers and torturers.

Some other research questions apply to youth literature in both Chinese and English. Is it possible to tell young people about Japanese wartime atrocities when popular writers and historians, whose opinions range from total denials to indignant condemnations, are still contending over many issues and facts? Is it possible to portray the violence and horror of Imperial Japan's atrocities honestly and sensitively for young children? Writers of Holocaust youth literature have tried multiple strategies to present the unspeakable horror without overwhelming young readers (Jordan, 2004), though it is still debated whether some of the writings risked watering down the inhumanities of the Nazis.

Why ask these questions, and do they matter? These queries point to a striking gap between mission and action in the education of American youth about "multiculturalism." To help young people learn about other ethnic or cultural groups and to enable people of diverse origins and backgrounds to see themselves in literature, teachers have children celebrate festivals honored by all kinds of cultures, and librarians display exquisitely illustrated world folktales. Festivals, folktales, as well as food and traditional clothing, are among the most ostensible and entertaining features by which you tell one culture apart from another. They are not, I would argue, defining or reliable features of some cultures. (I am Chinese even though my diet often consists of sandwiches and I rarely walk around in cheongsam.) Given the huge impact of the war against Japan on Chinese politics and culture, on the lives of the Chinese people, and on international relationships among China, Japan, and the U.S., it is a much less rewarding attempt to understand contemporary China and its people without knowledge of its World War II history. For some first- and second-generation immigrants from China, experience or knowledge of the war is also part of their heritage and cultural identity, and is thus meaningful to those Chinese-Americans as well.

Through a comparative study of juvenile literature and history textbooks about the Sino-Japanese War for American and Chinese young people, I plan to search for possible answers to these questions. I will measure the quality of information produced for young readers about the Chinese experience during the Pacific War, using such criteria as historical accuracy, cultural authenticity, literary appeal, and age appropriateness. I wish to show American and Chinese publishers, authors, teachers, and librarians who work with children gaps and flaws in the existing body of literature, as well as to illuminate ways for enrichment and improvement.

My family story displeased a classmate from Japan. The granddaughter of a man who suffered in the atomic bombing of Hiroshima, she sent me a raging email saying that "Chinese are worse than we Japanese." I was unable to engage her in an open discussion with me. By the time people in China and elsewhere reach an accurate understanding of Imperial Japan's role in the Pacific War, and a heightened awareness of its ongoing impact upon Asia, I hope more Japanese like her will, too, see that to confront history in its true and ugly form is part of understanding ourselves, something we must all do.

A final agenda item in my research is to collect more stories from my hometown about the Japanese invasion and the plague. Many complex factors, including poor scientific understanding and political disruption, have contributed to the well kept secrecy of our World War II history. For example, my townsfolk were unable to decipher the sophisticated germ war plan developed by Japanese medical scientists, who mostly received immunity from the American military in a dirty exchange of the scientific data concerning biological warfare weapons for immunity (Harris, 2002). When the bombs did not explode, some of them went so far as surmising, it was perhaps a miracle blessed by local goddesses and gods! Story tellers will pass our unforgettable history on to the children of my town, and position themselves in a larger historical and international picture to show who they really are and what responsibilities they owe to people of the past, present, and future. Stories will travel far away to nourish other young people whose true appreciation of a multicultural society will benefit a world where tolerance, understanding, and peace are still wanting.

(1) Chang, I. (1997). *The Rape of Nanking: The forgotten holocaust of World War II.* New York, NY: BasicBooks.

(2) Harris, S. H. (2002). Factories of death: Japanese biological warfare, 1932-1945, and the American cover-up (Rev. ed.). New York: Routledge.

(3) Jordan, S. D. (2004). Educating without overwhelming: Authorial strategies in children's Holocaust literature. Children's Literature in Education, 35(3), 199-218.

(4) Sullivan, E. T. (1999). The Holocaust in literature for youth: A guide and resource book. Lanham, Md: Scarecrow Press.

(5) Toshi Maruki from HarperCollins Publishers. (2006). Retrieved June 29, 2007, from http://www.harpercollins.com/authors/17599/Toshi_Maruki/index.aspx

(6) Zhao, Y., & Hoge, J. D. (2006). Countering textbook distortion: War atrocities in Asia, 1937-1945. Social Education, 70(7), 424-430.

(7) 南京大虐殺の図(1975年). (2005). Retrieved June 29, 2007, from http://www.aya.or.jp/~marukimsn/kyosei/nanking.htm

1. Dedicated to campaigning for nuclear disarmament and world peace, Toshi Maruki and her husband Iri Maruki collaborated on paintings of other atrocities, including one created in 1975 about *the Rape of Nanking* ("Toshi Maruki," 2006; "南京大虐殺の図," 2005).

Adrienne Yi Ling Chuck
Student, College Undergraduate
Middlebury, Vermont, USA

The Causes of Japan's Disregard and Denial of its War Crimes

Although they occurred over half a century ago, the atrocities committed by Japan during World War II is still a volatile issue discussed today. Whether or not Japan has repented for the crimes it committed, and whether or not adequate reparations have been made to the victims, are the matters being debated. Unlike most other perpetrating nations, Japan has managed to avoid a large amount of international scrutiny for its crimes. Both the cultural traditions of Japanese society and a series of post-war events that led the Japanese to forget their war crimes are the cause of this. The consequences of losing WWII, the alliance between Japan and the United States, and the Japanese government's unwillingness to educate its people have created an isolated environment for the Japanese public, leading them to disregard and deny the WWII atrocities.

The Consequences of Losing WWII

One of the main reasons why Japan did not feel the guilt involved with committing an atrocity is because they felt victimized after the war. World War II ended with the bombing of Hiroshima and Nagasaki, which were widely publicized and achieved worldwide sympathy for the victims. The bombings caused a diversion of international and domestic attention from Japan's unjust acts during the war to the rebuilding of the bombed cities. The Japanese also felt victimized because of economic consequences from losing the war. The public's response to the Tokyo Trials was to reject the validity of the sentences instead of denouncing the behavior of the accused officials.

As Richard Falk puts it, the trials were seen as "an acknowledgement imposed by the victors in the war, and not by the Japanese government or the Japanese people."[1] They called the accused military officials the "victims of the War Crimes Trials," and developed a "surge of compassion"[2] for them. Instead of being shunned by the Japanese public, the accused criminals were welcomed back to their nation with honor and acceptance.

After the Second World War, the Japanese blocked out the memory of the loss by focusing their attention elsewhere. For the Japanese, "the end of the war meant an end to the hardship of war and a concentrated turn to the many, and often painful, changes accompanying democratization."[3] Many civilians had anti-war and anti-nationalistic feelings, believing that the government's propaganda drove the support for the war. So the Japanese developed a pacifist constitution and worked on rebuilding their nation through new democratic privileges. Their change in focus towards economic development was "based on their own sufferings, in other words, on the memory of the Japanese people as victims."[4] Although the nation recovered through taking a peaceful route, their aversion from war made them forget their crimes. The memory of the atrocities started to fade as the nation became economically stable during the 1960s. Later, the Japanese grew "tired of ongoing discussions of responsibility and compensation for things that happened more than a half-century ago. Many seem[ed] also to be seeking a positive identity and role in the world appropriate to the global superpower Japan had become."[5] Japan chose to turn its back on the past and to focus solely on the future.

The Alliance between Japan and the United States

The alliance between Japan and the United States that diverted international attention away from Japanese war crimes, leading to a lack of guilt on Japan's part, was a result of the Cold War and the U.S. occupation. The Cold War affected the international community's scrutiny of Japanese war crimes. The United States was pleased that Japan adopted democratic ideals so willingly and "valued Japan's position as a strategic ally during the Cold War."[6] China, one of the countries victimized by Japan, was a Communist nation and therefore an enemy in the U.S.'s eyes. The Western nations were not about to break the alliance they had with Japan by antagonizing it to come to terms with its crimes. In addition, after WWII, China was in the midst of a civil war and "both the Chinese governments purposefully neglected the incident as they focused on establishing their political and economic strength."[7] International focus was not on Japan's war crimes.

Despite the restrictions and censorship it imposed on Japan, the occupation played a significant role in Japan's denial. Trade and relations between the U.S. and Japan flourished. Compared to the Nuremberg Trials, the Tokyo Trials were much more lenient, perhaps because the United States felt guilty for dropping atomic bombs on Hiroshima and Nagasaki. Only a few very high-ranking officials like General Matsui (responsible for the Nanking Massacre) were prosecuted to represent the larger portion of perpetrators.[8] And even so, others who were considerably more responsible for war crimes went free. As Kato Shuichi says, "ministers of General Tojo's Cabinet, the equivalent of Hitler's, returned to power quietly as political leaders in postwar Japan; ex-officers of the Tokko (special police), the Japanese counterpart of the Gestapo, came to hold quite influential positions in the administration after the war."[9] The Asian victims were not given the same media attention that the Jews were given after the war. Richard Falk even goes so far to say that "racial, ethnic, religious, and cultural factors made most Americans feel more affinity with European victims than with Asian victims."[10]

The United States also hid evidence of certain atrocities. In the case of Unit 731, General Douglas MacArthur traded with Japan to get the experiments' documents and prevented international exposure of the crime. His defense was that he was trying to protect the U.S. from the Russians, who might have purchased the data and waged biological warfare.[11] The scientists who had conducted terrible experiments on prisoners were integrated back into Japanese society as professors at top universities or esteemed scientists.[12]

Japan's Reluctance to Educate Its People

Japan, as the perpetrating nation, did not go to many lengths to educate its people of the atrocities. The government either neglected to reveal information or destroyed the proof right after the war. It has never undertaken on its own initiative any trial of any person for war crimes, a sharp contrast with German attitudes toward Nazi misconduct.[13] The government also placed pressure on those who knew about the atrocities to keep quiet. Saburo Ienaga, a professor who has written history textbooks, explains that despite the new freedoms of expression granted by the U.S. occupation, all post-war textbooks were reviewed and censored by the Ministry of Education. In 1983, Ienaga wrote that Unit 731's "cruel experiments" on thousands of Chinese "were murder," and the examiner response was: "No credible scholarly research—articles or books—have yet been published on this issue; it is premature to discuss it in a textbook."[14] The government went to the same lengths to control the flood of international coverage entering the nation. Foreign newspapers and magazines were confiscated before they reached Japanese readers.[15] The flood of new information revealing Japan's war crimes came only after the death of Emperor Hirohito, the nation's leader during WWII, in 1989. It wasn't until the death of the Showa Emperor that victims could speak of their suffering.[16]

The fact that very few perpetrators came forward to confess their crimes also fueled the public's denial of them. In many cases, the perpetrators did not believe themselves to be criminals. As Ienaga puts it, pre-war Japanese society was "inculcated with militarism through the school system" and "the steady diet of chauvinistic information encouraged jingoism."[17] Japan's aggressive military nature helped justify the various acts of brutality. There were also aspects of Japanese pre-war culture that led to an intense racism towards other Asian nations. Hora Tomio, Fujiwara Akira and Yoshida Yutaka wrote about "the oppressive nature of Japan's pre-war military system and the emperor-centered nationalist ideology, which led to a contempt for the Chinese people."[18] Concerning the rapes of the comfort women and civilians in Nanking, Kasahara Tokushi suggests that the "sexual abuse of women" was "deeply rooted in pre-war society."[19] The mentality of women as property rather than human beings mirrors the underlying chauvinism in Japanese culture. The Japanese public's welcome of returning veterans also reinforced their mindset of innocence. After the war, there was little mea culpa for Japanese soldiers as victimizers of other Asian nations. No one was accused for the Nanking massacre, the biological experiments on human bodies, or for the deportation of the Koreans to be used as forced labor in the Japanese mines, where many of them died.[20]

Many soldiers did not feel guilty. After the Tokyo Trials passed, there were not many accusations made until the late 20th century, when victims of war crimes finally spoke out. However, to speak out was to be a traitor to Japan. Until the 1980s, when much more information on the atrocities was revealed, many perpetrators had gotten off free.

Journalists contributed to Japanese amnesia because they did not think that it was their responsibility to report such events. Despite new postwar freedoms of speech and limited government censorship, the "writers felt that it was neither their place nor duty to write about issues that would denounce Japan's reputation, and they most likely did not have the verified information to do so."[21] Proof of the atrocities was hard to obtain, and in some cases, the writers believed that writing about the issue was inappropriate. Most post-war literature did not involve politics or history, perhaps because it contradicted all the pre-war Japanese propaganda. There was a trend amongst post-WWII writers in which they would "put up a front of ignorance, on the pretext that as writers they know nothing of politics, or just leave the pursuit of the emperor's war guilt to the Communist Party."[22] After the war, there were articles written on the atrocities in WWII, but as Van C. Gessel says that in "the war writings from the postwar perspective treat Japanese war atrocities, either to deny or defend them or to reflect on their meaning."[23] The results of this were that the war crimes became hidden, ignored, or skewed stories in Japanese history.

Consequentially, the Japanese public had no means of getting such information. Unlike the Germans, who were forced by the Allied powers to witness the Jewish concentration camps, the Japanese were not forced to realize the crimes of their nation. They were unaware of the events that took place overseas. Without a distribution of information from the international community, government, or domestic journalists, the Japanese public had no way of knowing. Kato Shuichi observes that "any sense of duty to know the past on the part of the educated public has failed."[24] Coming from an aggressive military culture, the Japanese people "considered Japan's crimes of the 1930s and 1940s as merely regrettable side effects of the war. For the Japanese people, they were, although unfortunate, understandable and therefore excusable."[25] In the eyes of the Japanese, aggression was merely a battle tactic, and at most an unfortunate byproduct of war.

Disregard Escalates to Denial

During the latter part of the 20th century, especially after the death of Emperor Hirohito and the flood of new information covering the atrocities, various points of view on the matter arose in Japan. Both pacifist and revisionist writers started to pay attention to the war crimes. Although there were groups that wanted to expose and preserve the memories of WWII such as the Nanjing Incident Study Group, many radical revisionist groups wanted to keep the atrocities hidden. In the 1980s, Fujioka Nobukatsu founded the Liberal View of History Study Group and the Society for the Making of New School Textbooks in History. In the mid 1990s, groups aimed to "correct" Japanese history.[26] His motto was that if "Japanese are not proud of their own country, they will not be respected in the world."[27] He insists that the accusations of comfort women are "a grand conspiracy for the destruction of Japan...The comfort women were professional prostitutes, earning more than a general in the imperial Japanese army, or as much as 100 times the pay of their soldier customers."[28] According to the Fujioka Society, these women were driven by greed and the desire for money. Fujioka is not the only one who takes a rightist view. Itakura Yoshiaki, a Japanese historian stated that the actual number of "illegally murdered" Chinese in Nanking was between 13,000 and 19,000, a huge difference compared with China's official number of 300,000.[29]

What worries many victim countries is that this ideology of preserving Japan's reputation is a popular one in Japan and particularly appeals to the current Japanese younger generation. In 1997, Fujioka's first two volumes of History Not Taught in Textbooks "became two of Japan's top ten best-sellers."[30] Kobayashi Yoshinori's comic book Sensoron, "On War," "became one of the main topics of intellectual debate in Japan in 1998 not only because of its effort to justify Japan's part in World War II but because it was popular among the young."[31] The result of these history revision movements is the incorrect education of an entire generation that will continue to deny responsibility for their nation's actions in future years.

Japan's amnesia of its war crimes is a result of its unique postwar situation: the consequences of losing the war, the alliance between Japan and the U.S. and the inefficient education of the Japanese public. The lack of international scrutiny has played a large role in that it has not placed pressure on the government to make its crimes known. The inherent traditions in Japan also led some Japanese to view the crimes as effects of war instead of as human injustices. Meanwhile, Japanese citizens who have grown up without the knowledge of any war crimes don't know how to deal with the accusations. Japan's denial has placed strains on both international relations and national unity. What can Japan do to better this situation?

First of all, the nation should have no apprehensions to issuing a formal, written apology. Secondly, the government should make an effort to educate their people about the truth of the matter. They cannot stifle the viewpoints of the rightist groups aimed at revising history textbooks, but the Ministry of Education would be smart to approve textbooks that are internationally accepted. This in turn, would create a new identity for the Japanese public, instead of an evasion of responsibility. Thirdly, any artifacts that had been stolen during the Japanese occupation should be returned to the original countries. These actions would at least force Japan to admit its wrongdoings and gear the country towards a more peaceful and just future.

Bibliography

(1) Buzan, Barry, "Japan's Future: Old History versus New Roles." International Affairs

(Royal Institute of International Affairs 1944), 64.4 (Autumn, 1988): 557-573. JSTOR. Middlebury College, Middlebury, VT. 19 October 2006. <http://www.jstor.org/jstor>.

(2) Hein, Laura and Selden, Mark, Censoring History: Citizenship and Memory In Japan, Germany, and the United States. Armonk, New York: M.E. Sharpe Inc., 2000.

(3) Ienaga, Saburo. "The Glorification of War in Japanese Education." International Security, 18.3 (Winter 1993-1994): 113-133. JSTOR. Middlebury College, Middlebury, VT. 19 October 2006. <http://www.jstor.org/jstor>.

(4) "Japan," Encyclop?dia Britannica. 2006. Encyclop?dia Britannica Online. 9 December 2006. <http://search.eb.com/eb/article-23185>.

(5) Li, Fei Fei, Robert Sabella and David Liu, Nanking 1937: Memory and Healing. Armonk, New York: M.E. Sharpe Inc., 2002.

(6) Schlant, Ernestine and J. Thomas Rimer, Legacies and Ambiguities: Postwar Fiction and Culture in West Germany and Japan. Washington, D.C.: The Woodrow Wilson Center Press, 1991.

(7) Williams, Peter and David Wallace, Unit 731: Japan's Secret Biological Warfare in World War II. New York: The Free Press, 1989.

(8) Yang, Daqing, "Convergence or Divergence? Recent Historical Writings on the Rape of Nanjing." The American Historical Review, 104.3 (June 1999): 842-865. JSTOR. Middlebury College, Middlebury, VT. 19 October 2006. <http://www.jstor.org/jstor>.

Citation list

1. Li, Fei Fei, Robert Sabella and David Liu. Nanking 1937: Memory and Healing. Armonk, New York: M.E. Sharpe Inc., 2002. 11.

2. Schlant, Ernestine and J. Thomas Rimer. Legacies and Ambiguities: Postwar Fiction and Culture in West Germany and Japan. Washington, D.C.: The Woodrow Wilson Center Press, 1991. 105.

3. Schlant, 7.

4. Schlant, 255.

5. Hein, Laura and Mark Selden. Censoring History: Citizenship and Memory In Japan, Germany, and the United States. Armonk, New York: M.E. Sharpe Inc., 2000. 58.

6. Li, xxiii.

7. Li, xxiii.

8. Schlant, 255.

9. Schlant, 255.

10. Li, 29.

11. Williams, Peter and David Wallace. Unit 731: Japan's Secret Biological Warfare in World War II. New York: The Free Press, 1989. 135.

12. Williams, 236-240.

13. Schlant, 255.

14. Ienaga, Saburo. "The Glorification of War in Japanese Education." International Security, 18.3 (Winter 1993-1994): 113-133. JSTOR. Middlebury College, Middlebury, VT. 19 October 2006. <http://www.jstor.org/jstor>. 127.

15. Li, 85.

16. Hein,. 25.

17. Ienaga, 115-116.

18. Yang, Daqing. "Convergence or Divergence? Recent Historical Writings on the Rape of Nanjing." The American Historical Review, 104.3 (June 1999): 842-865. JSTOR. Middlebury College, Middlebury, VT. 19 October 2006. <http://www.jstor.org/jstor>. 855.

19. Yang, 856.

20. Schlant, 255.

21. Schlant, 102.

22. Schlant, 180.

23. Schlant, 216.

24. Schlant, 253.

25. Schlant, 45.

26. Hein, 56.

27. Hein, 26.

28. Hein, 60.

29. Yang, 852.

30. Hein, 25.

31. Hein, 81.

Victor Fic
Freelance Writer and Broadcaster
CBS News/Seoul
Seoul, South Korea

Japan's War Guilt: East Asia's Cold Dawn

Every day, the sun rises in East Asia first. Each dawn, its golden rays slowly seep into the dark night sky until the light turns the heavens bright. Unfortunately, the morning in many East Asian people's hearts is cold. Instead of a heartening sense of amity and cooperation, frigid feelings of resentment cause the day to fall short of a new beginning.

The chief reason is not meterological, but ethical. A certain island nation guilty of colonizing a dozen of its neighbours -- and killing millions of them — in an arc of aggression stretching from Pyongyang to Rangoon remains a moral pariah. In 1945, WW 2 in East Asia ended with the Japanese high command quietly signing a surrender document aboard the battleship USS Missouri's gray deck in Tokyo Bay while Asians cheered the sounds of their shackles falling off. Yet Japanese officials and their society have largely failed to analyze how and why they waged war — nor have they properly atoned.

The several ramifications are deep and negative. This essay is the fruit of a professional journalist's years of study and reflection on this cardinal subject. It scrutinizes how lingering, sometimes raging, mistrust of Japan has undermined or compromised the spread of liberal ideals such as cooperation and democracy in no less than four germaine areas: Japan's relations with its Korean neighbors, its ties to America, its interaction with the world community and finally Japan's sense of democratic self hood — a too often overlooked sphere. The analysis melds three variables. These are political analysis of how countries relate; the human factor, which comprises feelings of hurt or trust; and finally some personal experiences, too, which highlight the color and telling details in a subject about real people, who deserve to be chronicled as such.

Part 1: Japan and its Neighbours

I see them every Wednesday afternoon standing at the Japanese embassy's front gate when I leave my office next to that facility to buy lunch. They are a group of elderly women who gather weekly to hold placards and shout slogans demanding that Japan apologize and compensate them for forcing them into sexual slavery. Most are in their 70's or higher. The faces which were smooth as rose petals when the Japanese forced them into servitude are now creased with lines that bespeak the leaden passing of decades during which their pain and anger tore at them inside. But they all wear pink, blue, yellow or green hanboks (tranditional Korean dresses) and resemble a human rainbow. During the rainy season, liquid bullets pelt them. The summer's humidity causes visor-clad supporters half their age to guzzle cans of isotonic drinks. Yet they have appeared regularly for over ten years. Clearly, when an octogenerian heart is set on winning justice, even wobbly legs can turn to iron.

The embassy is a squat, four story structure of brown bricks. The flag that it flies is fastened to its roof so that it is not fire bombed. From my office's sixth floor corner window, I note the emblem is self sequestered like someone who suspects he has much to be ashamed of. Most conspicuous are security features: a long, high wall, the buses of security police parked 24 hours per day and above all the camera. It's a rectanbular, metal contraption festooned to the brick work that scans the front through a red lens. The Japanese officials within — they never greet or console the protesters — view their ex-victims through that mechanical, bloodless eye.

Given Tokyo's well documented refusal to apologize or to compensate the comfort women, relations between Japan and both Koreas remain strained. South Korean polls conclude that about two thirds of Koreans distrust their ex-colonial overlord.

Does that surprise anyone? During the 1965 normalization talks between Seoul and Tokyo, the Japanese negotiator yelled that Korea deserved all it got and that Japan had done wonders there. Rather than paying Korea direct compensation, Japan opted for $800 million worth of aid, some of which built the Pusan-Seoul expressway on which Japanese imports speed to the capital's markets. The big winner? Japanese industry.

In 1996, Japan proposed a "forward oriented" relationship predicated on a final, concrete apology after which Korea would foreswear insisting on contrition. Kim Dae-jung, the South Korean president, accepted the deal in early 1998. This analyst doubted if it would work straight off. That spring, at a closed session of the leading Korean Institute of Defense Analysis convened so that I could present my views, I predicted that Japan would take, but not give. While living in Japan during the mid-90's, I observed that the country was renationalizing. For Korea to expect real remorse then was akin to demanding a man on a down escalator head up. In addition, I noted that Japan wanted Korea to lift import restrictions on Japanese popular culture products. Finally, it seemed apparent that with China ever stronger, Tokyo sought to woo Seoul as a counterweight. It seemed far sighted to predict that if Seoul fell for Tokyo's siren song, the former would project weakness — and one day feel betrayed.

Isn't that exactly what transpired? President Kim stopped fighting for the comfort women and in return Japanese Prime Minister Keizo Obuchi apologized, but within a few years, Japanese revisionist comments were again making headlines. Now Japan is minting money in the Korean market with no real concession (although it has failed to swing Korea away from the northern collusus that borders it). In 2003, Korean officials used the very expression "feel betrayed."

What are the concrete implications? To start, it is hard for Japan to actively defend the Korean peninsula. Japanese ground troops cannot be stationed there, with the burden falling on Koreans and Americans, even though Korea is Japan's protective buffer. Therefore, the national security equation is skewed such that the small and distant protect the strong and near.

However, Japan earns hundreds of millions of dollars in Korea. There is little wrong with profiting when one invests. But is it honorable to take from a bowl when one does not cook?

In addition, the unresolved tensions infuse unrelated issues with hostility, jeopardizing resolution. For instance, the two countries are at loggerheads over ownership of Tokdo/Takeshima island. Nationalists in Japan will push their claim to assert their power, garner publicity and shift Japan rightward. Meanwhile, Korean leaders feel equal compulsion to stand up to the "bullying." The relatively minor issue could be shelved or defused through a co-ownership scheme, but for yesterday's fire burning in too many bellies on both sides.

Plus, the two Koreas will be united one day. Decades apart will ensure that the physical Demilitarized Zone will give way to an invisible -- but equally cleaving — mental version. What will suture that broken Korean heart? Unfortunately, one glue could be anti-Japanese sentiment. Is it hard to picture pan-Korean politicians and an eager public will stomp their feet on the common ground of resenting Japan? This will not only hinder human and economic ties, but could additionally trigger a panicky or opportunistic backlash from Japan. It will engender symbolic and substantive standoffs, higher defense spending and also block or slow the emergence of a united East Asian community modeled on North America or the new Europe.

Finally, isn't it unnatural for two neighbours who have shared so much culture to be so alienated? Japan's bedrock culture largely entered that island nation from China through an ancient Korean kingdom called Paekche. Japan is to Korea and China as Italy is to Greece as the son is to the father. Yet in 2003, South Korean high schools preparing to send their pupils to Japan cancelled the sojourns the betrayal. In contrast, after the war, over 2,000 French and German cities twinned to exorcise the demons of hate from their collective soul. Japan and Korea cannot attain this. While one cannot quantify friendship, what reasonable person or competent diplomat abjures it? With historical animosity unresolved, however, Koreans continue to categorize Japan as the country that is closest on the map — but farthest away in spirit.

Part 2: Japan and the World

In 1956, Japan joined the United Nations. Its gift was a large, bronze bell. When struck, its curved and inscripted shell would emit deep gongs resonating through the air that symbolize a spreading peace. However, Tokyo conspicuously failed to join in UN peace-keeping operations (PKO) because suspicion deriving from its wartime rampage prevented its troops from venturing abroad.

After the 1991 Iraq War, which Japan did not join in, the US pressured Japan to do more for international peace. However, when Tokyo proposed legislation to permit Japanese soldiers from joining in PKO, Asians grabbed the megaphone. Singapore's first minister, Lee Kuan-Yew, intoned that tempting Japan to venture abroad was like offering liquor filled chocolates to an alcoholic.

While Japan does, in fact, have personnel serving under the blue UN flag now, it remains an econimic giant, but political dwarf. The world's second largest economy, one that has benefitted so copiously from the international system's openness, does too little to maintain it. This is unprincipled, ensures global hotspots do not cool as readily and generates tensions with those smaller, trusted countries that take risks in the hell's kitchen of world geopolitics.

Part 3: Japan and America

Boosters of the Japanese-American relationship often smilingly assert that the cowboy and the geisha have an ideal alliance. However, a dark clould now hangs over the alleged love fest. The US Congress has just passed legislation that calls upon Japan to resolve the comfort women's plight.

This is welcome because Washington and many Japan experts do not engage Japan's war crimes with the same fervor shown for studying — and usually lionizing — the country's schools or industry. Too many American scholars and journalists have deliberately or implicitly allied with their Japanese counterparts to turn Hiroshima into a shrine of Japanese nuclear martyrdom, largely overlooking the redress movement's efforts to similarly recall and honor the victims of Japanese fascism. Again, note how many Americans pen tear-stained or self-accusatory words about the bombed Japanese city compared to the very few who specialize on the sex slaves. Therefore, the new law somewhat rights the imbalance.

So what is the downside? Expect it to fuel resentment in Japan. The right wing there will denounce the measure as Japan bashing and wielding it as a crowbar to leverage the public mood toward backlash. However, sober Japanese experts argue that only "gaiatsu" or outside pressure produces results. Tokyo does not act, but reacts. This is partly because elite, control bureaucrats dominate public policy. The press is house broken through the "press clubs" system of journalist-officialdom implicit collusion that discourages tough minded reporting. The public has displayed the "higaisha ishiki" (victim mentality) stemming from the A-bombs.

Unfortunately, this is a long term, lose-lose scenario. Even as the US ramps up the pressure to get results on war responsibility because Japan evades it, the Japanese public feels arm twisted — and becomes less likely to "surrender" the next round. Japanese-American relations will be tenser and more retributive overall. For those who prize harmonious ties, Japan must be a more open society under equitable, pro-active leaders starting with the long neglected issue of imperial guilt.

For now, however, we can expect a Japan that tilts right. Note that the war time generation that can testify to its abuses is dying. The China challenge will encourage many Japanese to vote conservative. The tired economic field yields the harvest of desperation. A thoughtless — easily manipulted — younger generation hears mainly demagogues like Shintaro Ishihara because the progressives are cowed or deracinated. The forced congressional act will combine with these trends like a new ingredient splashed into a toxic cocktail and produce an illiberal drink.

Finally, this seasoned diplomatic observer asks, "What if Washington pushes Japan toward a more muscular foreign role without Japan atoning?" Then the US will be resented in Korea and China especially because the very country that America sees as a sheriff these others adjudge to be a villain. Seoul and Beijing usually see Washington as breaking Tokyo's chauvinism, but that appraisal could turn negative if neo-con pressure on Japan to "do more" is unmatched by exhortations that it "win trust." In America, this is an often overlooked, but seminal, dimension of the history issue evident to those here.

Part 4: Japan and Itself

Finally, does the Japanese public value democracy? It is not mechanical. Instead, democracy issues from attitudes toward human rights, truth telling and justice that animate courts, colleges and the media, making it like an acorn which — if nurtured — transmutes into an oak tree. Sadly, post-war Japan is closer to the seed than its full culmination. Administrative vice ministers have heaved or elbowed the national parliament and even prime ministers out of the dohyo (sumo ring) of political competition. Although some journalists like Katsuichi Honda dig for the truth, most are agents in the process of national consensus formation (nemawashi), relaying information from the top without sufficient probing. The schools focus on passing exams, not developing confidence, debate skills or worldliness. Overall, Japan's twin ideologies have been Japanism, or militant groupism, and GNPism, or unfettered industrial expansion. What if Japan faced its war guilt? To be sure, this would be akin to water and sunshine striking the germ. Imagine a Japanese prime minister who is a moral leader, activist collegians, a press corps that is a watch dog rather than temple dog and a court system that protects victims of appalling rights abuses. Wouldn't these be symptoms and cause of a new Japan that is confidently democratic?

The Japanese people would win, for philosophically and practically they would live at an exalted level, with students receiving a liberal tutoring. East Asia would advance as wounds heal and Japan bridges orient and occident. The US would also prefer a credible ally which stands shoulder to shoulder in defending peace rather than pledging to roll bandages and write checks. However, with the past unresolved, the democratic acorn remains embedded in rocky soil.

Conclusion

The best thing about today's dawn is that if it disappoints one, another follows tomorrow. Japan can still honor its victims. Geoffrey Chaucer's lament that "past is prologue" is partly true as the human condition (ningen joken) is partly lapidary, but it is also false because reasonable men can lead themselves from the desert of conflict into the pasture of peace. Will Japan experience this epiphany? If so, it will usher in a warm dawn.

Joe Goodwill
Writer/Researcher
Vancouver, British Columbia, Canada
Currently Master of Arts Graduate Student

2007 marks the 70th anniversary of the Nanking Massacre – one of the darkest events in the history of humanity. Yet as I write this essay, the perpetrators of this atrocity still have not acknowledged responsibility, apologized, made amends or offered compensation. Tony Blair recently stated that "Japan is putting its past behind it."[1] However, this will not do. It will not do because, as Iris Chang warned us, quoting George Santayana: "Those who cannot remember the past are condemned to repeat it".[2] And it will not do to forget the past, because to do so would be to continue to ignore a pressing moral imperative – one that cannot any longer be ignored because if we do ignore it, all of humanity is pulled down to a level that is less than we can and should be. And that degradation of the human spirit is the true cost of continuing to deny the holocaust that was the Nanking Massacre.

As a group, we human beings are unique within all the universe. As such, we are one great, diverse family. Imagine someone looking down at the beautiful blue and green earth from the heights of the heavens. Such a being would not see many separate groups – we would look like one great family, blessed with a beautiful planet to share. True, we are scattered throughout all the earth, but we are a family. And the thing about families is that we sink or swim together. When some human beings rise to great heights, they pull us all up with them, so that we all rise closer to the heavens. And when some human beings sink to unspeakable depths, they pull us all down with them, so that we all sink closer to the infernal depths. This is why it is a pressing moral imperative for the Japanese to apologize for the Nanking Massacre, once for all, unequivocally — with all their hearts and with all their humanity. For until they do so, we, the human race, each and every member of the great family of man, are one and all less than we should be.

The horrific crimes committed against innocent Chinese civilians by Japanese troops in Nanking in 1937 are a haunting example of the vilest depths to which humans can descend. This was conclusively documented by Iris Chang in her meticulously researched book, *The Rape of Nanking: The Forgotten Holocaust of World War II*. It was illustrated with horrific photographic evidence, attesting to the slaughter of between 200,000 and 370,000 Chinese civilians and prisoners of war by Japanese troops in Nanking. In a six-week orgy of mayhem and horror, men, women and children were slaughtered without mercy. Humanity, it seems, took a leave of absence from the Japanese army. Many people were hacked to death, others were buried alive, still others were burned alive in mass slaughter pits or were used as bayonet target practice. Japanese soldiers competed to find the most horrifying ways to kill innocent women and children, while their comrades-in-arms grinned and applauded.

Some 20,000 women and girls were raped, including young children. For this reason, this shameful period of history is sometimes referred to as the Rape of Nanking. Often, gang rape was merely a prelude to a brutal and sadistic death, and many were dispatched with a bayonet thrust up the vagina. No mercy was shown to anyone. Even the smallest of children were not spared savage deaths at the ripping end of a bayonet. One Japanese solider, Azuma Shiro, recalls:

"There were about 37 old men, old women and children. We captured them and gathered them in a square. There was a woman holding a child on her right arm and another one on her left. We stabbed and killed them, all three, like potatoes in a skewer."[3]

All in all, the Japanese troops displayed a level of brutality seldom equalled – not even in the bloodiest, most depraved moments of our human history.

These demonic deeds are an affront to all of us, a dark smear on the soul of our common humanity that degrades us all. Therefore, it is imperative that the perpetrators make amends. To do this, the Japanese must now demonstrate to us the heights to which the human soul can ascend, by having sufficient courage, dignity and compassion to take responsibility for their deeds, to apologize, and to offer compensation. Only then will the Chinese be able to demonstrate the most sublime heights of all – by accepting the apology, and moving forward in a spirit of forgiveness and cooperation. Forgiveness is not possible without an apology – and without forgiveness, the harm done will fester like an open sore forever more.

It might be thought that the rift created by the atrocities of Nanking is so broad that it is beyond human capacity to transcend it. However, there is a recent example of one group in our human family achieving such transcendence. In South Africa, after generations of repression, the black majority in the country finally took back their country. In a miracle which confounded all of the prophets of doom, this transition was achieved without descending into the heart of chaos, with the whites peacefully handing back the country, and the blacks gracefully accepting it. And once democratic elections were held and a black government was installed, the new government did not exact revenge on their former oppressors.

Instead, a Truth and Reconciliation Commission was established to give people – even the vilest mass murderers – the chance to take responsibility for their sins and apologize to their victims or relatives. Time after time, criminal and victim met face to face, human oppressor facing up to human victim, and tried to work together to come to terms with the horrific crimes of the past.

South African psychologist Pumla Gobodo-Madikizela asserts that acknowledging misdeeds and expressing remorse for them are the most crucial signs of restorative justice, which seeks to restore the best interests of all by addressing the needs of the victim, the broader community, and even the offender.[4] This crucial need for acknowledgement and remorse was the guiding principle behind South Africa's unprecedented Truth and Reconciliation Commission. South Africans attempted to make up for past sins by facing them, taking responsibility for them, and apologizing. Even more profoundly, some of the victims accepted these apologies so that they too could heal, transcend the past, and go on with their lives. As Jann Turner, a woman whose activist father was assassinated by the apartheid regime in South Africa, has said, quoting Maya Angelou: "History, despite its wrenching pain, cannot be unlived, but if faced with courage need not be lived again."[5] Human beings are capable of terrible crimes, as the Nanking Massacre so vividly showed. However, they also have the ability to reach up and attempt to brush the robes of angels, as the Truth and Reconciliation Commission illustrates.

The attempt at reconciliation in South Africa met with varied responses – sometimes it was very successful, sometimes not so. But what is important is that the attempt was made. And surely this is part of the reason why South Africa has not followed the example of some of its neighbours to the north, and descended into internecine chaos. Instead, black and white citizens continue to work together to overcome the legacy of the past, and strive to walk together into a brave new future. To even attempt such repentance and forgiveness is surely to attempt to soar as high as the human soul can go. It is incredibly hard for those who have sinned against their fellow human beings to confess and apologize, and surely even harder for those most sinned against to dig deep within their hearts and to find the strength to forgive. The path of remorse, apologies, forgiveness and rebuilding is not an easy path – but at least South Africans are on it.

Tragically, the same cannot be said for the Japanese people and their Asian neighbours. Japan has failed to acknowledge and express remorse for the atrocities its soldiers committed against the Chinese during the Nanking Massacre – apparently out of some misguided notion of honour. Yet surely true honour consists in taking responsibility for our actions and owning our mistakes. But instead, one Japanese government after another has refused to acknowledge Japanese guilt for the Nanking Massacre. And as Elie Wiesel, Nobel Laureate, expressed it, "... to forget a holocaust is to kill twice"[6]. Yet while some few Japanese acknowledge responsibility, the authorities refuse to do so. Japanese novelist and Nobel Prize Laureate for Literature Kenzaburo Oe said in 1994: "Japan must apologize for its aggression and offer compensation. This is the basic condition, and most Japanese with a good conscience have been for it. But a coalition of conservative parties, bureaucrats and business leaders opposes."[7] Sadly, the denial of the Japanese authorities persists to this day, and it comes with a terrible cost. It means that there can be no healing, and no moving on.

Japan will not have the luxury of putting its past behind it until such time as it has dealt with its past, thus giving China a chance to forgive and heal. For it is not possible to forgive those who do not acknowledge guilt or ask forgiveness for their sins. To refer again to South Africa's Gobodo-Madikizela: Forgiveness usually begins with the person who needs to be forgiven. This means that there must be something in the perpetrator's behaviour, some "sign," that invites the victim's forgiveness. The most crucial sign is an expression of remorse.[8]

And once the perpetrator gives sign, meaning once Japan apologizes, then China can forgive, and the two countries will reconcile. Then these two nations can again be friendly neighbours, not enemies. Moreover, the tension that currently sours relations between Asian countries and Japan will be resolved, which will lead to greater regional stability and peace.

It will not be easy – Japan must to truly listen to, and truly hear, the suffering it caused to Chinese people. As one expert on truth and reconciliation expresses it: "… perpetrators and bystanders in the apartheid era learned to listen to each other in many painful public hearings. Real empathetic hearing of a neighbour's story of officially imposed suffering is an indispensable step towards reconciliation." [9]

How can this situation ever be resolved? The answer surely lies in continuing to speak for those who cannot – the dead, the raped, the tortured, and the bereaved – until Japan finally steps up with dignity to take responsibility for its deeds, apologizes and makes compensation. Iris Chang did more than her share to speak for the victims. Columnist George Will wrote as follows about her work: "Something beautiful, an act of justice, is occurring in America today … Because of Chang's book, the second rape of Nanking is ending."[10] This is indeed true – the denial of the Rape of Nanking amounts to a second rape, a second transgression against all that is good in the human soul. Chang gave enormous meaning to her life by using much of it to fight back against this second rape. For as one philosopher has expressed it, the meaning of a life "resides in how we spend it. We might wish we had more to spend, but meaning emerges from how we spend, not how much we spend".[11]

Sadly, we no longer have Chang to fight this fight. However, the work of the Iris Chang Foundation helps to keep the consciousness of the Nanking Massacre alive. This in turn helps to keep the unremitting pressure on Japan to do the right thing. The second rape of Nanking must end. The terrible history of the Nanking Massacre must be courageously faced and acknowledged, so that its wrenching pain will never happen again. Japan has shown us how low the human spirit can descend – now we wait with optimism for Japan to step up and show us how high it can ascend.

1. Tony Blair, "What I've Learned." The Economist, 2 June 2007: 26-28.

2. http://www.irischangmemorialfund.org/Brief_Biography.htm

3. BBC News, http://news.bbc.co.uk/1/hi/world/asia-pacific/223038.stm

4. Dennis Sullivan & Larry Tifft, *Restorative Justice: Healing the Foundations of our Everyday Lives.* 2nd edition (Monsey, New York: Willow Tree Press, Inc. 2005) 2.

5. http://www.jannturner.co.za/films.php

6. http://irischangmemorialfund.net/Essay_Contest_2006/ICMEC_main_1115.html

7. From "Denying History Disables Japan," *The New York Times Magazine*, July 2, 1995.

8. Pumla Gobodo-Madikizela, A Human Being Died That Night: A South African Story of Forgiveness. Quoted on http://www.religion-online.org/showarticle.asp?title=2954

9. John W. de Gruchy, Reconciliation: Restoring Justice. Quoted on http://www.religion-online.org/showarticle.asp?title=2954

10. http://www.irischangmemorialfund.net/Brief_Biography.htm

11. David Schmitdz, "The Meanings of Life." David Benatar (Ed) *Life, Death & Meaning*. New York: Rowman & Littlefield Publishers Inc., 2004.

Bibliography

(1) Blair, Tony, "What I've Learned." *The Economist*. 2 June 2007: 26-28.

(2) De Gruchy, John W., *Reconciliation: Restoring Justice*. Fortress.

(3) Gobodo-Madikizela, Pumla., *A Human Being Died That Night: A South African Story of Forgiveness*. Houghton Mifflin.

(4) Iris Chang Memorial Fund web site.

(5) Schmitdz, David, "The Meanings of Life." *Life, Death & Meaning*. Ed. David Benatar. New York: Rowman & Littlefield Publishers Inc., 2004.

(6) Sullivan, Dennis & Larry Tifft, Restorative Justice: *Healing the Foundations of our Everyday Lives*. 2nd edition. Monsey, New York: Willow Tree Press, Inc., 2005.

Carol Leung
Graduate Student
Sunnyvale, California, USA

Lost Conscience: Japan's Denials of its Past

In an insult to tens of thousands of Chinese who were victims of Japanese aggression in World War II, a group of Japanese conservative lawmakers announced on June 9, 2007 that they will urge China through diplomatic channels to remove from Chinese war museums what it calls "unjustifiable" photos showing the Japanese military's wartime atrocities ("Lawmakers" par. 1). By requesting the removal of so-called "unjustifiable" photos, hard evidence of Japanese war crime from the war museums, Japanese politicians have again tried to erase the entire atrocities from public awareness. This incident, another example of Japanese collective amnesia and denial of its war crimes, highlights this issue of great tension and animosity between Asian countries and Japan stemming from their unresolved past. At the commencement of the 70th anniversary of the Nanking Massacre, the extent of the atrocities is still debated between China and Japan. As Japan continues to evade its responsibility for its horrendous war crimes, one wonders how the two countries can ever bring the dark chapter of their histories to proper closure. Yet, in fact, the solution is not arduous. As that saying goes, with great power comes great responsibility: Japan, now an industrialized world power, is more compelled than ever to take full responsibility for its past conduct. When confronted with its past, Japan should acknowledge its wrongdoings in World War II. At the minimum, the Japanese government should issue an official apology and pay reparations to its victims in Asia. And most importantly, Japan must educate its future generations about its wartime conduct during World War II and take full responsibility for its war crimes.

For a long time, because of Cold War politics, Japan was able to evade its responsibility for its horrendous war crimes. Following World War II, the United States wanted to replace the leadership responsible for Japanese aggression, but with the advent of the Cold War, Washington was mindful of Tokyo's support. As a result, the United States government allowed postwar Japan to be administrated by its prewar bureaucracy. Unlike Germany, where the Nazi government was replaced and numerous Nazi officers were brought to trial, many high-ranking wartime Japanese war criminals returned to power and prospered. In 1957, Japan even elected a man who had been imprisoned as a suspected class A war criminal as prime minister (Chang 182). In addition, the decision by the United States government to exonerate Hirohito as a war criminal had a long-term impact on the Japanese understanding of the war. "In exchange for Japan's surrender, the U.S. government granted Hirohito, the emperor of Japan, and all members of the imperial family implicated in the war immunity from trial" (Bouissou 43). Hirohito, as many historians believe, was the mastermind behind the atrocities committed by the Japanese imperial forces in World War II. Therefore, the decision to grant immunity to Hirohito and the decision to keep him on the throne after the war severely impeded the Japanese people's awareness of their country's war crimes.

Today, as a result of not being punished for its wartime conduct, the Japanese government repeatedly demonstrates a lack of remorse for its past. Up to this date, the Japanese government still does not fully repent for its war crimes and continues to deny the atrocities that they committed during the war. For example, former Justice Minister Shigeto Nagano denied that the Nanking Massacre had occurred, claiming it was a Chinese fabrication ("Scarred" par. 41). In September 1986, Fujio Masayuki, the Japanese minister of education, made a comment during an interview that the Nanking Massacre was just a part of war (Chang 203). And earlier this year, the Prime Minister of Japan denied that there were coercions in the recruitment of comfort women during World War II. In sum, the Japanese government over and over again has denied its war crimes and tried to distort historical facts, causing angry protests from China, South Korea and other victim countries.

Another debate between Japan and its neighboring countries is the Japanese history textbook controversy. Through textbook censorship, Japan deliberately obstructs important historical information about Japanese aggression from its education system. For example, as Chang points out, "the text of standard history books neglects to mention the casualties on the other side or Japanese war atrocities, while it consists largely of pictures of the U.S. atomic bombing in Japan" (Chang 206). Clearly, the Japanese government tries to whitewash Japanese war crimes in World War II and hide the truth from younger generations. In addition, despite official protests from China and Korea, Japanese Prime Ministers continue to visit Yasukuni Shrine, a temple that houses millions of war dead, including the 14 convicted as World War II criminals by a 1948 war tribunal. The frequent Yasukuni Shrine visits by the head of government indicate that Japan refuses to come to terms with its evil past and continues to disregard the feelings of its neighbors.

The consequence of Japan's denial of its war conduct is the mistrust of its neighboring countries. As debates over Japanese war conduct and textbook controversy go on, relations between Japan and its neighbors continue to be strained. According to Professor Gavan McCormack, an orientalist specializing in East Asia at Australian National University, he states that in South Korea, a nation with the most vibrant democracy in Asia, 90 percent of people do not trust Japan, and in China hostility and suspicion is widespread (McCormack par. 3). As the questions of history remain unresolved, it is difficult to see how Japan can have closer relations with China and South Korea when it is at odds with all its neighboring countries.

While mistrust exists between Japan and its neighboring countries stemming from the legacy of the World War II, there are increasing suspicions from Asian countries on Japanese renewal of its militarism. At its worst, the mistrust between Japan and its neighbors will continue to grow and military competition among nations will be unavoidable. On the other hand, as Professor Koji Murata points out, cooperation between Japan and China is essential for regional stability in Asia. It is necessary for Japan, for example to cooperate with China in order to address the North Korean issue (Chen par. 17). Therefore, the tension and animosity between Asian countries and Japan will no doubt undermine the stability and peace in the region.

With no remorse and self-reflection on its evil conduct, Japan will never be trusted by the people in Asia and the world. In some cases, the heated disputes between Japan and other Asian countries over Japan's wartime past has led to economic loss for Japanese businesses in Asia. The latest dispute between Japan and China in 2005, has erupted into anti-Japanese protests across China and Chinese boycott of Japanese goods. As China, a nation with 1.3 billion people and a booming economy, offers the greatest potential market in the world, the loss of the Chinese market will be a blow to Japanese multinational enterprises financially, and this in turn can seriously hurt the Japanese economy. In addition, failing to gain trust from its victim countries could cost Japan the support that it needs in order to elevate itself to a permanent seat on the United Nations Security Council. China, one of the council's five permanent members, strongly opposed Japan's bid for the security council in 2005 and told Japan to "face up to its World War II aggression before aspiring to a bigger global role" (Trull par. 1). Without taking full responsibility on its past conduct, Japan will never be recognized as a world power and be allowed to take a bigger role in the international community.

Only when Japan completely repents and atones for its evil acts can Japan finally be recognized as a responsible member of the international community. Nevertheless, it is still possible for Japan to be recognized as a great world power in 21st century. When confronted with the record of its past conduct, Japan should acknowledge its wrongdoings and fully atone for its war crimes. In order to regain trust and respect from its Asian neighbors, Japan needs to take full responsibility for its war crimes by issuing an official apology and offering reparation to its victims. Most importantly, Japan must educate the young generation about the war and not distort any historical facts of its past.

In order to foster a better relationship, Japan and its neighboring countries can adopt measures to ease the tensions over their disputed past. One way to achieve this would be for the Japanese government to declare it a crime for anyone who denies atrocities that the Japanese committed during the war. To stop hurting the feelings of its victims, Japanese officials should stop visiting the Yasukuni Shrine, or else set up a separate site for World War II war dead. To avoid controversy on the content of history textbook, Japan can cooperate with Chinese and Korean educationists to create textbooks, as France and Germany have done.

Currently, progress towards resolving the disputed past is stalled between Japan and its Asian neighbors. Yet, the situation can be improved if the international community gets involved by voicing their opinions on the issue. When a significant number of countries express their views and advocate for victim's justice, Japan will have no choice but yield to the diplomatic pressure to take its first step towards acknowledgement of its past conduct. Therefore, it is important to bring awareness about Japanese aggression during World War II to the general public in the world. Yet, the history of Japanese aggression in Asia is mostly unknown to the Western world. Students in America and Europe learn a lot in their history class at school about World War II and the Holocaust. But, few if any of the students know anything about the Japanese atrocities in Asia. To bring forth the awareness of the Japanese atrocities committed in Asia during the Pacific war, one can start by talking to friends, classmates and co-workers who do not know about the history of Japanese aggression. Asian community groups in the United States and other part of the world can organize events such as conferences or workshops on related topics to foster constructive discussion on history. In addition, people with creative and production skills can create multimedia, documentary films or movie clips to disseminate the message of the victim's desire for justice around the world through the internet. Once people learn more about the sufferings and hardships of the victims, they will be able to comprehend the scope and latitude of the atrocious behavior that was done by the Japanese military forces in World

War II.

As Elie Wiesel, Holocasut survivor and Nobel Peace Prize winner in 1986 says, "to forget a holocaust is to kill twice" (Chang 16). To deny its wrongdoings in World War II, Japan has deprived its war crime victims a fair justice. With denials comes its cost, so the Japanese government risks ruining its relations with the international community. Economically Japan will suffer great loss in losing its neighbors' markets. And morally Japanese people will forever carry the burden of their past and cannot move forward in history. In order to bring this dark chapter of Japan's history to a closure, we must fight to help the Japanese find their collective conscience, if not their good sense, and to accept responsibility for their grim past.

(1) "Lawmakers group to seek removal of China's anti-Japan photos." Kyodo News. 9 June 2007 <http://www.japantoday.com/jp/news/408948>

(2) "Scarred by history: The Rape of Nanjing." BBC News 11 April 2005, 29 June 2007 <http://news.bbc.co.uk/2/hi/asia-pacific/223038.stm>

(3) Chang, Iris. *The Rape of Nanking*. New York: Penguin Books, 1997

(4) Bouissou, Jean-Marie. *Japan: The Burden of Success*. Boulder: Lynne Rienner Pulishers, 2002

(5) McCormack, Gavan. "Rewriting an ugly past." the age.com.au 15 August 2005, 29 June 2007 <http://www.theage.com.au/news/opinion/rewriting-an-ugly-past/2005/08/14/1123957950490.html>

(6) Trull, Chelsea. "China opposes Japan's bid for security council." The Michigan Daily. 14 April 2005. 29 June 2007. <http://media.www.michigandaily.com/media/storage/paper851/news/2005/04/14/News/China.Opposes.Japans.Bid.For.Security.Council-1430322.shtml>

(7) Chen, Xuefei. "Role of nationalism in Sino-Japanese relations" People's Daily Online. 16 Feb. 2007, 29 June 2007 <http://english.people.com.cn/200702/16/eng20070216_350573.html>

Wei Li
Staff Member
Intellectual Property Office
Guangdong Province
P. R. China

A Winter to Remember

The winter of 1937 was definitely the coldest in the history of Nanking, China. That December, the ancient city felt icy wind, saw the chilling bayonets of Japanese troops and the blood of virtually all Nanking residents, old and young, men and women, and heard the harrowing cry of Chinese civilians mixed with the gruesome laughter of Japanese soldiers, all for six weeks. That was a humiliation of the Chinese nation, and indeed of human nature itself: the Nanking Massacre, or in the words of the great writer, truth seeker and human rights defender Iris Chang, *the Rape of Nanking*.

The Nanking Massacre 70 years ago was merely one episode among a long list of atrocities that the Japanese aggressors commited in China during 1931-1945, or in a larger view, throughout Asia during the World War II. Other major Japanese atrocities in China included the Unit 731 germ and chemical experiments on humans, the sexual enslavement of women ("comfort women"), and countless "Pits for Tens of Thousands of Bodies" (pits containing enormous numbers of murdered or tortured Chinese people, many of whom were buried alive by Japanese soldiers.)

I first came to know about the Nanking Massacre at the age of 11. At that time, my school organized my class to see the film Massacre in Nanking (Tu-Cheng-Xie-Zheng in Chinese). During and after seeing the film, almost all the students, including me, cried and wept. The film's graphic exposure of truths as later described in Iris Chang's ***The Rape of Nanking, the Forgotten Holocaust***, gave me nightmares for days. From that day on, I firmly remembered the winter of 1937. Later, as I grew up, I knew about more Japanese troops' crimes in China and in the rest of Asia during war times. The more I knew, the more deeply I felt chilled over humanity's capability for evil and power.

Considering how all those acts with their horrible details, not to be seen among wild beasts in nature, were factually done by humans, it is reasonable enough to believe that, given the circumstances, humans, such as the Japanese soldiers, may commit evils more perverse than in an ordinary person's wildest imagination. This insight is probably painful yet indeed important. It prompts us to examine what atrocities humans have done in history, and to remember such history to prevent it from happening again.

George Santayana argues that, "Those who cannot remember the past are condemned to repeat it". His choice of the word "condemn" is meaningful in that he regards the "repeat" of the past as a punishment. As I consider it, the punishment is, on the surface, for forgetting the past, but in the root, for underestimating the possibility of human evil. The perpetrators of historical atrocities, unless demonstrating true, real, authentic remorse, are most likely to commit those evils time and time again, against the same victims and others. The victims, then, have to remember those atrocities they suffered to warn themselves against the perpetrators' future acts; if not, the victims are subject to the ruthless condemnation in Santayana's argument.

The winter 70 years ago saw the unimaginable evil of the Japanese aggressors and, in a sense, of any aggressors. As Chinese people, if we do not wish any place to be massacred by the Japanese or by any foreign forces, we have to remember the dark, cold winter of 1937. In the same logic of avoiding being "condemned to repeat it", if we do not wish our daughters, sisters and wives to be forced into sexual slavery, we have to remember that the Japanese enslaved over 200,000 Chinese, Korean and other Asian women as prostitutes. If we do not wish any of our fellow citizens to be subjects for germ warfare experiments, we have to remember that the Japanese army had the special Unit 731 to systematically kidnap Chinese people for such inhuman experiments.

Farce of the Japanese Denial

The massacre of over 200,000 Nanking civilians, and the sexual enslavement of over 200,000 Asian women, among other atrocities that Japanese troops commited, took place over decades ago, and Japan as an aggressor was defeated in 1945. In a sense, however, even today, the massacre and the enslavement still do not completely end. The reason is that the Japanese government, until today, has not made a definite, formal, open apology, nor reparations for its atrocities; on the contrary, from time to time, the Japanese Government, especially its right-wing politicians, jump up to deny the historical occurrence of the massacre and the sexual enslavement. As Elie Wiesel, the Nobel Laureate put it, "... to forget a holocaust is to kill twice." In a similar vein, I would state that, to deny those atrocities is to continue them right now and to prepare for new atrocities through conspiracy.

The denial of historical truths started in Japan as early as half a century ago. In the 1950s, the Japanese government started to examine and adapt textbooks, hence giving rise to the "Textbook Issue", which constantly causes tension between Japan and other Asian countries including China and Korea. In the 1990s, Japanese right-wing politicians formed the so-called New History Textbook Compilation Committee. In the new century, this committee aggressively promoted the deletion of the Nanking Massacre and sexual enslavement of women from Japanese textbooks. In 2001, among six published editions of textbooks, four omitted the specific number of Nanking Massacre victims, and two renamed the holocaust the Nanking Episode; more ridiculously, some of them even blamed Japan's aggressive war on China, and glorified the war by identifying the purpose of the Japanese invasion as "liberating" Asia.

In recent years, months or even weeks, people across the world have watched one farce after another performed by Japanese "scholars" and government officials, who attempted to deny the Nanking Massacre and the sexual enslavement of Asian women including

Japanese women. Some might acknowledge the existence of the massacre, but claimed that the number of victims was less than 20,000; however, for people in the whole civilized world, even if the number was just two thousand, the heinous details would still powerfully testify to the unlimited possibility of evil in humanity. Such denial by Japan certainly incurred protests and condemnations from China, Korea and some other countries.

In March, the Japanese Prime Minster Shinzo Abe, along with his Cabinet members, claimed that the sexual enslavement of women "had no proof". In the same month, Abe expressed apology for the comfort women's suffering, but still refused to acknowledge those women were "forced". In June 2007, Japanese right-wingers placed in the Washington Post a paid advertisement, denying the comfort women issue, stating that those women were not "forced" into prostitution, and even shamelessly claiming that some women earned more money than Japanese army officers. This time, the farce by Japan proved to be too disgusting, hence arousing the indignation of more and more people in the world, including law makers in the U.S. Congress.

Costs of the Denial

Japanese politicians might take pleasure in performing the farce of denying Japan's past atrocities. However, they must pay for playing the game. The denial will cause Japan to bear a series of costs.

First, the denial undermines Japan's national morality. Diverse forms of denial may help to produce large quantities of Japanese children ignorant of history, finally giving rise to a deceived and self-deceiving Japanese generation. The Japanese politicians, by denying facts, are leading Japanese children down a perilous path. By absorbing those distorted "facts", Japanese students will have difficulty in living in harmony with Asia. Moreover, the Japanese government has to lead in telling lies and compromising moral integrity. In so doing, it helps to promote a culture of dishonesty and deception in Japan, and that definitely detracts from Japan's national morality building.

Second, the denial humiliates Japan in the international community. Constant denial has partly ruined Japan's national profile worldwide. The denial of the Nanking Massacre and the comfort women issue serves only to make Japan a state showing no remorse for its past atrocities. In other words, the rest of the world, especially those countries invaded by Japan, in light of Japan's lack of remorse for its past atrocities, always have reason to believe that Japan will commit those evils again, given the chance. Today, Japan chooses to deny its past crimes, and tomorrow, the possibility is that it may commit new crimes and again simply deny them. Japan has been seeking the status of a permenant member of the UN Security Council. However, it would be hardly possible that world security should be entrusted on a country which committed inhuman crimes but always refuses to acknowledge and apologize.

Third, Japan's denial serves to demonize itself. Some Japanese may argue that exposure of the Nanking Massacre with its heinous details is to purposely demonize the Japanese race as a whole. Yet exactly who is demonizing the Japanese? In truth, it is nobody else but those Japanese politicians that have most effectively demonized Japan. If Japan's aggressive war along with its atrocities, including the Nanking Massacre, was launched by Japan when it was possessed by a demon, but today Japan loudly denies those atrocities and even glorifies the war itself, then we can gain the insight that the demon has never been dead but is still alive inside Japan, ready to rise, roar, and run amok again. Therefore, nobody is demonizing Japan, except the truth-denying Japanese politicians, who successfully enable the world to see Japan as a "demon" with no remorse.

Finally, Japan's current denial will incur the long-term rancor of people in those invaded countries. Today, as I know it, more and more Chinese people, especially youngsters, have developed a strong anti-Japanese sentiment because of Japan's denial of the Nanking Massacre, the comfort women issue and other atrocities. Many people even boycott Japanese products. Unless the Japanese government comes up with a definite, formal, open apology and makes reparations, the rancor towards Japan as a whole nation will never diminish. However, a lamentable phenomenon may be that, because Japan has so far already been so reluctant and unwilling to apologize, on that day when Japan cannot but apologize in future circumstances, the Chinese rancor will still continue for decades.

Outlook of the Future

In December 2004, Li Xiuying, a survivor of the Nanking Massacre, passed away at the age of 86 in Nanking. She was among the last few witnesses of the massacre. On December 19th, 1937, she was seven months pregnant, fought against Japanese soldiers trying to rape her, and hence received 37 sword cuts. She was finally saved by a U.S. doctor Mr. Robert Wilson, but the expected baby died. As time goes by, more and more Nanking Massacre witnesses like Li Xiuying are leaving us. Meanwhile, Japan still has not made a sincere and formal apology for its past atrocities and provided compensation., We cannot hear the footsteps of the day of Japanese apology coming in the near future

The outlook for a Japanese apology seems gloomy. However, even in the darkest days for American blacks in the 1960s, Martin Luther King still had a great dream; later, his dream came true. Similarly, I also have a dream today. I have a dream that one day the Chinese and the Japanese may fully resolve all historical problems, and restore their Tang Dynasty (618-907) friendship, whereby both countries have sincere, authentic respect for and trust in each other.

Rabindranath Tagore, the Nobel Laureate uttered the famous message: "Man's history is waiting in patience for the triumph of the insulted man." Coldly, I watch Japan performing farces of denial in the international community; calmly, I see Japan paying all the costs of its denial; and confidently, I wait for the triumph as prophesized by Tagore and the day of Japanese apology and reparation, as well as the day of true China-Japan friendship.

Robert Thomas Marcell
Matriculating Graduate Student
University of Chicago
Omaha, Nebraska, USA

The Rape of Nanking:
Still Salient in East Asian Politics

Japan carries not only the legal burden but the moral obligation to acknowledge the evil it perpetrated at Nanking.

— Iris Chang

In April 2007, the Premier of the People's Republic of China, Wen Jiabao, visited Japan. It was the first such visit that a Chinese leader made to Japan in nearly seven years, and it was, in the premier's opinion, a success.[1] The trip saw Wen jogging with the elderly, playing baseball with university students, chatting it up with a local farmer, and delivering a speech before the Japanese parliament, called the Diet. The speech that Wen delivered is as noteworthy as the visit itself, for it had been twenty-two years since a Chinese leader spoke before Japan's Diet. Given all this, one might justifiably conclude that the visit was an important first step in improving Sino-Japanese relationship. Summing up his feelings of optimism, Wen ended one of his speeches with a poem: "Spring has come. The sun shines brightly. The cherry trees blossom proudly and the snow and ice have melted."[2]

Nevertheless, lying just beneath the apparent success of Premier Wen's visit was very real tension. Security was tight throughout the premier's stay in Japan, and, as if to justify the high security, Japanese ultranationalists drove through the streets with loudspeakers decrying China and the Chinese. Moreover, judging from interviews conducted in both China and Japan, the visit also seems to have had little effect on the popular attitudes each country holds towards the other. Many people wrote the visit off as being little better than a publicity stunt, or otherwise treated it cautiously. It is telling though, that despite his optimism, Wen made it clear that China remains wary of the possible reemergence of Japanese militarism, especially in light of certain recent developments in the political culture and government of Japan.

Meanwhile, Japan's Prime Minister, Abe Shinzo, desires that Japan play a larger role in global affairs. The idea of Japan having not only its economic strength, but strong political, or worse yet, military influence in international affairs has met with staunch resistance from Japan's Asian neighbors. Indeed, the fact that Japanese troops are in Iraq has even split the country of Japan itself with controversy, as such a force strikes many as a circumvention of the Japanese constitution, wherein Article 9 renounces the country's right to wage war.[3] In any event, it is clear that without continued and earnest efforts on the part of both nations, a cloud of distrust will overtake Premier Wen's brightly shining sun, hate will wither his proudly blossoming cherry trees, and mutual antipathy will dirty his melting snow.

When considering the current state of affairs in East Asian politics, the question that naturally seems to arise is, "Why is it that Japan and its neighbors seem so polarized against one another? Why can't they just get along?" The roots of the political problems of today, however, are more than one hundred years in the making, harkening back to the First Sino-Japanese War of 1894-95. Even more important than this first war in terms of its modern reverberations is the Second Sino-Japanese War, beginning officially in 1937[4] and lasting to 1945. The Japanese invaded China and killed, looted, burned, and raped their way across the country for approximately fourteen years, but have, to this day, failed to give an acceptable, official apology for their aggressions, nor have they made more than a pittance worth of compensation to their numerous victims. Instead, Japan has denied and downplayed its actions in China and the rest of Asia. Regarding their 1937-1938 massacre at Nanking, the denial has been more fierce and obstinate than almost anywhere else. The ghosts of the war still haunt East Asian politics today, some seventy years after the fact, and the reason for this is because of Japan's refusal to take responsibility for its past.

THE RAPE OF NANKING

On July 7, 1937, a Japanese soldier went missing outside of Beijing. The disappearance of this single soldier, later found unharmed, set into motion a horrible series of events that would, before the end of 1945, cost China some twenty million sons and daughters. Of those twenty million killed, an estimated seventeen to eighteen million were unarmed civilians. The majority of those who died in the war were not killed directly, but rather, indirectly by preventable famine and widespread disease. Nevertheless, Japan had a hand in the direct killing of more or less 4,000,000 Chinese, all but about 400,000 of whom were civilians. However, Japan has yet to deliver a heartfelt apology or any real compensation to those of its neighbors who suffered under the bloodstained boots of Japanese expansionism. To add insult to massacre, many of the Japanese in governmental and academic positions have grotesquely transformed the Japan of the 1930s and 40s so much so that even the fabricators themselves seem to believe that their wartime role was that of the victims.

The killing energy of the Japanese army swept right across China during the Second Sino-Japanese War – kicked off in 1937 by the Marco Polo Bridge Incident briefly delineated above – but it is perhaps best epitomized in the gruesomely well-documented story of Nanking. In the December 1937, the Japanese Army entered the old capital of Nationalist China, Nanking. For six weeks, they looted there thousands of homes, brutalized and raped tens of thousands of men and women, and executed or murdered upwards of 300,000 innocent people. The massacre was splashed across the front pages of some of the major newspapers of the day, but, after the close of World War II, lay largely forgotten by the West for nearly sixty years.

In 1997, however, historian and journalist Iris Chang wrote *The Rape of Nanking* and forced the sleeping memory to the forefront of Western consciousness. Her book was important historically, to be sure, and her work in finding the German John Rabe's diary incalculably significant, but the book's true value was in its re-exposing the massacre to the English-speaking world. It opened up to the West the fierce debate that has been raging in the East ever since the end of the war. Since Iris Chang's best selling book, some dozen or more works have been published on the massacre in English – many of which make explicit reference to her and her research.[5] Big companies like the History Channel have produced documentaries on the incident. Numerous scholarly articles and consumer magazine articles have been written about it as well. In 2007, the documentary film Nanking was originally inspired by Iris Chang's book. Another upcoming movie is actually based off her book, and expected to release in 2008. Nevertheless, Japan continues to deny or deemphasize the events that took place in Nanking.

THE DENIAL

For years, Japanese right-wingers have dismissed the Rape of Nanking as Chinese fabrication meant to embarrass or discredit Japan – even in the face of extraordinary evidence to the contrary. Those who have spoken up for historical truth within the country have been bullied, harassed, and, in some cases, even killed. The Japanese Ministry of Education has stamped out or softened any mention of Japanese atrocities in textbooks for many years, and, to a lesser but still quite frightening degree, continues to do so to this day. It is disheartening, for instance, to learn that Japan's current Prime Minister, Abe Shinzo, headed the Japanese Society for History Textbook Reform before his election – a group that since its foundation in 1997 has attempted to revise Japanese history in order to promote Japanese patriotism at the cost of historical accuracy.

There is no doubt that the denial continues. In June 2007, members of Abe's party, the Liberal Democratic Party, claimed that there was no evidence to prove that the Japanese had participated in mass killings in Nanking during the war. In retort to the global interest in Nanking's massacre, catalyzed by Iris Chang's book and the recent release of the movie Nanking, Nakayama Nariaki, the leader of the group, said that they would not let "lies and deceit be spread around the world."[6] Their outspoken denial comes on the tail of Chinese Premier Wen Jiabao's speech to the Japanese Diet, where he urged "Japan to face up to its World War II actions."[7] Clearly, the Liberal Democratic Party is not listening. Similarly, in direct retort to the American movie Nanking, Japanese filmmaker Satoru Mizushima is producing a documentary called The Truth about Nanjing, wherein he hopes to prove that the first movie was "based on fabrications and gives a false impression."[8] The debate today is as healthy as ever before, and, thanks to Iris Chang and the stir she created, it is global as well.

It is important to stress that Japan, as a whole, does not condone nor agree with the political right wing's fringe (and erroneous) beliefs about history. Roger B. Jeans argues this point very well in his article "Victims or Victimizers? Museums, Textbooks, and the War Debate in Contemporary Japan."[9] Historians like Ienaga Saburo have also challenged the government about their historical revisionism from within Japan, with Ienaga suing the Ministry of Education over the issue in 1970 and winning. However, because the groups that believe that the Nanking massacre was either fabricated or exaggerated have controlled and continue to control the Japanese government, the official stance of Japan remains decidedly right wing on the issue, as exemplified by the Liberal Democratic Party's June 2007 report against the Rape of Nanking.

An official, heartfelt apology and compensation effort from Japan to its neighbors will only be possible when new, truly liberal government comes to power in Japan, or when international pressures from the West, or domestic pressure from within Japan itself, manages to sway the dominant, conservative party's views. Meanwhile, the Rape of Nanking – and the Second Sino-Japanese War more broadly – continue to hamper relations between Japan and the rest of East Asia. The cost of Japan's denial has been great so far, but it only continues to grow with the passing of the years. Saving perhaps the immediate postwar years, there has never before been a more urgent need or more appropriate time for Japan to make amends than right now.

THE COST

The immediate and continuing cost of denying the Rape of Nanking and the other atrocities committed by Japan in the Second World War is a moral one. It is a blot against the Japanese people that simply cannot be erased until it has been addressed. It is a festering wound in the East Asian heart that upsets people as individuals, and nations as a whole. This cost is an eternal one, too, and will continue exerting its dark influence on East Asian affairs for however long it is until Japan caters to its moral duty and seeks reconciliation with its East Asian neighbors. Seventy years is a long time, but one hundred and seventy years will not be enough. Ignoring the issue will not make it go away.

Related to the moral cost is the cost that the survivors of Japan's massacres have paid. The cost for the survivors has been in their live-lihoods, their physical health, and their emotional and psychological well-being. Rape victims, like Japan's "comfort women," have had to live with years of stigmatism even in their home countries. Orphans have had to grow up without ever knowing their parents or siblings. Unlike the moral cost, the lifespan of the survivors is limited, and run-ning out. If Japan hopes to redress the issue, it should not wait until all of its war criminals and former soldiers die out – because all the vic-tims will be dead by then, as well. It may be less embarrassing for Japan to wait ten, twenty more years before apologizing, but the gesture loses potency and sincerity with every year, and survivor, that passes.

Disengaging oneself from the human element, the moral outrage and the individual pain, one can see that there is yet another cost in Japan's denial. It is the political and economic cost. For twenty-seven years after the end of the war, Japan and China had an extremely tense relationship. Only in 1972 did the two countries normalize relations. To this day, however, they remain wary of one another. With political and economic issues of worldwide importance happening in East Asia, the mutual distrust Japan and the rest of Asia have for each other is downright dangerous. Japan and China have been increasing bilateral trade with one another over the past decade. Meanwhile, North Korea has been developing nuclear missiles technology, so the fears go. In Japan itself, its desire to revise its pacifist constitution is being met with widespread protest primarily because of its history, and its unwillingness to acknowledge that frightful past for which it is responsible.

THE FUTURE

Despite Premier Wen's poetic assertion that "spring has come," there is clearly much left to do before such optimism is warranted. Japan's Prime Minister Abe's visit to South Korea and China, and Pre-mier Wen's visit to Japan, are steps in the right direction. Japan-China talks on their shared past, such as those ongoing talks that both coun-tries hope to have completed by 2008, are also a step forward.[10] How-ever, the position of some groups within the Liberal Democratic Party who claim that the Rape of Nanking is a fabrication is a step back-ward. Claims that "the past can't be changed" and "should be forgotten" are not only dangerous, but also steps backwards.

Like Premier Wen's "spring has come" assertion, it would be naive to preempt the future by suggesting that holocausts like the Rape of Nanking are behind us in this 21st-century world. They are not behind us. And perhaps they never will be behind us. All we can do, as human beings, is remain guarded against them, and the governments that might perpetrate them. For this reason, a remilitarizing Japan is a grave threat to its neighbors so long as it continues to deny its past. Only by acknowledging its past will Japan find acceptance in the East Asian community.

---

1. Nishiyama, George. "China's Wen pitches friendship as Japan ties thaw." Reuters. 13 April 2007.
http://www.reuters.com/article/worldNews/idUST32494820070413?pageNumber=1
2. Ibid.
3. Buckley, Sarah. "Japan extends its military reach." BBC News. 10 December 2004.
< http://news.bbc.co.uk/2/hi/asia-pacific/4078815.stm>.
4. Although 1937 is officially the beginning of the Second Sino-Japanese War, Japan invaded China as early as 1931, when it took control of Manchuria. It annexed the Korean peninsula in 1910.
5. To list just a few, there has been The Nanjing Massacre in History and Historiography by Joshua A. Fogel; American Goddess at the Rape of Nanking: The Courage of Minnie Vautrin by Hua-ling Hu; They Were in Nanjing: The Nanjing Massacre Witnessed by American and British Nationals by Suping Lu; and Documents on the Rape of Nanking, edited by Timothy Brook.
6. Nishiyama, George. "Japan ruling MPs call Nanjing massacre fabrication." Reuters. 19 June 2007.
< http://www.reuters.com/article/latestCrisis/idUST214128>.
7. "China PM seeks war reconciliation." BBC News. 12 April 2007.
<http://news.bbc.co.uk/2/hi/asia-pacific/6547199.stm>.
8. Schilling, Mark. "Docs offer rival visions of Nanking." Variety. 24 January 2007.<http://www.variety.comindex.asplayout=features2007&content=jump&jump=story&dept=sundance&nav=NSundance&articleid=VR1117958065&cs=1>
9. This article can be found in The Journal of Military History 69 (January 2005): 149-95.
10. For more information, see: Hogg, Chris. "Japan-China talks on shared past." BBC News. 26 December 2006 < http://news.bbc.co.uk/1/hi/world/asia-pacific/6209283.stm>

Delroy Oberg
Teacher
Boondall, Australia

History, Historiography, and the Art of Denial

"Those who can make you believe absurdities can make you commit atrocities."

— **Sissela Bok** [1]

The histories of countries run by totalitarian governments have relied on persuasion of the people, by the people, for the people – so they would say. The methods of persuasion may be brutal, or more subtle and insidious. Limiting information, withholding education, purveying falsehoods, reinventing language, rewriting history – all these are ways a powerful minority can use to persuade the gullible minority that black is white, and two plus two equals five.

Patriotism is also a powerful persuader. Yet the demise of such governments in recent decades testifies to a "People Power" that demands truth, freedom, respect and equality.

French playwright, Ionesco, states that "It is the enemies of History that, in the end, make it." [2] Hitler will never be forgotten for his contribution to world history; and, despite revisionist denials, historians – even German historians - would mostly view him in the same light.

However, writing history is never a simple process. The determination of what is fact and what is fiction is difficult enough in the present; so who can be sure what really happened seventy years ago? Some primary sources will be as deceptive as the known villains who wrote them. Who can be trusted? What credentials qualify a person to be an historian? What attributes should disqualify him?

This is the dilemma of those who, like Iris Chang, seek to understand the Japanese Government's paradoxical position concerning its role in World War II, and especially in the Sino-Japanese conflict. "A people denied history is a people deprived of dignity,"[3] and the treatment meted out to the Chinese people of Nanking deprived them not only of dignity but, in 300,000 cases, their lives.

Chang's book, *"The Rape of Nanking,"* was her attempt not only to tell the world what happened, but most importantly to convince Allies and enemies alike that it really did happen; for the official Japanese position is still enigmatic, ambiguous, and unremorseful. The enigma lies in their denial that this tragic event in history ever took place, despite much evidence to the contrary, the subject matter and conclusions of the Tokyo Trials, and the research and publications of their own historians and scholars.

HISTORICAL REVISIONISM AND THE TOKYO TRIALS

Historical revisionism is an academic term that should be restricted to history reviewed in the light of new, concrete and reliable evidence. Instead it is often used to cast doubts on whether certain events in history actually occurred. Its exponents may have personal agenda – political, racial, religious, or a combination of all three. The Ku Klux Klan in the United States fits this descriptor.

For the purposes of this essay, we are looking at what is called "HOLOCAUST DENIAL." It first related to Hitler's persecution of the Jews. Later Harry Elmer Barnes extended "holocaust" to refer to the role of Japan in World War II. That is, he denied that the Japanese committed the atrocities that are attributed to them by eyewitnesses, journalists, historians, and victims[4]. Deniers do not just rewrite history; they expunge what they do not want the world to know from the records.

HOLOCAUST DENIAL

It was in the interests of both the German and Japanese Governments to deny the atrocities they had committed if they wished to avoid punishment and retribution. They destroyed as much evidence as possible, but not everything. Living documents bore convincing and compatible witness.

The conclusions of the trials at Nuremberg and Tokyo did not favour "the enemy." The reason why Iris Chang's book still needed to be written so long after the Tokyo Trials finished (in 1948) is that Germany and Japan responded very differently. The former admitted that what had happened, had happened. The worst criminals were executed. Others received life sentences. Furthermore, Germany could not falsify the facts, for their holocaust denial is a criminal offense. The history books cannot be rewritten to cover up the past.

On the other hand, Japan emerged from the Tokyo Trials still with a chip on its shoulder and convinced of its victimization. It saw no need to apologize or make reparations. Former war criminals were promoted. Executed Class A criminals were honoured at the Shrine. Ironically they had unlikely support for their denial – and it came from America.

GENERAL DOUGLAS MACARTHUR

Twenty-five Japanese military personnel and politicians were convicted as Class A war criminals. They had committed crimes against peace. Of these, only seven were executed. One of them was IWANE MATSUI, the General with most influence in the events of Nanking – though his version of events is hardly to be trusted. He was there from December 17, 1937 and, from his diaries, it is clear that he was aware of the raping and looting that had already occurred in just four days. He claimed not to condone it. Why, therefore, did the massacre continue for another five weeks? In 1940, the Government decorated him for his part in the war. On December 23, 1948, he was hanged for it at Sugamo Prison in Ikebukuro. He was seventy-one!

The Emperor at that time, HIROHITO, had called Matsui out of retirement to lead the army in the invasion of Nanking. Therefore, if Matsui had condoned the atrocities, it was logical to assume he was acting under orders from the Emperor, who was the Commander-in-Chief of the armies.

PRINCE ASAKA, Hirohito's uncle, held a position where he was in charge of the funds obtained by looting. Again, the Emperor appears to have quietly condoned both the looting and the mass murders by which the loot was obtained.

DOCTORS from KYUSHU UNIVERSITY, who performed experiments including vivisection (without anaesthetic) on a group of American survivors of a plane crash in May 1945, were also tried and sentenced. Justice appeared to be happening.

GENERAL DOUGLAS MACARTHUR was presumably assigned to Japan for this purpose. A much decorated American hero, he had a long and varied experience of front line conflict, as well as peace time clean-up operations. Thus he was proactive in the aftermath of the Trials. Some of his actions and decisions were very strange.

He overturned many of the sentences set down by the Judges at the Trials. This included the twenty-three medical personnel who conducted the vivisections and, if the victims were still alive afterwards, killed them. All were sentenced: five to death, four to life imprisonment. MacArthur commuted the death sentences, and all were free within ten years.

At times MacArthur circumvented the system entirely. Any Japanese criminal who surrendered to the Americans and came to his attention was never brought to trial.

The most significant group under his "protection" was the royal family. One of MacArthur's first acts was to assure Hirohito that he need not abdicate. Indeed, he contrived without scruples to ensure that not one member of the royal family was brought to trial. Assisted by Brigadier General Bonner Fellers, he aimed "to protect Hirohito from the role he had played during and at the end of the war" thus allowing "the major criminal suspects to coordinate their stories so that the Emperor would be spared from indictment."[5]

Did MacArthur have an ulterior motive — patriotic, but nevertheless perverse? For example, he granted immunity to any of the doctors who would disclose the results of their experiments with germ warfare to America. Was this part of his assignment? The fact that he was hurriedly withdrawn from his position by President Truman in 1951 (one suggested reason was insubordination) would hopefully indicate that he was acting unilaterally, and very, very unwisely.

Regardless of motive, the outcome was unsatisfactory. Professor Herbert Bix, author of the book, "Hirohito and the Making of Modern Japan," believes that Hirohito should have abdicated and been tried. In an ABC TV interview by Jennifer Byrne for "Foreign Correspondent" (5/09/2000), Bix maintained:

- *Hirohito's wartime record resulted in the rewriting of history and truth;*
- *the enemies collaborated to change the truth;*
- *the truth did not come out during the war crimes trials in Tokyo because of the desire to protect the Emperor.*[6]

To conclude, Bix believes that there was a "culture of denial,"[6] and America was as guilty of it as Japan.

THE YASUKUNI SHRINE.

This shrine, now infamous rather than famous, was built in 1869 under the Meiji regime to honour those who lost their lives in defence of the Emperor. Their names were written in the "Book of Souls," and they were considered martyrs.

After World War II, these records needed updating. In 1969, the decision was made that even Class A war criminals deserved to be honoured, and fourteen of them, including General Tojo, were included. By 2004, 1,068 of the names in the book (out of nearly 2.5 million) were known war criminals. The Shrine's pamphlet states that these war criminals were "cruelly and unjustly tried" by a "shame-like tribunal of the Allied forces."[7]

Clearly those who run the Shrine refuse to show remorse or make apology for Japan's war crimes. However, it is interesting that none of the post-war Emperors, including Hirohito, have paid official visits to the Shrine since the war criminals have been honoured; and even in recent months the visits of prominent people to the Shrine have caused controversy. It suggests that there is some hope that the Japanese may express more explicitly a sense of shame for what they did during the war. Meanwhile, the unfavourable coverage given by the Japanese media (and it has come to the attention of our papers also) indicates that there is a public conscience that needs to be satisfied.

THE SILENCE OF THE TEXTS

"We need not waste time and effort
answering the deniers and contentions.
It would be never ending to respond to
arguments posed by those who freely
falsify findings, quote out of context
and simply dismiss....of testimony.
Unlike true scholars, they have little,
if any, respect for data or evidence.
Their commitment is to an ideology
and their 'findings' are sloped to
support it."[4]

Japan did literally rewrite the history books. It proceeded by a process of scrutiny and selection. One of the early guidelines was to expunge all references to Nanking, the Sino-Japanese War, and the War in the Pacific. In the fifties, there were a number of controversies arising from this censorship and distortion of truth.

For example, Japanese historian, SABURO IENAGA, wrote a textbook which the Government, in denial, censored. Ienaga sued the Ministry of Education on the grounds that his freedom of speech had been denied him. His integrity was respected much more by those outside his own country. He was nominated for the Nobel Peace Prize in 2001[8].

Other Japanese academics have been less ethical, squandering their talents and their professional integrity in perpetuating the myth of Japan's innocence.

KOBORI KEIICHIRO, Professor at Meisie University and Emeritus Professor of Tokyo University, wrote the FOREWORD to TANAKA MASAAKI's book, "What Really happened in Nanking?" and seems to be on the right path. He damns those "charlatans" who "invent or intentionally misrepresent history and, regrettably, there is little we can do to stop them."[9]"Some 'historiographers'," he tells us, "make no effort to choose words that most closely resemble the truth."[9]

He offers a perception of history that is sound, but misplaced and misleading. As an academic he says the things he ought to say, and says them very well. As a patriot, he is blind to the fact that every accusation he levels at other historians is exactly what he himself is guilty of.

If follows that if he praises Masaaki as an historian (which he does when he describes him as one who "presents judiciously reasoned arguments"[9] and recommends his book, he is being either very dishonest or sadly deluded. The Tokyo Trials inspired people to invent history – the specific period referred to being the Nanking Massacre, which he described as having been "manufactured".[10] The trials were responsible for preventing Japanese freedom of speech. Now it is time for scholars to have their day. They cannot "sit by in silence while the minds of the people of the world were being clouded by vicious Chinese Propaganda."[11] Conveniently ignoring confessions and admissions of atrocities by those who perpetrated them at Nanking and elsewhere, Keiichiro paints a pathetic portrait of the Japanese as victims. In highly emotive language, he claims:

> "Wrested of freedom of speech, they were
> powerless to object to the shower of baseless
> slanders and charges of nonexistent war crimes
> that fell upon them. During the Occupation,
> which spanned nearly seven years, the sins
> committed to Japanese military in Nanking,
> products of their inventors' imaginations, were
> persistently and repeatedly broadcast throughout
> the world. This propaganda was spectacularly
> successful; it was embraced as fact by the
> international community, and engendered an
> inexorable, undeserved prejudice."[12]

It is to Iris Chang's credit that Keiichiro and Masaaka consider her book a turning point in the public attitude to Japanese propaganda. Tanaka Masaaki refers to her as a "problem."[12] His greatest problem is really his academic ineptitude. His bias is obvious. His evidence is unconvincing, and his methods of reaching a conclusion unscientific and contrived. "Would an officer as honourable and ethical as Gen. Matsui have ordered or sanctioned the massacre of 300,000 Chinese?"[13] he asks, rhetorically manipulating his audience into an unthinking and uninformed "No." Indeed, as soon as such a device is used, the writing falls short of history to become emotion and imagination.

Masaaka paints a poignant description, much better suited to creative writing than objective history, of the good Matsui visiting hospitals and bringing cheer to the ill. Matsui, of course, painted the picture first in his diary, and made sure that it was made public.

Masaaka does not quite call him a saint, but he describes Matsui as "without question, the most illustrious Japanese officer of his time."[13] When Tanaka journeys to Nanking at his hero's request to see how the town is faring, his report is positive. Of course. In seven months, there was ample time to clean up and bury the bodies.

UNCOMFORTABLE COMFORT WOMEN

When the academic elite are so biased and deluded, it is easy to understand why denial succeeds in convincing the hoi polloi. One still blinkered area continues to be the acknowledgement and compensation of women who were taken by force and made to work in army brothels. One method of denial was quite ingenious. Lists of the women "working" for the Japanese were fabricated to give their areas of employment as being "nurses" or other respectable careers. They were not referred to as prostitutes, a term which the women would have been quick to dispute anyway. They called a spade a spade, which is to say they called rape, rape. They have written themselves back into history with their vigorous campaigns to expose their situation for what it was, but so far have not met with great success.

CONCLUSION

What must be determined from the events described is that the debate is far from being concluded. In war, all sides kill, maim, and do things they would never have imagined in civilian life. Iris Chang's book describes soldiers competing in competitions to see who could lop off a hundred heads the fastest, with no thought for the human being on the ground who trembled as he awaited his turn.

The photographs and Chang's texts show women and children were not spared the massacre. The reader could feel the tension that women and young girls must have experienced dreading the summons to report to the Japanese, and knowing what that would mean. One cannot even believe the Japanese then killed most of their rape victims to spare them suffering. They appear to have done it because they did not regard the Chinese as anything more than animals. In fact, in wartime an animal is probably treated better, for it can feed an army.

But then, there are those terrible tales of cannibalism.

Should any reader find these things absolutely impossible to believe, then that person is substantiating the need for Chang's book, and for the commemoration of the event that, now after seventy years, still stands as one of the worst blots on the history of mankind.

1. Bok, Sissela, "Secrets," 1983. Quoted in *The Pan Dictionary of Contemporary Quotations*, Ed. Jonathon Green, p. 323

2. Ionesco, Eugene, 'Notes and Counter-Notes.' Quoted in *The Pan Dictionary of Contemporary Quotations*, p. 16

3. Kwami Nkrumah, quoted *Africanity Redefined: Collected Essays of Ali A. Mazrui*, Vol. 1, p. 3

4. "Holocaust Denial", http://www.en.wikipedia. Org/wiki/Holocaust_denial

5. "International Military Tribunal for the Far East," p. 7, http://www.en.wikipedia.org/ wiki / International _Military _Tribunal _for _the _Far _East

6. "Foreign Correspondent," ABC Interview with Jennifer Byrne, 5/09/2000, pp. 1-2, http://www.abc.net.au/foreign/s220033.html

7. "Yasukuni Shrine", p. 3, http://www.en.wikipedia.org/wiki/Yasukuni

8. Chang, Iris, *The Rape of Nanking.* London, Penguin Books, 1998, pp. 216-217

9. Tanaka Masaaki, *What Really Happened in Nanking. The Refutation of a Common Myth,* p.5, http://www.ne.jp/asahi/nuko/tamezou/nankin/whatreally/index.html

10. Ibid, p. 6

11. Ibid, p. 8

12. Ibid, p. 11

13. Ibid, p. 16

Thomas Park
CTY Distance Education Instructor
Graduate Student of Educational Technology
Johns Hopkins University
Baltimore, Maryland, USA

The Nanking Massacre: Following the Flow of Information

After the occupation of Nanking in December 1937, the Imperial Japanese Army conducted an eight-week campaign of death and destruction, unleashing unthinkable acts of cruelty upon the local Chinese populace. Hundreds of thousands of prisoners-of-war and civilians were raped, tortured, and murdered, alternately with ruthless caprice and with systematic efficiency. Seventy years have passed since this dark event, yet the Nanking Massacre remains an unresolved issue. Despite an abundance of eyewitness accounts and primary sources, historical interpretations of the incident vary considerably, bending to political influence and succumbing to a haze of misinformation. The Nanking Massacre remains a point of contention between China and Japan, tensing international relations and threatening the stability of the region. To successfully resolve this tragic chapter, a close examination of the flow of information before, during, and after the Nanking Massacre is required.

There is no greater illustration of the maxim "knowledge is power" than the rise of Japan in the 1800's. In centuries prior, the rulers of Japan adopted an isolationist policy, repulsing any attempts at interaction by Europe, even as the latter underwent the Industrial Revolution. It was not until Commodore Matthew Perry, in a show of technological superiority, sent a flotilla of steam-powered "Black Ships" into present-day Tokyo Bay in 1853 that Japan opened its borders and established diplomatic relations with the United States and the rest of the world. "As we are not the equals of foreigners in the mechanical arts, let us have intercourse with foreign countries" (Chang, 1997) became a familiar refrain among the nation's advisers. Japan quickly capitalized on its forced membership into the global community by sending its best students to study science abroad, infusing the nation with the latest advances in research and technology. Students were also sent abroad to study the British Royal Navy and the Prussian Army, and in exchange, European advisers were invited to organize and train the Japanese military.

Thanks to this new flow of information, the Japanese experienced unprecedented economic success, modernizing its infrastructure and developing industries in textiles, steel, and foreign trade. With the economy expanding and the population booming, Japan set its eyes on the arable land, coal and iron ore, oil, and other natural resources that its neighbors possessed. In 1876, a small naval fleet dispatched from Japan coerced Korea into accepting an unequal treaty, echoing what occurred in Tokyo just two decades earlier. Some in the Hermit Kingdom hoped that the treaty, which opened three Korean ports to Japanese commerce, would result in the influx of new technologies that could help them to defend against European imperialism. Japan's embrace of education and technology paid dividends in China and Russia as well. 1895 saw the Japanese triumph in the First Sino-Japanese War and gain the Liaodong Peninsula, Formosa, and the Pescadores Islands, in addition to unimpeded control of Korea and access to China's ports and rivers. Japan added Manchuria and half of the Sakhalin Islands to their spoils following the Russo-Japanese War in 1905.

Right-wing ultranationalists, buttressed by the military, choked the free flow of information within Japan by securing control of its government and educational system during this time. Under the pretext of Peace Preservation Laws, the government censored the media, filtered public opinion, spied on its citizens, and arrested dissidents (Yoshida, 2006). The government promoted the ideals of the emperor as a deity, Japan as a sacred land, and the Japanese as a master race. It instilled in the populace contempt for the Chinese people through skewed news reporting and propagandistic education, setting the stage for the atrocities in Nanking. In the late 19th century, the Ministry of Education declared that the primary objective of Japanese education was not the edification of students, but the good of the nation. The Imperial Rescript on Education issued by the Emperor in 1890 emphasized unconditional obedience to the Empire. Students were required to memorize the 315-word code of ethics and recite it each morning in class. Schools operated like military academies and brutal pecking orders were established. Teachers and students alike were subjected to harsh discipline and continuous indoctrination. A 1928 British War Office report noted, "During these impressionable years, they have been walled off from all outside pleasures, interests, or influences. The atmosphere of the narrow groove along which they have moved has been saturated with a special national and a special military propaganda" (Chang, 1997).

Textbooks on history, geography, ethics, and language were transformed into propaganda tools, distorted to reinforce the notion of the Japanese as a superior people and justify the expansionist policy of the government. A single narrative, chosen by the government to reflect whatever distorted reality it desired, was distributed to the schools. After the Japanese invasion of Manchuria and installation of a puppet regime, the 1936 edition of the sixth-year geography textbook stated, "Our country endorsed Manchukuo's independence as soon as it became independent... and has been making a substantial effort to develop this nation and to maintain peace in Asia" (Yoshida, 2006). The 1941 edition of the sixth-year national history textbook summarized aggressions in China with, "In July 1937, at the Marco Polo Bridge near Beijing, Chinese troops fired on our army, which was conducting maneuvers. In addition, some even assaulted our residents. Therefore, in the interest of justice, our country decided to send the military to rectify China's mistaken ideas and to establish eternal peace in the East" (Yoshida, 2006). By controlling the flow of information in such a manner, the government manipulated the Japanese public into not only condoning, but endorsing, barbarous acts by the Japanese military in Asia.

Seventy years have passed since hundreds of thousands of civilians were tortured and mutilated in Nanking, and the haze of misinformation surrounding the event has not yet lifted. Many leaders in Japan have subsequently whitewashed the Nanking Massacre and other atrocities committed by Imperial Japan. The Ministry of Education, responsible for screening and approving all textbooks for use in schools, has played a recurring role in this "second tragedy." In 1965, the Ministry rejected the textbook New Japanese History by Saburo Ienaga, claiming it contained "too many illustrations of the 'dark side' of the war, such as an air raid, a city left in ruins by the atomic bomb, and disabled veterans" (Masalski, 2001). The Ministry's recommendation that Ienaga soften descriptions of Japanese wartime activities in his 1982 textbook submission was much-publicized, resulting in an outcry among the victimized nations and formal diplomatic protests by the Chinese and South Korean governments.

In 2000, a coalition of conservative scholars named the Japanese Society for History Textbook Reform received approval by the Ministry of Education for its New History Textbook, which offered a revised view of Japanese history that downplayed the severity of the Nanking Massacre and interpreted Japanese imperialism in Asia as liberation from European powers. A passage from the 2005 edition simply stated, "[Japan] occupied [Nanking] in December... Note: At this time, many Chinese soldiers and civilians were killed or wounded by Japanese troops (the Nanking Incident). Documentary evidence has raised doubts about the actual number of victims claimed by the incident. The debate continues even today." The approval of the New History Textbook once again sparked protests and further contributed to strained relations between Japan and its neighbors.

The obscuring of history is not limited to textbooks. Within the academic community, the Nanking Massacre remains a stifled area of study that many scholars avoid due to an atmosphere of intimidation. Yet others actively tamper with historical documents, such as Masaaki Tanaka, who made approximately 900 manipulations in Iwane Matsui's wartime diary before publishing it in 1985 (Chang, 1997). Those who do scrutinize the atrocities risk threats on their careers and even their lives. For example, in 1988, Nagasaki mayor Hitoshi Motoshima

125

was asked to speak on the Emperor's role in World War II, to which he replied, "Forty-three years have passed since the end of the war, and I think we have had enough chance to reflect on the nature of the war. From reading various accounts from abroad and having been a soldier myself, involved in military education, I do believe that the emperor bore responsibility for the war" (Buruma, 1994). Reaction to this statement was fierce. Motoshima was removed as advisor to the Liberal Democratic Party Prefectural Committee and many conservative organizations took to the streets in protest. In 1990, Motoshima was shot by a member of a radical right-wing group in retribution.

In contrast, Takami Eto, a senior member of Japan's ruling party, claimed in 2003 that the estimate of 300,000 dead during the Nanking Massacre was a "fabricated lie" and chastised past prime ministers who apologized for Japan's actions in China and Korea. His beliefs are reflected by many other people in positions of power. After publishing a cartoon that depicted Japanese soldiers massacring Nanking civilians in a 2004 issue of a weekly magazine, Japanese publisher Shueisha bowed to pressure from forty conservative assemblymen, issuing an apology and striking it from the book version (Gamble, 2004). Unfortunately, coerced censorship such as this occurs frequently in the private sector as well. In 1988, Shochiku Fuji Distribution removed from the Japanese release of the Last Emperor thirty seconds of film depicting the Nanking Massacre, claiming the scene was "too sensational." Film critic Takehiko Nakane speculated, "I believe the film's distributors and many theater owners were afraid these right-wing groups might cause trouble outside the theaters. Some of these people still believe that Japan's actions in China and during the war were part of some sacred crusade" (Chang, 1997). In 1999, publisher Kashiwashobo canceled its contract to translate Iris Chang's *the Rape of Nanking* and bring it to Japan because the author refused to add notes and remove photographs as requested specifically for the Japanese edition. The Japanese publisher's editor-in-chief declared, "It's biased, prejudiced and like wartime propaganda" (Carvajal, 1999).

Time and time again, the truth is threatened by a campaign of disingenuous claims and baseless denials. Unimpeachable facts, photographic evidence, and primary accounts from Chinese victims, Japanese soldiers, and third-party witnesses are suppressed. This censorship shares a continuity with the propaganda that enabled the Japanese to perceive their victims as subhuman and describe their path of calamity as divine destiny. In order to regain the trust of its neighbors and give this tragic chapter a dignified resolution at last, the Japanese government must free the flow of information into Japan and promote open discourse among the media, academia, and general public. No longer can details of the Nanking Massacre be cut from films and sanitized in books. Courageous individuals, like Saburo Ienaga and Hitoshi Motoshima, and conscientious organizations such as the Center for Research and Documentation on Japan's War Responsibility must be celebrated, not vilified. Schools must educate future generations of Japanese about the true Nanking Massacre and the lessons that can be learned from it. This, even more so than an official apology from the Japanese government, will prove beneficial to East Asia. While an apology may be merely a reactive diplomatic measure from a government figure, opening discourse on the Nanking Massacre demonstrates genuine acceptance that permeates all levels of Japanese society.

Those outside of Japan must also raise awareness of "the forgotten holocaust" and keep it in the global consciousness. Not only does the Nanking Massacre mark a significant event in our past, but it serves as a sober warning of what becomes possible when the flow of information into and within a nation is restricted. *The Rape of Nanking* has acted as a catalyst in bringing the issue to the foreground throughout the world, and all people can contribute to this momentum. Prior to the Rape of Nanking's publication, no full-length nonfiction narrative of the massacre existed in English. Since 1997, over a dozen books have reached the English-speaking market, and several films are in production as well. After reading Iris Chang's work, Ted Leonsis was inspired to produce Nanking (Heath, 2006), which won a documentary film editing award at this year's Sundance Film Festival. Educators should follow the lead of schoolteacher Graeme A. Stacy by incorporating the Nanking Massacre into their social studies curricula. Stacy's resource guide, entitled Human Rights in the Asia Pacific 1931 — 1945: Social Responsibility and Global Citizenship, was created in conjunction with the British Columbia Ministry of Education and made available to teachers throughout British Columbia, Canada, in 2003. We do the victims of the Nanking Massacre the ultimate honor by remembering what occurred in those bleak winter months so many years ago and passing the history onto others in this way. The Nanking Massacre offers lessons from which, regardless of nationality, we can all learn.

---

(1) Buruma, I. (1994). The wages of guilt: Memories of war in Germany and Japan. New York: Farrar Strauss Giroux.

(2) Carvajal, D. (1999, May 20). History's shadow foils Nanking chronicle. New York Times.

(3) Chang, I. (1997). *The rape of Nanking: The forgotten holocaust of World War II.* New York: Penguin.

(4) Gamble, A. (2004, December 4). Japan, media still deny Nanking massacre. Chicago Sun-Times.

(5) Heath, T. (2006, July 31). Ted Leonsis takes a sharp turn. Washington Post.

(6) Masalski, K. (2001, November). Examining the Japanese history textbook controversies. Japan Digest.

(7) Yoshida, T. (2006). The making of '*the rape of Nanking*': History and memory in Japan, China, and the United States. New York: Oxford University Press.

Michael D. Sepesy
Graduate Student
Cleveland, Ohio, USA

The Costs of Denial

Japanese human rights abuses during the second world war, as enumerated by the late Iris Chang in her best-selling book *The Rape of Nanking: The Forgotten Holocaust of World War II*, distinguish themselves as perhaps some of the most egregious atrocities committed within twentieth century combat and beyond. Yet, despite repeated unofficial apologies for wartime aggression by government leaders, Japan refuses to demonstrate the sincerity of its remorse by paying reparations to the victims of the nation's war crimes. Furthermore, Japanese officials have consistently undermined their professed sorrow and their own efforts for reconciliation by stubbornly resisting a full condemnation of and break from their nation's sullied past. While in office, former Prime Minister Junichiro Koizumi made annual visits to Tokyo's Yasukuni Shrine, a site that honors convicted war criminals as well as other deceased soldiers, in direct defiance of warnings by the Chinese government and his more diplomatically minded predecessor Kiichi Miyazawa. In addition, as recently as April 2007, Japan's current prime minister Shinzo Abe, who, in a rare move to reestablish Sino-Japanese relations, chose to make his first official trip to China as opposed to Washington, D.C., later commented that there was no proof that thousands of Chinese and Korean women and girls were abducted and forced into prostitution as "comfort women" for the Imperial Army—an assertion made in spite of the number of survivors who have spent decades demanding an official apology sanctioned by Japan's parliament.

Abe eventually retracted the statement, but his enigmatic stance on the severity of Japanese war crimes reflects the resistance of Japa-

129

nese nationalists to accept full accountability for the scope and ferocity of the Imperial Army's offenses. Paradoxically, such nationalist maneuvers to defend Japan's honor by whitewashing, distorting or erasing history injure not only the victims of Japanese misdeeds, but also the very reputation and regional relationships that revisionists and progressive thinkers alike hope to salvage.

That Japan's evasion of proper restitution continues to negatively affect the victims of that nation's atrocities is self-evident. Chang herself provides examples of Nanking survivors who have dwelt in poverty as a consequence of their experiences with the Imperial Army while Japan's economy (aided by the United States) has flourished. Moreover companies that participated in setting up concentration camps and torturing prisoners remain protected by the Japanese courts. According to an April 2007 report from the Xinhua News Agency, the Japanese Supreme Court overturned a decision to reward damages and an apology to two laborers and three families of deceased victims interned by the Nishimatsu Construction Company during the war.[1] Since the Chinese government stated in the Sino-Japanese Joint Statement of 1972 that it would not seek reparations from Japan, a move made to improve political relations, plaintiffs in China and Korea have sought to sue for retribution on an individual basis, as with the Nishimatsu lawsuit, their argument being that the 1972 agreement with Japan was only valid at the governmental level. With this latest decision, however, Japan's court was adamant: the Sino-Japanese Joint Statement negates both China's ability to seek restitution and that of its citizens.[2] Regardless, then, of its leaders' words of regret and repentance, Japan has, through its judiciary's actions, crystallized the country's official policy in dealing with those affected by the torture, rape, germ warfare, and murder with which the Imperial Army ravaged its Asian neighbors—namely, that Japan holds corporate interest above human life, and the "bottom line" above responsible behavior; and such a policy will undoubtedly reopen old wounds and stoke the already smoldering coals of resentment. For one nation to affirm to another nation that its citizens' lives are worth nothing is to court ill will and poison further diplomatic relations.

Of course, Japan's evasion of adequate international justice and failure to make proper restitution to its victims is not unique. An examination of the actions of both Allied and Axis countries both during and after the second world war, as well as the oppressive measures taken by colonial powers globally, reveals that not only was the twentieth century marked with widespread war crimes by countries as diverse as France, the Netherlands, Great Britain, and the United States (and the more typically vilified Germany, Italy, and Soviet Union) but also that in the majority of cases, the offenders either justified or rejected allegations of wrongdoing, and guilty parties remained unpunished. However, Japan is in a somewhat unique position in that it has benefited greatly from postwar reparations itself. Following the inexcusable obliteration of Nagasaki and Hiroshima, the United States helped rebuild the country's infrastructure, albeit with the cost of restricting Japan's degree of independence from American coercion.

This position as a recipient of aid affords Japan an opportunity that it chooses to routinely squander. The Japanese could take a leadership role in promoting conscientious global citizenship and distance themselves from other nations' shameful evasions and dismal human rights histories by formally apologizing in a manner suitable to victims' wishes (and not solely Japan's own), and by resolving, without the spur of legal action, prodding, or force, to implement a compensation strategy that would be acceptable to recipients and once and for all place old war crimes in the past. To courageously renounce the international tradition of disgraceful self-preservation that the rest of the world espouses and to stand on the side of justice might usher in a new era of disclosure and global commitment to humane principles. Viewed from an interpersonal perspective, if an individual violates the law and, when confronted, attempts to hide and lie about his actions to avoid punishment, any moral system would condemn him as a villain and a coward. By contrast, if such a person, regardless of his transgressions, confesses his crimes, exhibits genuine remorse, and accepts the consequences of his misdeeds, he regains at least a portion of his integrity.

Yet, instead of unburdening its collective conscience by assuming its responsibility to its victims and willingly extending a hand of mercy, Japan has, like a stubborn tortoise, withdrawn its compassion within an isolating shell of nationalism, and in so doing has forfeited regional stability and doomed the country's own aspirations. Concerning the perception of Japan among its Asian neighbors, a 2005 Kyodo News survey elicited responses from 1000 or more citizens from each of three nations: China, Japan, and South Korea. Researchers conducted the poll at a time when then Prime Minister Koizumi was preparing to once again visit the Yasukuni Shrine; and the results showed that both China and South Korea experienced a marked increase in the number of citizens holding an unfavorable opinion of Japan (83 percent and 75 percent respectively, both figures up from a previous survey).[3] Moreover, approximately half of all Chinese and South Korean respondents felt that the resolving of historical tensions between their respective countries and Japan would improve relations.[4] Given that the survey was comprised of a rather modest sampling, the outcome supports the notion that Japan's conduct during World War II continues to resonate as a factor in its reputation today, and that reaching a final settlement on the war crimes restitution issue would likely alleviate much of the friction in the region.

Unless a country explicitly acknowledges its human rights abuses as unlawful and rejects such actions clearly and emphatically without equivocation, the message left unspoken, expressed intentionally or unintentionally, is that such a nation privately grants itself the right to justify similar behavior in the future. Until a country can submit its behavior to the same justice that that state would wish for itself and abide by the penalties deemed necessary, its relationships will suffer from mistrust, residual bitterness from injured parties, and an eroded level of international respect. The United States has yet to learn this lesson, while Japan, though familiar with it, continues to ignore it. The consequences of not squarely addressing inhumane treatment matters is to risk appearing, directly or indirectly through rationalization, to condone such criminal behavior, and to perpetuate brutal and barbaric practices internationally by failing to promote justice as a prerequisite of civilized society, even when that justice balances its scales against one's own country.

Ultimately, Japan's circumvention of extending any tangible monetary symbol of regret to survivors of the Imperial Army's aggressions confounds the nation's own ambitions. For example, Japan has the aim of one day winning a position as a permanent member of the United Nations Security Council but faces stiff opposition from the Chinese government. In fact, in the same Kyodo News poll, 87 percent of Chinese and 85 percent of South Korean participants came out against Japan's bid for permanent member status.[5] This resistance, one could argue, may not be unrelated to Japan's historical record. Likewise, more than half a century after World War II and with a renewed sense of patriotism, Japan wishes to revisit its constitution and rebuild its military to strengthen the country's ability to protect itself. One need not be particularly creative to imagine the reaction of those nations with victims still attempting to receive recompense for the last time a patriotic Japan boasted a strong military presence. If Japan chose to allay its neighbors' anxieties by purging itself of its past and paying survivors and their families, its desire to shake off the shackles of postwar restrictions placed upon it, and to do so without its prompting suspicion and antagonism from its neighbors, might be realized. But Japan's courts continue to rule against reparation. Such decisions leave wounds open, subtly excuse the Imperial Army's barbarism, and reinforce animosity. As a result, Japan secures for itself assured conflict with surrounding countries whenever that nation displays an urge to be more independent, to upright itself in strength, or to make any move that may call to mind the ghosts of its former colonial will-to-power.

To be sure, victims and their relatives have sought new approaches with which to break through Japan's fortress of defiance. Survivors and those representing the deceased have undertaken legal proceedings in their own countries, since Japan will not recognize these cases within its own borders. Some plaintiffs have investigated mirroring the successes of Jewish Holocaust survivors by looking toward the United States' courts to conduct litigations. In light of Japan's ruling against individuals seeking redress for atrocities, however, the promise of such ventures is dubious unless survivors can gain the notice and support of American voters, who might then pressure their elected representatives to enact legislation or persuade state officials to encourage more cooperation from the Japanese government. As Chang suggests in *The Rape of Nanking*, the late 1990s saw rising U.S. interest in holding Japan responsible for its war crimes, and the surge in visibility culminated in HCR 126, a House resolution intended in part to call for an apology from Japan for the mistreatment of prisoners of war and other victims, such as the "comfort women" and survivors of Nanking, and to force Japan to pay restitution to all concerned.[6] Despite being sponsored by 78 House representatives, the resolution failed.

Since the United States is the country with perhaps the most influence on Japan, strategies involving the U.S. may seem more viable to reach survivors' goals, although America's current lack of credibility with regard to questions of human rights may subvert our country's efficacy in engaging Japans' sympathies. Nevertheless, should tactics of negotiation not prove effective, America's clout in the world market and leverage in the U.N. might prove useful tools where moral example fails. It should be noted that the U.S. itself also entered into a treaty in 1951 that absolved the Japanese of war reparations, thus not guaranteeing success for those wishing to utilize the U.S. justice system. Immediate legal solutions notwithstanding, perhaps the single best method of causing Japan to reevaluate its position is to adopt the most potent weapon wielded by the postwar Jewish population— to engage the public imagination through the arts, and specifically film. The sheer volume of material on the Nazi Holocaust has ensured that the words and images depicting its tragedies will forever burn into the public's memory. To date there have been only three films depicting the dramatic events of the Rape of Nanking, each project meeting with mixed results, and all of them released primarily to Chinese audiences. The power of film is that, when done well, it most viscerally and instantaneously fuses ideas with raw emotions, and transforms cold facts into images that reach people's hearts—and it is from the human heart and its compassion, its outrage, its sorrow, that people can be moved to act toward positive change.

One thing is certain: to gain harmony in Asia will require more concessions from Japan for its war crimes than simply rhetorical assurances. The actions of Japanese higher courts have continually undermined the sentiments expressed by passing administrations. To apologize without offering assistance is an empty gesture. Unless Japan looks forward to being dogged by decades-old disgraces, to being greeted with misgivings by its neighbors, and to having its goals thwarted into perpetuity by the begrudging descendants of its uncompensated victims, its offerings of peace and good faith must be as visible and real today as its reign of carnage was seventy years ago within the walls of Nanking.

1. Xinhua News Agency. "Japanese Court Decision on War Reparations Slammed." China.Org.Cn 28 April 2007. <http://www.china.org.cn/english/news/209388.htm >

2. Ibid.

3. Kyodo News. "Ex-PM Urges Koizumi Not to Visit Yasukuni." China Daily. 19 June 25, <http://chinadaily.com.cn/english/doc/2005-06/19/content_452685.htm>

4. Ibid.

5. Ibid.

6. "Expressing the Sense of Congress Concerning the War Crimes Committed by the Japanese Military During World War II." HCON 126 IH. 25 July 1997. Sponsored by William O. Lipinski. The Library of Congress.

<http://thomas.loc.gov/cgi-bin/query/D?c105:20:./temp/~c105yHfQYD::>

Works Cited

(1) "Expressing the Sense of Congress Concerning the War Crimes Committed by the Japanese Military During World War II." HCON 126 IH. 25 July 1997. Sponsored by William O. Lipinski. The Library of Congress.

<http://thomas.loc.gov/cgi-bin/query/D?c105:20:./temp/~c105yHfQYD::>

(2) Kyodo News. "Ex-PM Urges Koizumi Not to Visit Yasukuni." China Daily. 19 June 25 <http://chinadaily.com.cn/english/doc/2005-06/19/content_452685.htm>

(3) Xinhua News Agency. "Japanese Court Decision on War Reparations Slammed." China.Org.Cn 28 April 2007 <http://www.china.org.cn/english/news/209388.htm >

Lillis Taylor
Graduate Student China Studies
University of Washington
Seattle, Washington, USA

I am a twenty-seven year old white female from Birmingham, Alabama. I grew up in a town full of ghosts. The civil rights movement shaped lives all across Alabama and often the nucleus of the battle was centered in Birmingham. Lives were brutally battered and destroyed. There was no regard for sex or age. And yet, with time, the battle was won. That battle was before my time. Often, my mother thinks the battle was before her time as well. She was an elementary school student during the 60's, and her middle-class, church-going family kept her sheltered and out of the fray. During my formative years, I went to school and played with black boys and girls. I thought nothing of it and wasn't aware of my hometown's important social history until I encountered lingering racism in the news or, occasionally on the streets. My parents taught me the difference between right and wrong and how absurd it is to judge people based on physical differences. When I first learned and later read about slavery, the Underground Railroad and brave freedom fighters such as Harriet Tubman, Sojourner Truth, Frederick Douglas and educators such as George Washington Carver, I was mystified by the crazed actions of one race against another, but I was lifted up by their brave stories. This was my first taste of the world's imbalance.

When I was nine years old, I went to visit my father in Northern Japan where he was teaching English and trying to write the next great American novel. After a month of exploring the wonders of rural Japan, hiking among pristine streams and waterfalls, traipsing about in rice paddies and plucking rosy apples from branches hanging with ripe fruit, my father asked me if I wanted to spend a year in a Japanese school among Japanese children. My summer had been magical and I was delighted at the prolonged opportunity. Each day, I attended a fourth grade class. My teacher, Sato Sensei spoke almost no English. During my year among Japanese peers, I made many mistakes and grew deeper with understanding from them. The experience of another culture instills compassion because your eyes are open and only the emotionally blind are incapable of compassion. My year in Japan was a rich, colorful year and it shaped my sense of wonder and excitement. I learned to listen carefully, to perceive and to be patient. I fell in love with Japan. I fell in love with the resolve of the people. I fell in love with the sense of duty, honor and calm that I felt from every soul I met.

After my fourth grade year, I returned to Alabama with a devotion to Japan rooted in my whole being. I grew up and moved to Seattle to pursue a degree in Industrial Design. After graduation, I started working for a company with manufacturing ties in Shenzhen, China. And thus, a new devotion started to evolve. This devotion sprang from a different soft spot in my heart. My love for Japan grew from the beauty and the culture I had experienced at a tender age. My love for China grew from an idea that there was a grave imbalance. I watched as my white-collar co-workers experienced one world within the comfortable realm of product design and as my blue-collar counterparts in China slaved under very different conditions in order to produce the ultimately useless items that we designed for Americans to purchase for amusement. I felt that, somehow, my Chinese counterparts were being wronged. In every facet of life, culture was telling me that China was a simmering pot of opportunity, wealth and power. It seemed the time to make a change, and so, I quit my job and left for a yearlong teaching contract in Wuhan, Hubei Province.

That was exactly one year ago today, June 23rd 2006. A year ago, I didn't know of the Nanking Massacre and I had never heard of Iris Chang. I regret that it took so long to learn of the tragedy that occurred at the hands of the Japanese, but I am thankful to have the opportunity to write about it now. Because I love Japan so, it is extremely important to me that the wrongs of the past be recognized and atoned for.

In my mind, it is no accident that the Holocaust inflicted by Nazi Germany on the Jewish population of Europe during World War II is the first genocide that school children in America learn of. Based on what I have read about the Rape of Nanking, the atrocities occurred during the second Sino-Japanese war, which was fought in tandem with the Second World War. And thus the Japanese were committing crimes against humanity at the same time as the Nazis in Europe, if not earlier, and yet, after the war, the results of the Tokyo tribunal were very different from those of the tribunal in Nuremburg, Germany.

In Germany, many of the Nazi generals and sympathizers were put to death after court proceedings that were presided over by a multinational panel. In Tokyo, the power in the courts was still on the side of the Japanese. In order for justice to come, it is necessary for China to stand united against this terrifying history and speak up. The Chinese government must do its part as a strengthening world power to request honest telling of history and Japan's role in it. Although the truth of the Massacre was obscured by many of the Japanese participants after the war, China's government, led by Mao Zedong, further hampered justice when it suppressed history in order to strike a tenable diplomatic accord with Japan. Japan must risk likely shame and accept with honesty and integrity the complete history of its involvement in genocide during the second Sino-Japanese War. From my time spent in Japan, I know that society is imbued with a sense of honor and duty and that in the best of times, these traits bring out a great loyalty, but this loyalty can be disfiguring to the overall goal of love of country if it is stubborn and held in higher regard than compassion for fellow humans be they fellow countrymen or old foes. It is often this loyalty for country that leads to great lapses in judgment the world around. The greater good for humanity should be each citizen of the world's guiding principle.

China must stand united and speak up about the painful scars left by the Massacre. At the time, China was a victim, but the country is victim no more. China has shown the world what she can do on her own. The people are strong and there is a determination that has built a strong economy and a self-sufficient infrastructure. In regards to past wrongs, to take the stance of a victim would weaken China's ability to bring justice to those real and fallen victims of the Massacre. It is important that brave souls like Harriet Tubman and Sojourner Truth speak up. Iris Chang was a brave soul. She should not be the only one to stand up and demand action from the Japanese. In her time, she asked for recognition of the atrocities and recompense. Because of her constant research and her lone voice in the storm, she lost huge pieces of her soul, and we lost a shining example of bravery and strength.

The compassionate people of the world need to work harder to bring such atrocities as the Nanking Massacre to the rest of the world's attention because these acts against fellow man are devastating. They continue to occur and each time, it is a more humiliating realization that we let it happen again. Bosnians and Serbs. Rwanda's Tutsis and Hutus. Israelis and Palestinians. Sunnis and Shiites. Muslims and non-Muslims in Darfur, Sudan. There is too much apathy and the genocides continue as comfortable citizens in comfortable countries concern themselves with blocking out the truth as it appears on the nightly news and in newspapers and on the radio. Iris Chang raged against the apathy for so long and so alone that she lost her strength and herself.

Iris Chang's demise is an additional tragedy, piled on the imbalance of the still-suppressed truth of Japan's acts after the second Sino-Japanese War. Enough blood has been shed. It is time for compassion on all fronts. The world's youth are tired of the mistakes of our predecessors, especially those who hold office and busy themselves in bureaucracy and neglect the task they were elected to contend with: the righting of wrongs and the protection of victims of genocide and hatred.

Imagine a world where Asia is united. What a powerful image that creates. So much of the world's population resides in Asia and it is time these people had a united voice. There is no way for Asia to truly unite until Japan confesses the wrongs perpetrated by its powerful army during and before World War II. But there is also a roadblock if China is not willing to come to the table ready for honesty. Victim and Foe must relinquish these roles alike and work towards a relationship of unity that does not rely on differences in order to create boundaries. It is time for honesty, openness, strength, integrity and forgiveness. It is time for individuals to really see each other when walking down the street. It is time for compassion. It is time for balance. And it will always be time for remembrance of the mistakes we've made so that we never make them again.

Jerry Jun-Yen Wang
Graduated from University of Minnesota
Minneapolis, Minnesota, USA

The Nanjing Massacre:
On Japanese who deny and others who accept the truth

In the middle of December, 1937, less than six months after Japan invaded China, the Japanese Imperial Army captured the city of Nanjing (or Nanking), the capital of the Nationalist government in China. In the following weeks, Japanese soldiers committed mass murder and rape, with as many as 100,000 to 350,000 Chinese killed, and up to 200,000 women raped (Ogawa, 2000: 42). Historians inside and outside of China remembered the atrocity as the Rape of Nanjing or the Nanjing Massacre [Nanjing Gyakusatsu in Japanese] (Morris-Suzuki and Rimmer, 2002: 157). Since then, Japan has refused to issue a full apology; moreover the Japanese government has allowed removal of the incident from some history textbooks. And some top officials have paid visits to the Yasukuni Shrine, a symbol to China and Korea of the wartime atrocities. These Japanese actions have increased tensions in this region and harmed Japanese economic relations.

Why does Japan continue to ignore or dismiss the wartime atrocities? This essay will look into the actions that the Japanese government has taken, the responses of Japanese civilians, the roadblocks that have prevented this atrocity from being officially recognized by the Japanese government, and offer solutions that may help the recognition of the atrocity by the Japanese government and thereby help the relations between Japan and China.

One may ask what has Japan done about the atrocities that were committed during the World War II. This has been up to those who have power in the Japanese government. For the majority of period after World War II and the Allied Occupation, the right wing, nationalists, and hardliner factions within the Liberal Democratic Party (LDP) had control of the Japanese government along with popular support from various sectors in society (Ogawa, 2000: 42). They denied any wrong doings by Japan during World War II and further questioned if the Nanjing Massacre and other atrocities such as the Comfort Women had even occurred, so as to defend Japan's pride or "saving face" (Ogawa, 2000: 46). In addition, veterans associations that felt the Japan's wartime actions were justified, "that Japanese wartime occupation actually freed Asian countries from Western colonial oppression" (Ogawa, 2000: 44). Moreover, together they felt Japan was a victim of Western power (two atomic bombs were dropped on Japan by the U.S. in World War II), not a victimizer of East Asia. They do not want "words such as 'aggression,' 'colonization,' and 'apology'" (Kishimoto, 2004: 29) in textbooks or letters written to victimized nations.

But in 1993, when for the first time a non-LDP political party, the Japan New Party, held control of the government, its leader, Morihiro Hosokawa, "became the first premier to formally recognize Japanese responsibility, using the term 'aggression' instead of 'advance' to describe Japan's wartime actions in Asia" (Ogawa, 2000: 44). And in 1995, then prime minister Tomiichi Murayama, also a member of a non-LDP party, Socialist Party, "was the first to use the word owabi (apology) in his 50th anniversary address commemorating the end of World War II… fulfilling a lifelong personal and Socialist Party goal to atone for Japanese aggression" (Ogawa, 2000: 44). However, when Murayama tried to have the Diet (the Japanese parliament) "pass a resolution expressing apology," it "was thwarted by members of the LDP… the final approved resolution expressed only fukai hansei (deep self-reflection)" (Ogawa, 2000: 44).

In the aftermath of several anti-Japanese protests in China in April of 2005, former Japanese Prime Minister Koizumi Junichiro, a member of the LDP, offered an apology at the Africa-Asia summit in Jakarta, addressing the actions that were done by Japan during World War II, "Japan, through its colonial rule and aggression, caused tremendous damage and suffering to the people of many countries, particularly to those of Asian nations;" and also addressing what Japan had done since World War II,

"with feelings of deep remorse and heartfelt apology always en-

graved in mind, Japan has resolutely maintained, consistently since the end of World War II, never turning into a military power but an economic power, its principle of resolving all matters by peaceful means, without recourse to the use of force " *("Excerpts from Japan PM's apology,"* 2005).

Several apologies were also made by high-ranking Japanese officials regarding the actions taken by Japan in World War II. However the three events mentioned above were personal apologies by politicians to victimized nations. In contrast, the Japanese government, over sixty years after the Nanjing Massacre, has not formally recognized the atrocity, nor apologizes, nor paid compensation to the victims. Many Chinese, Chinese-Americans, and others are demanding that the Japanese government formally recognize the Nanjing Massacre and other atrocities committed by the Japanese military during World War II, and accept responsibility towards the victims.

There is a deep meaning in the words used in the personal apologies. According to Kyoko Kishimoto, the word hansei could mean either "regret" or "apology," and there is a difference between them. Kishimoto wrote, "'Apology' implies full acknowledgement of a wrongdoing and willingness to take responsibility, whereas 'regret' recognizes the wrongdoing but does not necessarily take responsibility" (Kishimoto, 2004: 29). The stance that Japan is current taking is more of self-regret than to apologize to the victimized nations.

Chalmers Johnson comments on the Japanese government's failure to recognize its past atrocities and its failure to take action to uncover the truth in the present,

"Japan has no law covering war crimes, has never brought to justice any Japanese citizen accused of crimes against humanity, is the only advanced democracy whose government censors school history textbooks, and has consistently used its censorship power to suppress information about Japan's treatment of civilians and prisoners during wartime, including its army's killing its own citizens in places like Okinawa ".(Johnson, 2000).

This is a sharp contrast when compared to what Germany has

done after World War II to remember its own atrocity such as the Holocaust. Germany has included the Holocaust in their history textbooks, built memorials remembering the atrocities they committed in the past, and "compensated individual victims of the Holocaust directly." Germany also worked together with Poland to publish history textbooks for both sides to teach, a matter that Japan avoids to do with its neighboring nations (*Censoring History*, 2000: 25). For its action, Germany was praised by South Korean President Roh Moo Hyun for "the way it has settled its past and recovered trust by showing conscience, courage, and action" (Wakamiya, 2005).

One area that reflects the conflicts of recognizing and denying the atrocities is the issue of history textbooks published in Japan. These are "'screened' (i.e., censored) by the Ministry of Education to ensure that the subject matter is 'suitable' to be taught in elementary, junior high, and high schools" (Kishimoto, 2004: 35). This became a scandal in 1982 when the Chinese government protested after it learned that changes in the history textbooks were made "to deny Japanese responsibility for an aggressive war." Examples included changing "invasion" of China to "advance into" China, and "that references to Nanjing Massacre had been deleted" (Buruma, 1995: 126).

Japanese schoolteachers, students, and other grassroots' movements (or known as Progressives, considered as left-wing movements by the Japanese government) have continuously challenged the Ministry of Education and the government about the content in the textbooks, demanding the inclusion of wartime atrocities committed by Japanese soldiers during World War II (Buruma, 1995: 192-3). The great example may be the late Prof. Iegana Saburo (1913 ~ 2002), who sued the Ministry of Education in 1965 for deleting references to the Nanjing Massacre and Unit 731 from his history textbook. He claimed it was unconstitutional for government to censor textbooks. Ienaga faced an uphill battle against the government for over thirty years, many times he lost his case, and he was attacked by people from right-wing and subjected to death threats. In 1997 Ienaga had a small victory; the Japanese Supreme Court ruled that the Ministry of Education acted illegally in removing the contents from his textbook. However an earlier ruling in 1993 by the Japanese Supreme Court ruled that the government had the right to delete details about the

Japanese atrocity in World War II (Lewis, 2002).

To counter the movements from the left-wing, the right-wing nationalists are publishing their own textbook to serve their own agenda. These people are also known as the Revisionist and include politicians, scholars and celebrities. In December of 1996, University of Tokyo Professor Fujioka Nobukatsu founded the Japan Society for History Textbook Reform (JSHTR), which calls for rewriting the history textbooks to downplay the atrocities committed by Japan during World War II (Morris-Suzuki and Rimmer, 2002: 148). Manga (comic book) star Kobayashi Yoshinori, who was also a member of this society, published Sensoron (A Theory of War) in 1998, which "called the Nanjing Massacre and the enslavement of comfort women fictitious" (Jeans, 2005: 187). In 2001 the latest edition of history textbook by the JSHTR, The New History Textbook, was approved by the Ministry of Education (Takahashi – 2, 2004).

However, it is important to know there are other textbooks that are used, and the education system in Japan allows the local districts of boards of education to have the power to either adopt the textbooks by the JSHTR or not (Jeans, 2005: 191). This is shown in the summer of 2001 where 532 out of the 542 school districts in Japan (about 98 percent) choose not to adopt the JSHTR textbook, while only a handful of schools choose to adopt it (Jeans, 2005: 192). In 2003, there was about 0.13% of junior high schools using the JSHTR textbook "despite aggressive right-wing media campaigns" (Takahashi – 2, 2004).

The education system itself could contribute to ignorance about history. In Japan students focus on preparation for entrance exam into the prestigious high school or college for a successful later life. The emphasis is on rote memorization of materials for the exam (Ogawa, 2000: 46). In Who Rules Japan? Harold R. Kerbo and John A. McKinstry argued, "Japanese universities are not always the best places for objective, scientific debate on social and political issues." They also commented, "Japanese high school students have the best test scores for math and science in the world. But with respect to history and aspects of their own contemporary society, there are surprisingly large gaps in their knowledge (Kerbo & McKinstry, 1995:

161)." The content of the history textbook is very small. It "consists mostly of concise presentation of facts" without analysis of historical events. A combination of these factors may discourage Japanese students from discussing or having an opinion about certain events in history (Ogawa, 2000: 46). This is not enough to help younger Japanese generation to understand the effects on current relations between Japan and its neighboring nations caused by the atrocities committed in the past.

Another related source of tension between Japan and its neighboring nations is the official visits to the Yasukuni Shrine. This shrine, built during the Meiji Period and originally dedicated to honor those who had died during the Bosin War, was to include those who had died in the later conflicts in which Japan had participated. Among those enshrined include Koreans and Taiwanese that served in the Japanese Imperial military as colonial subjects "without consultation with family members" (Tanaka, 2004). The shrine also includes several Class-A war criminals from WWII who were convicted in the Tokyo War Tribunal (Jeans, 2005: 151).

The Class-A war criminals were placed in the shrine during the 1970's, and the head priests that oversaw the shrine included former members of the Japanese Imperial military. And the shrine also houses the Yushukan war memorial, which displays military weapons used by the Japanese military during WWII, such as the Mitsubishi Zero fighter (Wakamiya & Watanabe, 2006), and offers a "Japan is innocent" perspective on the causes of WWII. For example, the reason that Japan entered the war was to free itself along with other Asian nations from Western powers, a belief reflective of the Japanese right-wing (Marquand, 2005). In the past and present, when high ranking Japanese officials, including Koizumi, visited the Yasukuni Shrine, it usually drew massive protests from Chinese, Koreans, and other citizens in Asian nations (Takahashi – 1, 2004); but the Japanese see it differently.

The difference is reflected through a survey that was conducted jointly by Asahi Shimbun of Japan, the Dong-A Ilbo of South Korea, and the Chinese Academy of Social Science of China in March of

2005, which found 92 percent in South Korea and 91 percent in China were opposed to Koizumi's visits to the Yasukuni Shrine, whereas in Japan, 28 percent were against the visits, while 54 percent were in favor. When asked what they say the Yasukuni Shrine represents, 6 out of 10 South Koreans and Chinese saw it as a "symbol of militarism," where as 7 out of 10 Japanese saw it as a "facility to pay tribute to the war dead" ("Japan disliked by 60% of neighbors," 2005). Some questioned if Koizumi was true to his apology in Jakarta, since he had visited the Yasukuni Shrine several times before and after, leaving a bad impression to the Asian nations (Wakamiya, 2005). And there are growing oppositions to the shrine visits.

In the present there is continued protest from China and [South] Korea over the visits, the revised textbook, as well as territorial disputes (Miyazaki, 2005). This mistrust between Japan and China had caused friction between the two nations (there is mistrust between Japan and Korea as well). This became very apparent in the summer of 2004, when China hosted the Asian Cup soccer tournament. There the Chinese fans harassed the Japanese players and fans, and sat down or booed the Japanese national anthem (the title of the Japanese anthem is "Kimigayo," meaning "the Emperor's World"), which drew protest from the Japanese government (Takahashi – 1, 2004). In a response to Japan's bid to the Security Council in April of 2005, several massive protests erupted in China, where Chinese protesters threw objects at the Japanese embassy, burned Japanese flags, damaged Japanese business and called for boycott of Japanese goods, in which Japan's Trade Minister Shoichi Nakagawa called China "a scary country" ("Japan: China is 'scary country,'" 2005).

Some Japanese and others criticize that China uses the Japanese atrocities in World War II to incite nationalism so as to deter its people from other issues, and "intimidate Japan or… to highlight China's victim's status" (Morris-Suzuki and Rimmer, 2002: 160). They also say that China has committed atrocities towards its own people while denying it at the same time, such as the Tiananmen Square Massacre. Asked by Britain's Financial Times whether China would close the question of responsibility if Japan met all of Beijing's demands, Ian

Buruma replied, "Probably not... These outbursts of emotional and sometimes violent nationalism in China take place partly because they are the only expression of public protest the government allows" (Halloran, 2005). But these criticisms do not take the responsibility away from Japan for its actions committed in the past.

Scholars and publics inside and outside of Japan believe the government's stance on denying any wrong doing in World War II will do more harm to itself. This was reflected in a survey done in Japan in 1995 by Yomiuri Shimbun, where 70% felt that the Japan's action in China during World War II poses a threat to the development of more positive relations between China and Japan (JPOLL – 1). When Asahi Shimbun conducted a survey in Japan in 1997 about the compensation towards China, over half (58%) of those surveyed thought Japan had done "not enough" (JOLL – 2).

But Japan, even in the face of negative repercussion, has consistently refused to make an official apology by the government and allowed right-wing movement to continue to make their stance of "Japan as Innocent," while politicians and war veterans preserved as powerful voice in Japanese society.

We saw that Germany has taken a more direct approach than Japan in response to the atrocities they committed during World War II. Germany has admitted the atrocities, taught it in the textbooks, compensated the victims, and built memorials to remind future generations of the past. Social scientists and historians offer different perspectives on why Germany has been able to progress forward with its past.

One perspective is the regime changes that Germany experienced after World War II, where the Nazi party was completely removed from the German government. In contrast in Japan, particularly in the Reverse Course taken by the Allied Forces, many officials and members of the Imperial Government, including Empire Hirohito, were to remain in their position prior to the war and avoiding war criminal trial altogether. This post-war condition was best described by Robert M. Orr, Jr., "For the U.S. to exonerate Hirohito made it much more difficult for military leaders to conceive of their own guilt. Since the war was fought in the name of the Emperor, how could soldiers carrying out the will of the Emperor be guilty if the Emperor himself was innocent? (Orr, 1998)"

Another perspective argues that the geo-political situation such as economic needs and geographic closeness motivated Germany to reconcile with its neighboring nations, while Japan is caught in conflicts with both China and North Korea concerning economic and security matters, and its longtime alliance with the U.S. makes it stand out from the rest of East Asia (aside from South Korea) in terms of military and economic power, thus it didn't need a very close relations with its neighbors (Censoring History, 2000: 18-20).

Whatever the differences in the perspectives are, this does not mean Germany has the sense of shame and guilt and Japan has none (Censoring History, 2000: 10). We have seen Japanese individuals trying to preserve the truth about the wartime past, only to be blocked by politicians and their supporters.

In his words, Ogawa believed, "acknowledgement of guilt will enable Japan to assure without suspicion the greater role in regional and international arenas that it has sought in recent years" (Ogawa, 2000: 46); this statement could not be truer at a critical time as Japan bids towards a permanent seat in the United Nations Security Council. From the Asahi Shimbun poll conducted in April of 2005, 87 percent of South Koreans and 84 percent of Chinese opposed Japan's bid to the U.N. Security Council ("Japan disliked by 60% of neighbors," 2005).

But there are risks in confronting the past. On the eve of the death of Emperor Hirohito in 1988, the mayor of Nagasaki, Motoshima Hitoshi, commented that the dying emperor had responsibilities for the wartime suffering of the Japanese people. After Mayor Motoshima made his comment, he was attacked by his own party and the extreme right-wing, and in 1990 the mayor barely survived an assassination attempt by members of the right-wing (Buruma, 1994: 249-50). When both LDP senior member Koichi Kato and Fuji Xerox chairman Yotaro "Tony" Kobayashi each spoke against Koizumi's visits to the Yasukuni Shrine separately, members of the right-wing burnt down their houses (Clemons, 2006).

Foreign voices are also threatened by the right-wing; David McNeill, an American, did a radio show in Japan with his wife and they commented on the Nanjing Massacre; after the show was done, members from the right-wing showed up at the radio station and met with the station's managers. By pressuring the station's managers, the right-wing members demanded both McNeill and his wife to apologize for the comment on the Nanjing Massacre and to read an apology statement, which McNeil refused but had to comply: "We decided to read out some of the faxes - only one of which referred specifically to Nanking - and not to read the station's apology" (McNeill, 2001).

However threats from the right-wing should not discourage people from finding solutions. News reporters inside and outside of Japan have proposed several solutions to improve relations between China and Japan. One suggestion included conducting an international joint research of the history in the East Asia region (China, Japan, and Korea), promoting information disclosure and conservation of historical materials that were kept away after World War II, and encouraging public discussion on postwar compensation ("AAN Proposals," 2002). Others call to reiterate the Murayama statement (Wakamiya, 2005). And others believed that Emperor Akihito could have delivered the ultimate apology for the sixtieth anniversary of the end of World War II in the summer of 2005 (Halloran, 2005). Two editors, Wakamiya Yoshibumi and Watanabe Tsuneo, from competing newspapers in Japan, the Asahi Shimbun, and the Yomiuri Shimbun, called for a construction of a non-secular, national war memorial to replace the Yasukuni Shrine (Wakamiya & Watanabe, 2006).

At the end of this paper, I would like conclude with my personal thoughts. A true recognition of the wartime events is to take responsibility, not to deny it. This will be a true show of courage of preserving the truth, instead of following blind patriotism for the individuals involved. While all the actions above would not guarantee forgiveness from all the victims of the victimized nations, only by admitting to the atrocities committed in the past and paying the reparation to the victims could Japan relieve itself of its heavy burden of guilt, show the courage of confronting the past, gain the trust of East Asian nations, and move forward towards the international stage, just as Germany was able to do. In doing so, China would no longer attack Japan's past and use it as a nationalism rally cry; and with the possibility of greater support from forgiving nations, getting a U.N. Security Council seat would not be so unlikely for Japan.

---

(1) "AAN Proposals," The Asahi Shimbun Asia Network. Asahi.com 2002. March 28, 2005 <http://www.asahi.com/english/asianet/hatsu/eng_hatsu010707d.html>

(2) Buruma, Ian. *The Wages of Guilt: Memories of War in Germany and Japan*. Jonathan Cape, London. 1994

(3) *Censoring History: Citizenship and Memory in Japan, Germany and the United States*. Ed. Laura Hein and Mark Selden. M.E. Sharpe. Inc., Armonk, New York. 2000

(4) Chang, Iris. *The Rape of Nanking: The Forgotten Holocaust of World War II*. Basic Books, New York, 1997

(5) Clemons, Steven. "The Rise of Japan's Thought Police," WashingtonPost.com 27 August, 2006. June 29, 2007 <http://www.washingtonpost.com/wp-dyn/content/article/2006/08/25/AR2006082501176.html>

(6) "Excerpts from Japan PM's apology," BBC News Online 22 Apr, 2005. April 28, 2005 <http://news.bbc.co.uk/go/pr/fr/-/1/hi/world/asia-pacific/4471961.stm>

(7) Halloran, Richard. "Japanese apologies never seem to be enough." Taipei Times Online 02 May 2005. May 11, 2005 <http://www.taipeitimes.com/News/edit/archives/ 2005/05/02/2003252861>

(8) "Japan: China is 'scary country.'" CNN.com 12 Apr, 2005. April 12, 2005 <http://www.cnn.com/2005/WORLD/asiapcf/04/12/china.japan/index.html>

(9) "Japan disliked by 60% of neighbors." asahi.com 28 Apr. 2005. May 11, 2005 <http://www.asahi.com/english/Herald-asahi/TKY200504280161.html>

(10) Jeans, Roger B. "Victims or Victimizers? Museums, Textbooks and the War Debate in Contemporary Japan," *The Journal of Military History*, Vol. 69. January 2005. pg 149 – 95

(11) Johnson, Chalmers. "Some Thoughts on the Nanjing Massacre," JPRI *Critique* Vol.VII, No.1 (January 2000), Japan Policy Research Institute (JPRI), <http://www.jpri.org/publications/critiques/critique_VII_1.html> March 31, 2005

(12) JPOLL – the Japanese Public Opinion Database <http://roperweb.ropercenter.Uconn.edu>

1. Question: "Do you think the Japanese army's conduct in China and other Asian countries during World War II still poses a threat to the positive development of relations between Japan and China?"

2. Question: "Do you think Japan has compensated China enough for what it did in the past including World War, or not?"

(13) Kerbo, Harold R. and John A. McKinstry. *Who Rules Japan: the inner circles of economic and political power.* Praeger Publishers, Westport, Connecticut, 1995

(14) Kishimoto, Kyoko. "Apologies for Atrocities: Commemorating the 50th Anniversary of World War II's End in the United States and Japan," *American Studies International*, Vol. XLII, Nos. 2 & 3. June-October 2004. pg 17 – 50

(15) Lewis, Paul. "Saburo Ienaga, Who Insisted Japan Disclose Atrocities, Dies at 89," The New York Times Online 8 Dec. 2002. May 10, 2005 <http://www.nytimes.com/2002/12/08/obituaries/08IENA.html?ex=1115870400&en=62b69bdb6da44d3c&ei=5070>

(16) Marquand, Robert. "Koizumi's visits boost controversial version of history," Christian Science Monitor Online 21 October, 2005. January 16, 2007 <http://www.csmonitor.com/2005/1021/p01s04-woap.html>

(17) McNeill, David. "An unwelcome visit from the uyoku," New Statesman Online 26 February, 2001. June 29, 2007 < http://www.newstatesman.com/200102260017 >

(18) Miyazaki, Jamie. "Textbook row stirs Japanese concern," BBC News Online 13 Apr. 2005. April 14, 2005 <http://news.bbc.co.uk/go/pr/fr/-/hi/asia-pacific/4439923.stm>

(19) Morris-Suzuki, Tessa, and Peter Rimmer. "Virtual Memories: Japanese History Debates in Manga and Cyberspace," *Asian Studies Review*, Vol.26, Number 2. June 2002

(20) Ogawa, Shuko. "The Difficulty of Apology: Japan's Struggle with Memory and Guilt," *Harvard International Review*, Vol.22, Issue 3. Fall 2000. pg 42 – 6

(21) Orr, Robert M. Jr. "The Rape of History," *JPRI Critique* Vol.V, No.6 (July 1998), Japan Policy Research Institute (JPRI), <http://www.jpri.org/publications/critiques/critique_V_6.html> June 8, 2006

(22) Tanaka, Nobumasa. "Yasukuni Shrine and the Double Genocide of Taiwan's Indigenous Atayal: new court verdict," ZNet 27 July, 2004. January 15, 2007 <http://www.zmag.org/content/showarticle.cfm?ItemID=5937>

(23) Takahashi, Kosuke. "China vs Japan – It's not just a soccer game," Asia Times Online 7 Aug. 2004. March 31, 2005 <http://www.asiatimes.com/atimes/Japan/FH07Dh01.html>

(24) "Tortuous tangles over Japanese textbooks," Asia Times Online 26 Oct. 2004. March 31, 2005 <http://www.asiatimes.com/atimes/Japan/FJ26Dh01.html >

(25) Wakamiya, Yoshibumi. "Why Japan's apologies always fall flat," asahi.com 5 May 2005. Column. May 11, 2005 <http://www.asahi.com/english/column/TKY200505070217.html>

(26) Wakamiya, Yoshibumi and Tsuneo Watanabe. "Yomiuri and Asahi Editors Call for a National Memorial to Replace Yasukuni," JapanFocus.org 14 February 2006. May 22, 2006 <http://japanfocus.org/article.asp?id=524>

Essays of Honor

Mary E Whitsell
(an expatriate American living in the U.K.)
Moffat, United Kingdom

The Folly of Ignorance

Half a lifetime ago, I moved to Japan. I was young and ignorant and keen on learning an Asian language, and I knew that I could support myself in Japan by teaching English, as I had begun to study TESOL in college. I intended to acquire a working knowledge of Japanese, then go back to the States and complete my TESOL degree. As it turned out, I ended up spending seventeen years in Japan.

When I first went to Japan, I had little knowledge of Japanese history, and even less interest in it. Although I was aware that my grandfather and a few of the older members of my family were very anti-Japanese, their attitude struck me as racist and old-fashioned. If I had thought it through, I might have come to another conclusion: my grandfather had many Chinese friends and he raised his children to be open-minded and egalitarian. Still, I imagined that my grandfather's anti-Japanese stance must be due to prejudice and the war. But the war was behind us, and though I had Korean and Chinese friends whose parents occasionally mentioned the Japanese in a less than complimentary way, I felt that it had nothing to do with my generation. Given that, why dig into it?

My first year in Japan was revelatory. Like all newcomers to Japan, I quickly went from my 'honeymoon period,' when every new thing about the country is interesting and wonderful to my 'marriage period,' when all of Japan's faults and idiosyncrasies become oppressively tedious. One of the first things I noticed about the Japanese was a tendency for many of them to both admire and look down on foreigners. On one hand, we were seen as being worthy of emulation. Models in Japan tended to be Caucasian, and Japanese young people were keen to adopt western customs and fashions. Conversely, though, foreigners with their odd ways and brash manners were held in derision. People either loved us or hated us, and quite often they seemed to do both in equal measures. And there was an equally ambiguous attitude towards foreigners who did not look like foreigners as such: other Asians such as Chinese, Indochinese, or Koreans. A lot of Japanese people seemed to ignore them, or to treat them very much like second-class citizens.

I did not realize at the time just how much history had to do with Japanese attitudes to westerners and other Asians, and in fact, the world in general. And yet when I look back on that time, although I acknowledge that many people in Japan do try to minimize or whitewash Japanese wartime atrocities, most of the people I was fortunate enough to become friends with were quite the opposite.

In my wilful ignorance, I missed a hundred opportunities to discuss the events of the war. I am haunted by an experience I had one day during my first few months in Tokyo, in Kinokuniya Bookstore. I was in the history section, looking for a book for a friend, when an elderly Japanese man approached me. To this day, I do not know why he chose me to make this confession to, but in halting but passable English this man addressed me: "Japanese people do too much cruel thing during war," he began hesitantly. "Young people should know this: Japanese soldier do too much very bad, cruel thing to many peoples –." I was in a hurry and had no interest in what he had to say, so I brushed him off. Almost three decades later, I remember this incident with shame and regret; I would do quite a bit now to hear what that man wanted to say to me.

If I had listened to the people around me, I know that I would have learned a lot about Japan's past – and present. For instance, while I was attending a Japanese university as a research student, one of my professors was particularly fond of his Chinese students. He was old enough to remember, though not serve in, the war, and though his specialty was Japanese language and literature, he made it his business to study history – and he read both Chinese and Japanese history books. One day I heard him telling another foreign student that his Chinese and other Asian students were particularly dear to him because he saw their presence in Japan as a gift. "We were beastly to their parents," he commented, "and what do they do? They send us their children to educate, their finest minds. We have a great obligation to pay them back." Although I remembered this, the significance of it largely sailed over my head. '*The Rape of Nanking*' was nothing more than a phrase I remembered my parents mentioning, along with 'The Trail of Tears' and 'The Battle of the Bourne.' It meant nothing to me at all.

Another time, while apartment hunting in Yokohama, I was shocked to find that many of the properties for rent listed conditions for prospective tenants. While many of these were no doubt unfair, such as "No one involved in the entertainment industry" and "No self-employed people;" many were unabashedly racist: "No Europeans, Americans or Africans," one stipulated. "No Koreans or Chinese," another brazenly specified. Some were sneakier, but every bit as xenophobic: "No cooking with garlic. No clogs worn in apartment."

When I told my Japanese friends and a few of my students about these conditions, most of them were gratifyingly appalled. "You should have complained!" they told me angrily. "How dare they try to get away with that sort of thing?" One friend got particularly incensed: she actually went into one of the real estate agents, asked for the telephone number of several offending landlords, phoned them up and gave them hell. Afterwards, she was still infuriated. "We call ourselves international and yet people still have that attitude!" she spluttered.

During my fifth year in Japan, I joined Amnesty International. Although I was generally too busy to go to most of the meetings, I enjoyed meeting the other members and did my best to send out post cards about political prisoners and keep up with the agenda. One day, I happened to remark to one of the other members that I had met a group of Indonesian women in our town who were working as waitresses in a small restaurant and nightclub. These women strongly felt that they were not being paid well enough and that they did not have enough freedom outside working hours. I passed this story on as no more than a curiosity, but the Japanese woman I told it to reacted in horror. Exactly where was this restaurant? she wanted to know. Who employed them? How many of them were there? I told her, but asked why she was so concerned. For the first time in my life I heard the expression ianfu or 'comfort women.' "You should study more Japanese history," this woman bluntly advised me. "Then you would not need to ask such a question."

Shortly after this, I had to go to Korea to pick up my working visa. Because there was a delay in processing, I ended up spending three weeks there, and I used the time to do some sightseeing, travelling from Pusan up to Sorak, where there is a national park. I spent over a week in Sorak, staying at the youth hostel there, and I began to feel frustrated that I could not communicate with the people as I could speak no Korean. I soon learned, however, that elderly Koreans all spoke Japanese to some degree, and I began to spend a lot of time talking with them.

"Do you see these scars?" one woman asked me, pointing to long, raised welts on the backs of her legs. "I got them for refusing to speak Japanese when I was eight years old! I got them just for defying my teacher and talking to my friends in Korean!" Shocked, I expressed my dismay. "I hate this language we are speaking," she told me bitterly. "I hate the people who taught it to me. I hate the things they did – so many terrible things!" "What did they do?" I asked her. She burst into tears. "I cannot tell you!" I never dared to press this woman further, but I did mention what she said to some young Japanese men I had met during the course of my travels. They were all law students who were visiting Korea to learn Korean, and they were very upset, but not surprised, at what I told them. "She has a right to be angry," said one of the young men quietly. "So many terrible things were done here, even before the war."

During my seventh year in Japan, I attended a friend's wedding in Fukuoka. A mutual friend met me at the airport and while we walked from the terminal to her car, she told me that she had learned something very sad about Fukuoka Airport and how it was built. Perhaps I had heard this too? I had no idea what she was talking about.

"It was built with slave labor," she confided. "Allied POWs working without machinery, with their bare hands. A lot of them were sick, and even still they were worked to death." I expressed my surprise. "How do you know this?" I asked her. "I met one of them," she answered. "He and some others were walking around, trying to find the place where they were held as prisoners. I asked him if I could help them, and he told me what they were there for." This friend was several years younger than I, and when I think back on my experience with the elderly man in Kinokuniya, I cannot help but reflect that my friend was much better than I: she bothered to listen, so she learned.

"Do you believe that the emperor was responsible for the war?" one of my Japanese colleagues asked me in 1989, just before Hirohito died. I said that I had no idea, that he seemed an innocuous old fellow. My colleague snorted. "I think he's a fake. He puts on this air of being a bumbling old innocent who dabbles in marine biology, but he doesn't fool me: he's as guilty as hell. And America helped him!" That was another chance for me to learn something, but although I remembered this comment, I didn't pursue it.

All in all, I managed seventeen years in Japan without ever sitting down and reading about the events of World War Two. After we got married, my husband and I bought the book Japan at War: An Oral History by Haruko and Theodore Cook. This is an excellent book, though very disturbing in places, and we have both read it now, but we read it after leaving Japan. Once I started reading, I could not stop. And I was horrified.

Part of what I find so troubling is the awareness that many Japanese people tried to educate me about Japanese wartime atrocities. They were open to discussing the events of the war and they were anxious to learn my opinions. Prominent Japanese figures like Saburo Ienaga spent decades pushing for textbook reforms. Yet because they are Japanese, there are people who might be prepared to hate them because of their nationality, yet be more kindly disposed towards me. And knowing how wilfully ignorant I was for so many years, I realize that I must now make amends.

Recently there was a BBC program on the Rape of Nanking. We

were visiting friends at the time, and I asked them if we could watch it. "What is it the program about?" our friends wanted to know. I began to try and explain, and one of my friends interrupted me. "What? How many people? When did this happen?" she asked, incredulous. These friends are intelligent, educated people, and they had never even heard of the Rape of Nanking, comfort women, or Unit 731. I did my best to explain, but I think it was too much for them to take in. Indeed, it is too much for anyone to absorb in such a short time.

Our two children both attended a Japanese nursery school and public school. They are bilingual in Japanese and, like many children their age around the world, crazy about Japanese food, anime, and modern Japanese culture. They tend to ignore me when I try to tell them about the events of the war, but I still tell them. I know that I cannot simply drop hints, that I must not merely lecture them or try to present Japan to them as wholly evil, but it is wrong that they should have learned about slavery, the treatment of Native and African-Americans in the States, and the Holocausts perpetuated by Hitler and Stalin, yet have little or no knowledge of what the Japanese did in World War Two.

Denying what happened in Nanking, and indeed all over Asia, is wrong for so many reasons and on so many levels. It is wrong that the deaths of so many have gone unrecognized and that the crimes committed against them have gone unpunished. It is wrong that so many of the guilty were released for a price – whether that price was gold, knowledge, or the promise of cooperation – and that my own country allowed their release. And finally, it is wrong that the young people of Japan should learn about the tragedies Japan experienced during the war, such as the firebombing of major cities and the atomic bombs in Hiroshima and Nagasaki, but not the tragedies Japan caused.

Once, after a short trip to Korea, a young college-educated student of mine confessed something to me in tears. "I went into a shop in Seoul," she said, "and I was so pleased and surprised that the elderly woman there could speak Japanese. How wonderful that you can speak my language! I exclaimed. And then I asked her why she had learned it. And of course she told me! And all the way back to Japan,

I kept thinking about my teachers and the stupid, worthless history books they used. Why didn't anyone tell me that? If I had known, I would never have asked such a stupid question!"

The novelist Rutaro Shiba said: "A country whose textbooks lie will inevitably collapse." I happen to know that many people in Japan feel this way. They know that if the world allows the Rape of Nanking and similar atrocities to slip out of the public consciousness, they will have missed a rare opportunity for closure. And they know that ignorance of these dreadful events is not a foundation that can be built on.

Melissa K. Benson
Undergraduate, Berea College
Nicholasville, Kentucky
USA

Everyman's Duty:
Justice for the Victims of the Rape of Nanking

When reflecting upon the concept of justice, the image of Thetis, the Greek goddess, comes to mind. She stands blind to subjectivity with her scales delicately balancing right and wrong. It was believed that when Justice was disregarded, the matter would be dealt with by another member of the Greek pantheon, Nemesis. The word nemesis comes from another Greek word that literally means "to give what is due." In a spirit of divine retribution, she gave each party its just desert. In the modern world, we mortals must find our own sense of balance and redress. While this is an ongoing struggle for humanity, some wrongs seem to persistently evade correction. One of the greatest of these is an incident commonly referred to as The Rape of Nanking.

Long regarded the single most notorious Japanese atrocity during World War II, the incident has resurfaced as one of the most controversial issues of modern history in both Japan and China in recent decades[1]. Despite its notoriety in Asia, this massacre and rape of thousands of Chinese POW's and civilians remains a subject unfamiliar to the rest of the world. Unlike the Nazi Holocaust of the same time period, this tragedy has not made its way into many history textbooks in the United States. There has been no major motion picture depicting its horrors. Partially due to this lack of knowledge on the part of the average citizen of the world, this incident remains to this day a source of diplomatic tension between the two countries involved. The adage that knowledge is power also has the adverse affect if ignorance dominates.

159

The world first learned of the atrocities in Nanking from The New York Times, five days after the fall of the city on December 13, 1937[2]. The extent of the atrocities is a subject of debate, with the Chinese claiming a civilian death toll of 300,000 or more and Japan disputing the number being much lower. Some Japanese extremists even insist that the massacre was not illegal because it was military in nature or, worse yet, that it was Chinese propaganda and never happened at all. This is in spite of eyewitness testimony to the contrary. Sources of information include the diaries of foreign missionaries and journalists, survivors of the incident, and even Japanese solider accounts. The execution of Chinese soldiers who surrendered and civilians was well documented as well as the serial rape, regardless of the age of the women. Infanticide, torture, and mutilation were common. Evidence is available in the form of photography, film, as well as the written words. These images depict piles of bodies scattered by the side of the road, women forced to pose in a sexual manner for the camera, and severed heads on display. The carnage calls to mind the exploits of the infamous Attila the Hun.

Public sentiment in the United States was mixed - with most people being outraged by what they read, but others refusing to admit to themselves that the horrors were real. One subscriber to Reader's Digest wrote: "It is unbelievable that credence could be given a thing which is so obviously rank propaganda and so reminiscent of the stuff fed the public during the late war."[3]

Documentation also shows that the exploitation of the city continued after the initial six-week massacre. During their occupation of Nanking, the Japanese sought to crush the spirit of the Chinese and foreigners in a city while simultaneously sending a message of intimidation to anyone else who dared to oppose Japan. Their anger at the reports leaking out of the area was inflicted upon missionaries and other foreign nationals in the form of arson and flag desecration. Even the Nazis living there were subjected to harassment despite Hitler's alliance with Japan.

Opium which was once a drug done in secret by the wealthy was now sold openly to encourage use by the general population. Heroin was introduced and even used as payment for Chinese labor. Many succumbed to drug addiction to escape, even for a moment, the hell on earth in which they were living. The Japanese then used the crimes that often associated with widespread drug use as justification for their continued military presence. They were orchestrating the very violence they claimed to be there to stop.

The populace was further exploited by scientific experimentation. Chinese prisoners were fed and injected with various poisons like rats, then cremated to cover up the evidence. We know about this secret laboratory only because some scientists of the unit confessed their activities to American interrogators after the war.[4]

Women were again the targets of special attention. Once news of the mass raping of the citizens leaked out, the Japanese government dealt with this problem by encouraging and even assisting with the setting up of comfort stations. The houses were cramped and filthy. Food was not as plentiful as the sexually transmitted diseases. Women from China, Korea and other countries within the Japanese power were forced into this sexual service. The government has denied any involvement, claiming the houses were set up by private individuals. As transportation within all areas controlled by the Japanese military was strictly regulated, it is obvious that the military was aware.[5] With sexual purity being an important part of their culture, these women felt ruined by the things they were forced to do. Some of them were so ashamed and fearful of being ostracized that they hid what had happened to them.

If the people of Nanking expected to have closure after the end of the war, they were disappointed. While the Allied forces did conduct war trials and some of the people responsible either by action or lack thereof were punished for their crimes, many were not. In finding closure on this issue, apologies are needed not only from Japan, but also from the United States. As a result of a deal made with the US through General Douglas MacArthur, Hirohito was exempt from responsibility. In exchange for Japan's surrender, the American government granted him, the emperor of Japan, immunity from trial, so he was not called in as a defendant or even a witness.[6] He lived out his life as supreme ruler of Japan until his death in 1989. U.S. General Douglas MacArthur insisted that Emperor Shōwa (Hirohito) retain the throne. MacArthur saw him as a symbol of the continuity and cohesion of the Japanese people. Many historians criticize this decision to exonerate the Emperor and all members of the imperial family implicated in the war, such as Prince Chichibu, Prince Asaka, Prince Higashikuni, and Prince Fushimi, from criminal prosecutions.[7] It sent a message that this cruelty was an isolated incident carried out by some rogue individuals, which it was not. Whether Hirohito knew prior to the incident that the invasion of Nanking would be carried out in this fashion or if he did not find out until it had already begun is irrelevant. He certainly had the power as the Son of Heaven to stop it as did his Uncle who was in charge of the occupation at the time. Had he been stripped of his power the way Hitler's regime was, it would have sent a much different message to the world about how the Allied forces viewed their war time conduct.

The United States also returned documents to the Japanese that were evidence of its behavior without properly documenting them. Once the Cold War began, US foreign policy favored Japan over communist China, further isolating humanitarian efforts to get a formal apology and reparations. They encouraged China to accept the remilitarization of Japan which caused public sentiment to turn against the United States. In order to legitamize itself to the rest of the world, the People's Republic of China forgave Japan of its war crimes. This was a huge blow to the survivors whose honor had held on in the hopes of vindication. The victims of this tragedy found betrayal by the Allied Nations and their own government everywhere they turned. Their day of reckoning was not to be as they were shoved aside for political gains.

Japan refused to accept their actions. This denial of responsibility can clearly be seen in the editing of Japanese textbooks by the Japanese Ministry of Education in the 1990's. Wording was changed to soften the descriptions of what had occurred and to skew responsibility. This is unacceptable especially given the role the education has played in molding the psyche of the Japanese people in the past.

Japanese schools operated like minature military units.[8] Young men were taught that only the Emperor and his desendants were made in divine image. Their own lives were worthless except in service to the Imperial family. If your own life is worth nothing, how much is the life of your enemy worth? The emphasis on militarism and honor in death made the Japanese scornful to the Chinese who surrendered to them during the war. They believed that these people, to give up, were no better than insects. Knowing that education has this power to influence beliefs, it is vital that every effort is made to give a honest telling of these events and a sense that they were absolutely wrong.

Textbooks were not the only form of censorship taking place in Japan. In October 2004, the Japanese manga comic book "Kuni ga Moeru" or "The Country is Burning" by Hiroshi Motomiya was suspended from the manga anthology Weekly Young Jump because it "depicted the Nanjing Atrocities as 'real.'" Certain Japanese politicians and civilians wanted the manga censored or removed because they claimed that the incident never occurred and there was no proof of it.[9] This illustrates the fact that the Rape of Nanking has been portrayed in the minds of the Japanese as an event with questionable credibility. Until the Japanese people are confident that the facts are accurate, it is doubtful that this sentiment will change.

China continues to feel offended by the lack of proper shame in Japan for these events. Tensions have erupted since April of 2001 when Prime Minister Koizumi made it clear that he would visit a Shinto shrine for the men and women who gave their lives in WWII for Japan. The controversy stems from the 14 "Class A" war criminals who are buried there. After his visit, Koizumi offered words of contrition about Japan's behavior before and during World War II saying, "We should not engage in such a war ever again. I paid the visit to renew my pledge for peace."[10] Many Japanese feel the visit is appropriate as they should be able to mourn their dead. Protests took place in China and Korea as well in response to the visit. If Koizumi truly feels the way he says then, he should erect a memorial to the victims of WWII similar to what Germany has done with its holocaust memorial.

A resolution is currently before the House of Representatives to seek a formal apology from Japan for the comfort women. It is scheduled to be voted on July 30, 2007. This attempt by Congressman Honda to open up talks on these crimes is a good beginning, but does not go far enough. In pointing the finger at Japan, we must also look to our own culpability in delaying this issue's resolution in the past. By doing that, the US can set an example for the rest of the world that it holds itself to the same high standards as it expects from other countries. Japan's prime minister has been quoted as saying he will not accept the US resolution if it passes. Contrast this against Nagatomi Hakudo, a doctor in Japan, who has built a shrine of remorse in his waiting room. Patients can watch videotapes of his trial at Nanking and a full confession of his crimes.[11] There are voices in China and Japan who want a final peace on this issue, and to ignore them is to allow the wound to fester. Instead of putting a bandaid over a bullet hole, these goverments need to work with the International community to bring this issue to a close. It needs to be done for the good of the relations between the countries. It will shine as an example to the World community that this Japan is against human rights violations and is willing to put its money where its mouth is. This is a country that is a member of the United Nations. It is a worthy country that is capable of coming to terms with its past.

One only has to look at current events in Dafur to see that humanity has not learned much from the mistakes of the past. Inaction on the part of other countries in the defense of basic human rights is as bad as the overt actions of the oppressors. Until the United Nations has real meaning behind what it says, then proclamations are just words and resolutions just pieces of paper. The world community needs to pull together to put pressure on those who are violating human rights and not make exceptions to some behavior based on profitable treaties or how much money relief efforts will cost. If this does not happen, humanity will cease to be human and become only a political machine. Crimes against humanity must be stopped. The change must occur in the hearts and minds of people and begin with early education in what it means to be a good citizen of the world.

By continuing to argue over the number of victims and who

knew what when, the Rape of Nanking remains unresolved. The victims of these crimes are aging. Their opportunity for receiving an apology or reparations is rapidly coming to a close. The world must act now to ensure that they receive what they deserve. In order to learn from the past, people must be taught it in the first place. Japan's attempts to censor its own role in WWII in their textbooks should be stopped. Students in other parts of the world should be taught the lessons of this horrible tragedy in order to learn from it as well. Politicians should use their influence to encourage Japan's cooperation. A serious attempt at neutral scholarship should be made in order to avoid accusations that China is inflating the issue or that Japan is downplaying it. Modern day Japan should not be vilfied in the attempt to resolve these issues anymore than the modern day Southern US should be persecuted for the Civil War. It is not dishonorable to admit the mistakes of the past, but, to ignore mistakes and act as if they never occurred is.

Hollywood should produce a major motion picture depicting the struggle of these people. Something similar to Schindler's List could be done using John Rabe as the subject. The telling of his efforts to save 200,000 citizens of Nanking despite being a member of the Nazi party would bring attention to the common US citizen in a way no textbook could hope to. It would bring further exposure to it in order to make people care about these people. As of right now, Congressman Honda's efforts are not at the forefont of the news.

People who are aware of this issue should use their US civil rights of free speech, freedom of the press, and right to vote in order to exercise change. The average person can help by writing to their Congressman in support of Honda's resolution and others like it. Writing letters to the editor, publishing written works on the subject, and telling others about it will spread the word even further. Thanks to the world wide web, we have even more opportunities to talk and learn about this incident through web pages and blogging. These people deserve to be remembered. It is up to everyone, from John Q. Citizen to the governments involved, to do their part. There is no Greek goddess or any other deity waiting to exact justice for these people in this life. The power to do so is within each human being.

1.Yang, Daquin (PhD). A Sino-Japanese Controversy: The Nanking Atrocity As History. Harvard University, pg 14

2.Yang, Daquin (PhD). A Sino-Japanese Controversy: The Nanking Atrocity As History. Harvard University, pg 15

3.Chang, Iris. *The Rape of Nanking: The Forgotten Holocaust of WWII* (New York, 1997), pg 157

4.Chang, Iris. *The Rape of Nanking: The Forgotten Holocaust of WWII* (New York, 1997), pg. 164-165

5.Dologpol, Ustinia, Paranjape, Snehal. Comfort Women: An Unfinished Ordeal, Report of a Mission (International Commission of Jurists 1994),

6.Chang, Iris. *The Rape of Nanking: The Forgotten Holocaust of WWII (New York,* 1997), pg. 176

7.Dower, John, Embracing defeat, 1999, Bix, ibid.

8.Chang, Iris. *The Rape of Nanking: The Forgotten Holocaust of WWII (New York*, 1997), pg. 30

9.Wikipedia: The free encyclopedia. (2006, February 13). FL: Wikimedia Foundation, Inc. Retrieved February 13, 2006, from http://www.wikipedia.org

10.Growing Anger Over Japanese War Memorial Visit (August 2001), Christian Science Monitor retrieved from http://www.csmonitor.com/2001/0814/p7s1-woap.htm

11.Chang, Iris. *The Rape of Nanking: The Forgotten Holocaust of WWII* (New York, 1997), pg. 59

Edward C. DuBois
Graduate Student
SUNY at Albany
Middletown, New York
USA

"When you make a mistake, do not be afraid of mending your ways."

— **Confucius, Analects I.8**

In the years between 1931 and 1945, the Japanese military imposed a harsh and cruel control on much of Asia, especially China. The native population was treated with contempt, derision, and scorn, which more often than not culminated in bouts of rape, torture, and murder by the Japanese; the Rape of Nanking is perhaps the most well-known of these atrocities, but even this horrendous event has received relatively short shrift until rather recently, thanks in part to many activists and scholars throughout the world. This massacre, and the others like it, can at best be termed attempts at genocide; to simply label them as "mistakes" is to ignore the suffering and brutality which characterized the Japanese occupation. However, Confucius's suggestion still applies to the modern Japanese government: a nation so eager to exercise strength and honor must do so via an act of contrition, by admitting its own failures and mistakes during the 1930s and 1940s.

It takes great strength to face one's shortcomings and try to improve upon them. Courage is required to stand up to the criticisms which will inevitably follow. And, the greatest honor follows from atonement for wrongdoings and efforts to regain the trust and respect of others. Let Japan admit its own sins and apologize to all, for doing so will ease many tensions not just in Asia, but also the world over. Such an act would be the necessary scaffolding on which to build a bridge of reconciliation and resolution.

However, words alone would be insufficient in this case. Japan must prove that it is both cognizant and ashamed of its past behavior, or else the apology would be an empty gesture. Perhaps remunerations or reparations could be included in a plan by the Japanese government to extend the metaphorical olive branch to its victims and their descendants; I do not mean, of course, the crass and callous notion that money could ever replace a dead friend or relative, or that cash would be a strong enough balm to soothe years of suffering and hardship. But, the Japanese might consider using their own money to establish memorials, museums, or remembrance centers throughout Asia to represent[1] and admission of guilt,[2] a gesture of reconciliation, and[3] an attempt to educate others about the horrors of war, as well the dangers of racism and colonialism. Moreover, Japan might consider granting economic favors to its victimized neighbors, in order to help build strong ties of trade and friendship which would be mutually beneficial to all parties: although Japanese occupation made many lives miserable seventy years ago, the present Japanese government should do all in its power to help provide better lives for many in Asia.

> *"Faced with what is right, to leave it undone shows a lack of courage."*
> — **Confucius, Analects II.24**

What could be more right, nay, necessary, than endeavoring to uphold justice and humanity in the world? Certainly, trying to bring Japanese war crimes to light, especially the Rape of Nanking, is a noble task for any of us to assume. And, as Confucius mentions, to shirk our responsibility in the face of what is right would be both uncourageous and morally wrong. For a role model of courage, we could choose none better than Iris Chang. Her tireless efforts to bring the Rape of Nanking into the public consciousness resulted in her influential book, ***The Rape of Nanking: Forgotten Holocaust of WWII***. Iris was a talented author, amazing historian, and devoted humanitarian. Most recently, a vast number of courageous citizens (including Drs. Jesse Hwa, Wen-Husan Chang, and Nancy Lo, as well as Professor Ivy Lee, Sen. Diane Feinstein and Rep. Brian Bilbray of California)[1] have succeeded in an important venture: the declassification of thousands of pages of Japanese records pertaining to imperial war crimes. Through grassroots organizations and political activism[2], these men and women have taken a stand for justice and human rights, and have provided many opportunities for victims and their families to gain some sense of closure, as well as for historians and scholars to study this information and help us learn from the past.

These everyday people have displayed the exceptional dedication and courage required to change the world. We too can become courageous, and by following in the footsteps of these individuals, we can keep their vision alive: a vision in which Japanese war crimes are made public, as is an admission of guilt and a desire to atone by the present Japanese government; a vision in which the victims, their families, and their descendants are provided with closure and reconciled with their past; a vision which serves as a lesson for posterity, but also as a beacon of hope for those future generations — the hope that the world can be improved by common men and women with uncommon courage.

Essays, articles, projects, symposia, conferences, newspaper editorials, grassroots activism, political involvement, even casual conversations...., any or all of these things, could be the impetus for citizens of every nationality to take action. At the very least, they are all public outlets for our message to be heard: Get Involved. Learn. Act! Only through this motto can we spread awareness of Japan's heinous war crimes and ensure that the world learns from the past.

> *"The Master said, 'Men are close to one another by nature. They diverge as a result of repeated practice.'"*
> **— Analects XVII.2**

There is a certain kind of society, or brotherhood, to which all men belong. As Confucius illustrates in his aphorism, we are, by our very nature, designed to be amicable towards each other. What, then, drives us apart? There are those who exploit their fellow men, who prey on their insecurities and desires (however transient or illusory) in order to advance themselves and gain supporters. These characters develop from the necessary evils of civilization and politics, which are usually attended by war and propaganda. Suffice it to say that the Japanese war crimes were largely products of the 20th century Japanese mindset; Iris Chang calls it a product of "a thousand-year-old system in which social hierarchy was established and sustained through martial competition... [the warriors'] code of conduct was called bushido... So harsh was its code that its most notable characteristic was the moral imperative that adherents commit suicide if ever they failed to meet honorably the obligations of military service... Time did not erode the strength of the bushido ethic."[3] She also points to Japan's relative isolation for much of its history (it was forced into a "state of insecurity and xenophobic desperation")[4] as well as the Meiji government's proclamation that bushido should be the philosophy of every citizen and that Western technology and tactics must be adopted for Japan to succeed on the world stage.[5]

The newly strengthened and unified nation did not waste any time in showing off its capability; it sent gunboats to Korea in 1876 and fought with China in 1894, which garnered for Japan many trade and territorial concessions. Prosperity and success gave birth to arrogance, but increasing Western investments in China and boycotts of Japanese goods soon slowed the economy drastically. This desperation gave way to thoughts of military expansion, especially in China, in order to realize the propagandistic mission of Japan as well as to alleviate the starvation, depression, and over-population which had befallen the nation.[6]

Chang continues to tell us that in order to mobilize for the imminent Chinese war, "Japan had spent decades training its men for combat... toy shops became virtual shrines to war...Japanese schools operated like miniature military units... Teachers also instilled in boys hatred and contempt for the Chinese people, preparing them psychologically for a future invasion of the Chinese mainland."[7] This preparation is a prime example of the "repeated practice" which Confucius claims drives men apart. By mentally warping young Japanese boys, the government was laying the groundwork for their ability to rape, torture, and execute fellow men who had, in fact, become subhumans. The same sort of practice was at work contemporaneously in Nazi Germany.

The barbarity and inhumanity of Japan's actions during the Rape of Nanking only illustrate the success of Japanese indoctrination and preparation. The soldiers, officers, and generals who participated in this massacre (or at least turned the other way when it took place) were being driven away from their own humanity as well as the humanity of their victims. Sadly, though, it seems that the world has not learned enough of a lesson from this and other similar experiences. We can point out the recent violence in Darfur, as well as past violence in Bosnia and Iraq, to see that nationalism and racism are still a potent combination and often lead to rape, torture, murder, and genocide. But, this is nothing new to human history. We have not learned from our mistakes and our failures; perhaps this is why, as Santayana said, we are doomed to repeat our past.

> *"The Master said, 'It is these things that cause me concern: failure to cultivate virtue, failure to go more deeply into what I have learned, inability, when I am told what is right, to move to where it is, and inability to reform myself when I have defects.'"*
>
> **— Analects VII.3**

The government of Japan has been told what is right, not only by its neighbors in Asia, but also by the world as a whole. So far, it has demonstrated an unrighteous stubbornness and arrogance in its refusal to openly admit its past wrongs and attempt to rectify these injustices. Admittedly, the post-war environment of Japan was (and is) markedly different from that of Germany, as Iris Chang shrewdly observes:

"...the Germans have incorporated into their postwar political identity the concession that the wartime government itself, not just individual Nazis, was guilty of war crimes. The Japanese government, however, has never forced itself or Japanese society to do the same. As a result, although some bravely fight to force Japanese society to face the painful truth, many in Japan continue to treat the war crimes as the isolated acts of individual soldiers or even as events that simply did not occur." [8]

Some in Japan offer views that portray the island nation as the victim in WWII; they claim that the war was an attempt to liberate Asia from the stranglehold of the West, and point to the bombings of Hiroshima and Nagasaki as the freedom-loving nation's "reward" for its efforts. This version of history is present in Japanese history books, which conveniently ignore the events at Nanking, or else manage to glorify the utterly deplorable actions of the Japanese military. Other versions purport that the holocaust at Nanking was a Chinese lie, or try to nonchalantly write it off as "collateral damage," the likes of which are to be expected during a major war.[9]

Even in the face of vehement denial and attempts to downplay the massacre, some Japanese demonstrated exceptional courage in calling out the government to confront its past. Iris Chang's description of Ienaga Saburo's trial (in which he sued the Japanese government over the excessive censorship of history texts, and actually won) is an example of such bravery. However, even this landmark victory was not enough to stymie the dogged determination of the Japanese Ministry of Education in its attempts to whitewash history.[10] As a result of this, tensions in Asia are high and the calls for Japan to admit its culpability (especially that of the emperor and the wartime government) grow louder.

The time for silence and deception has come to an end; in fact, it began to crumble decades ago when brave citizens challenged Japanese tradition by demanding information about Nanking to be made widely available, and objectively so. In order to bring this regrettable chapter of history to its proper closure, the Japanese government must move towards what is right; it must apologize for its seventy-year silence about its war crimes, and demonstrate to the world sincere acknowledgment and regret for those terrible weeks in 1937.

Chang, Iris. *The Rape of Nanking: The Forgotton Holocaust of WWII.* New York: Penguin,1998.

Confucius. *The Analects, trans. D.C. Lau.* London: Penguin, 1979.

1. Nancy Lo, Declassification of Japanese War Crime Records in the U.S. Completed: a Tribute to the Late Dr. Jesse Hwa. *Chinese American Forum v.XXII*, No.4 (2007), p.10.

2. Ibid.

3. Iris Chang, *The Rape of Nanking: The Forgotten Holocaust of WWII*, pp. 19-20.

4. Ibid. p. 21

5. Ibid. p. 22-23

6. Ibid. 24-28

7. Ibid. pp.29-30

8. Ibid. p.200

9. Ibid. pp. 201-205

10. Ibid. pp. 206-208

Zahid H. Javali
Writer
Bangalore, India

Rape of Nanking is Not Anti-Japanese, But Anti-War

"I want the Rape of Nanking to penetrate the public conscious-ness. Unless we truly understand how these atrocities can happen, we can't be certain that it won't happen again."

— **Iris Chang**

Rape is a dirty word. It's a word that has inflamed the lives of many women, children, and cities. Take the Rape of Nanking in 1937 where Japanese troops are said to have ravaged more than 20,000 women in eight weeks. Much has been written about the Japanese and their war-time atrocities, but nothing much has been done to prevent such a massacre from happening in the future. Though people say the bombs on Hiroshima and Nagasaki were precisely in retaliation to these atrocities, there is no real official apology forthcoming from the Japanese politicians. Even if there were a few apologetic gestures, there has never been a full and final closure on this contentious issue. This incident alone makes us aware of what happens in periods of duress, anger, nationalism, and when people are let loose and given power without any limits.

A Brief History of Nanking

In December 1937, the Japanese army swept into the ancient city of Nanking. Within eight weeks, more than 300,000 Chinese civilians were systematically raped, tortured, and murdered, a death toll exceeding that of the atomic blasts of Hiroshima and Nagasaki combined. Even 60-year-old women were raped. After the act, they were often killed with bayonets slashing their throats or piercing their abdomens. In other instances, pregnant women were killed and their fetus ripped out. There were also cases of soldiers ramming bottles into women's vaginas. If a woman wasn't singlehandedly raped by one soldier, there were groups of soldiers who would often take turns raping her. That's not all. Entire families or groups of people were locked inside a house and burned to death.

Worried that the West was forgetting the atrocity, Chinese-American author Iris Chang compiled recollections from sources in China, Japan and North America and recorded them in her book, "*The Rape of Nanking: The Forgotten Holocaust of World War II*", which became the first full-length English-language narrative of the event to reach a wide audience. In her book, she writes that the defenders, when caught, were killed, their heads displayed on poles. Civilian prisoners were tortured, not treated much better than cockroaches. Officers held competitions to see who could chop off 100 heads first from the prisoners who were also used for target practice.

Nanking is not an Isolated Incident

In a shocking brief that's as much an intellectual artifact as a work of scholarship; Japanese historian Tanaka challenges the idea of Japan as a victim in WWII. And with good reason. Widespread cannibalism by Japanese troops in New Guinea, the shooting of 21 Australian nurses in cold blood and the sexual enslavement of Asian women for the pleasure of Japanese fighting men. Not to mention the premeditated murders of 32 civilians, including German missionaries, in 1943; Japanese plans for bacteriological warfare; and the use of prisoners as medical guinea pigs – all of these clearly showcase the Japanese affliction to war crimes.

In his book, Tanaka recounts how thousands of Australian and British POWs died in the infamous Sandakan camp in the Borneo jungle in 1945. Those who survived were forced to endure a tortuous 160-mile march on which anyone who dropped out of line was immediately shot. Only six escapees lived to tell the tale. Call it dehumanization of men at war without denying individual and national responsibility.

Coming in for even more criticism was the Japanese high command's plan for using cannibalism to feed their troops in the southern arc of their conquest plans. It wasn't just enemy troops who were on the menu, but low-ranking Japanese ground-pounders. Call it wooden-headedness, the source of self-deception is all about assessing a situation in terms of preconceived notions while ignoring or rejecting signs to the contrary. This is one quality that Japan seems to have been consistent with all these decades.

The large-scale Rwanda-style atrocities that occurred in Nanking only served to top the scale of genocides committed by the Japanese. Within a walled area of about 40 square kilometers, incredible crimes were taking place, akin to the treatment of "incubator babies" by Iraqi troops during the invasion of Kuwait or the dismemberment of children by the "Huns" during World War I.

Imagine if Germans continued to extol the virtues of their invasion of Western Europe and Russia! Or if they called the Poles liars for mentioning the Warsaw uprising or the horrors of Auschwitz! It is bad enough that so many Chinese died at Nanking (some Japanese and American apologists of the massacre continue to quibble about numbers of dead: let me ask them: does 40,000 dead make it acceptable versus 250,000 dead?). It is equally horrible that the Japanese government continues to deny compensation to the victims of that massacre and further insists in erasing all knowledge of the event (We have apologized enough). Others claim that the Chinese themselves caused millions of deaths during the communist regime as if to excuse the Nanking Massacre! One massacre should not be used to condone another.

The Second Rape

We are living in denial. The 'Rape of Nanking,' an important part of modern Chinese history, has disappeared from Japan's revised history textbook. The textbook from one publishing house has omitted a mention of the World War II atrocities committed by the Japanese in China, while the textbooks from four publishing houses only make a brief reference to it.

China estimates the total death toll at about 300,000. Japan has denied that the Nanking Massacre took place and some Japanese rightists plan to make a documentary to deny it happened. Allied trials of Japanese war criminals documented 140,000 dead. Some Japanese historians say the toll was less or deny the massacre altogether, alleging that victims were soldiers and not civilians. China saw rare street protests in 2005 after Japan approved an avowedly nationalist history textbook that made only a passing reference to Nanjing.

The bottom line is, the Nanjing Massacre and other Japanese atrocities are about as untrue as the existence of the Comfort Women (Chinese and Korean women kidnapped by Japanese soldiers so as to whore themselves among the Japanese military), and the Bataan Death March, where so many American and British military and civilians were murdered along the long walk to Japanese POW camps, none of which Japan has yet to come to terms with.

Japan has committed some of the world's worst atrocities in history (Nanking Massacre, unit 731, Baton Death March, Comfort Women, Pearl Harbor...) and they still refuse to apologize, compensate, or even detail the incidents in their history textbooks. What happened in Nanking (also spelled Nanjing) was terrifying, sobering and sad. It's the forgotten holocaust.

The advent of the Cold War led to a concerted effort on the part of the West and even the Chinese to stifle open discussion of this atrocity. Indeed, Chang characterizes this conspiracy of silence that persists to this day, as "a second rape." The 'holocaust' is throughout our history books, as it should be, but this " holocaust of the Pacific" will not be found there. That, in itself, is another tragedy.

The Argument Continues...

Using documentaries to spread different interpretations of history has become a common occurrence so far. In 1998, a film featuring the life of wartime leader Gen. Hideki Tojo -- which critics said tried to glorify Japan's wartime role -- was released simultaneously with the Chinese-Hong Kong film 'Don't Cry, Nanking', which portrayed the sufferings of a Chinese family in Nanjing during the 1930s.

This year will see the release of at least seven films on the Nanking Massacre. Chinese producers are making '*The Rape of Nanking*' (based on Chang's book), which is scheduled to wrap later this year. In a predictable counteroffensive, a group of Japanese nationalists in late January announced plans to make their own, Nanjing-denialist feature, 'The Truth About Nanjing'.

And then, there is the American version: "Nanking," a documentary (with dramatic readings by Woody Harrelson and Mariel Hemingway) which debuted at Sundance in January this year. It focuses on 22 European and American expatriates who stayed behind in the Japanese-occupied city, using their precarious influence to establish a "safe zone" that protected some 200,000 grateful Chinese residents.

The Fundamental Issue

The story of Nanking proves how the U.S. and other western countries' indifference to justice caused by geographical distance and political expediency could give a helping hand to evil's cover-up even to this day. It also shows how small this world is for evil to hide, and that it is never too late to stand up to inhumanity.

Don't compare China and Japan. Compare Japan and Germany. Both became democracies eventually. However, the German government makes schools teach about the holocaust so it can never be forgotten. They don't want their people to be ignorant of the crimes of their ancestors. In Japan, there is official amnesia. If only Japan listened to the pleas of the numerous Korean 'Comfort Women' who are asking again and again for compensation. If only Japan backed off from weak claims that Dokdo is their land. If only Japan taught the truth to its students.

Should Japan be Forgiven?

Should we give Japan a break? We've forgiven Germany, haven't we? Some rationalists say Japan has paid reparations eventually; not in terms of money but in helping China build things. What's more, they say if America has forgiven Japan, even after Bataan, and the Philippines have forgiven Japan, even after the rape of Manila, why

177

can't the Japanese be forgiven for Nanking? Agreed, the Japanese apologized to China in 1995, and some Comfort Women have won cases in Japan. But the real issue is textbooks. The Japanese Ministry of Education is a notorious haven for insipid apologists. If Japan has apologized, what's the outcome? When you repent, something's got to change. This has not happened for Japan, and this is the sole reason for anti-Japanese feelings all around Korea, China and the rest of Asia. Only the truth can set Japan free. Unlike Germany, Japan has not fully atoned for World War II atrocities. Reparations across the board are yet to be paid.

The Solution

This year marks the 70th anniversary of the Rape of Nanking. More awareness of this historical genocide could hopefully lead to some steps being taken to avoid such massacres in the future. Cross-border educational exchange programs for Chinese and Japanese students could encourage friendship and cultural sensitivity and lay the groundwork for achieving a better understanding among nations in future generations. In light of the recent stirrings of potentially destabilizing nationalist re-armament in China, Japan, Korea and elsewhere, we need more international cooperation and less accusatory finger-pointing.

The Rape of Nanking is for the whole world to remember. It is for the Japanese, for obvious reasons: that they may acknowledge their past. It is for the Chinese, for not so obvious reasons: that they may learn to understand and forgive (and maybe even eventually acknowledge their own past — as they would demand of the Japanese people.) It is for us all in the hope that soon we will each actively seek to stop such things from happening in the world today and ever again.

Author Iris Chang committed suicide in 2004. There is speculation that she was depressed and haunted by the very stories and images that she wrote so adamantly about. You could add another victim to the tally...

Iris Lee
High School Student
Chandler, Arizona
USA

Better Late Than Never

Sixty-three years after the Rape of Nanking, 300 Japanese intellectuals and nationals gathered in Osaka, Japan, while another 200, unable to gain admission, congregated outside. Their attraction was a conference titled "The Verification of the Rape of Nanking: The Biggest Lie of the 20th Century." Shudo Higashinakano, a professor of history at Tokyo's Asia University, took his position as the keynote speaker and began his dogged denial of the tragedy, even claiming that "there was no massacre of civilians at Nanking." To support his argument, he called on the "testimonies" of two Japanese soldiers who decried as liars the soldiers who confessed to the brutal, systematic murder of civilians. The listeners, who erupted in hearty applause, either consciously ignored or did not care that neither man was ever stationed in Nanking.

The 500 audience members represented a fairly small sector of the Japanese population, tabbed at 120 million at the time. Yet the sentiments they listened to, absorbed, and accepted as truth indicated that something was gravely wrong with the society in which they lived and the leaders that governed that society. Such a blind and total neglect of the facts only highlights the tragedy that spawned from the Rape of Nanking itself: the Japanese denial of its war crimes. It seems completely illogical and ignorant that people of the time – members of the "modern age" of intelligence and enlightenment – could deny such undeniable events. 30,000 Chinese women were not mysteriously raped by unknown perpetrators, and 300,000 Chinese civilians were not mysteriously slaughtered by similarly unknown perpetrators.

As the seventieth anniversary of the Rape of Nanking comes and goes, Japan has yet to fully admit to the atrocities it committed in Asia during World War II. It has taken baby steps, finally acknowledging that its soldiers killed 140,000 Chinese civilians during the war – a gross understatement. Historians attribute this unabashed prevaricating mainly to the American and Chinese leniency that followed WWII. The United States, out of the war but diving into yet another with the Soviet Union, sought to build up a strong and stable ally in Japan to counter the communist forces pushing eastward from Stalin's empire; the People's Republic of China and the Republic of China had too many stakes placed in the battle for Japanese trade to dare to criticize the nation they were striving to please. Furthermore, the American government was mired in controversy for bombing Hiroshima and Nagasaki, rendering it unable to demand Japanese reparations without coming under fire for its own war crimes. As a result, postwar Japan escaped reparations and ultimately, responsibility.

Many historians and observers have drawn parallels between the Rape of Nanking and its Jewish counterpart, the Holocaust. The most glaring distinction is the attention the two have received – the former has been dubbed "The Forgotten Holocaust" by conscientious historians while the latter has been enshrined as a tragedy that, by default, touches the life of every human with its weeping, bleeding hands. Undoubtedly, the victims of the Holocaust deserve all the restitution and every bit of attention their experiences have received. But this only justifies the indignant attitudes of the Chinese people – both at home and abroad – toward the Japanese denial of the Rape of Nanking and the world's shutting its eyes.

The Chinese, along with some non-Chinese who have the sense of justice to recognize the occurrence and significance of the Rape, have learned ponderous lessons from the atrocities committed in Nanking and elsewhere. They have learned of the danger of an absolute ruler – such as Emperor Hirohito. Young Japanese boys were raised to become warriors, willing to die for their emperor, calloused to "kill, rape, maim, starve, and humiliate" (Chang 232-233). It was only natural that such a cohort of soldiers would impose such a juggernaut on the land of the country that had tried to force the beloved emperor to pay tribute.

Those who understand the Rape of Nanking have also learned of human nature at its worst and at its best. While Japanese soldiers participated in killing contests, used Chinese men for bayonet practice, and murdered babies in front of their mothers, some brave people treated the wounds of the injured, provided safe places to sleep, and actively fought the perpetrators. Most of these saviors were foreigners who had been living in China for one reason or another – to spread the Gospel, to teach, to practice medicine. Because of Japanese reluctance to kill nationals of Western countries, the foreigners who did not flee were relatively safe from the atrocities and formed a small underground network to help the Chinese civilians.

The world as a whole has seen the repercussions of the Rape of Nanking magnified by Japan's denial; China and Japan have understandably seen many of the more obvious consequences. The most pervasive and, simultaneously, the most dangerous is a heightened sensitivity to the slightest possible offense or disrespect, especially on China's part. Over the past few decades, although the tension has cooled somewhat due to the passage of time, relations are still somewhat fragile. Occasionally, anti-Japanese sentiment flares more dramatically than it would in other cases. Even before the Osaka conference mentioned earlier, the Chinese Foreign Ministry had urged the Japanese government to halt the gathering, and in its wake, spokesman Zhu Bangzao said on national television: "The event harmed the feelings of the Chinese people and interfered with the normal development of China-Japan relations." The masses were quick to organize, forming protest groups that emotionally denounced the conference.

There also resides a deep, potent danger in Japan's denial: the terror that "the history of three hundred thousand murdered Chinese might disappear just as they themselves had disappeared under Japanese occupation and that the worlds might actually one day believe the Japanese politicians who have insisted that the Rape of Nanking was a hoax and a fabrication" (Chang 200). Should Japan succeed in erasing this tragedy from the perception of the world – and such atrocities go unpunished – the world runs the risk of suffering a repeat. The Japanese denial of its war crimes and the general acceptance of this denial only demonstrates to others seeking justification of their own perverse doings that to commit such acts will not necessarily bring just ramifications.

At this point in history, Japan's full recognition of and public apology for its wartime atrocities are long overdue. Although the conservative forces in the Japanese government may find it hard to swallow their pride and reveal to their people that the textbooks and reports have been grossly understating the facts for years, it is the only way to rectify the situation. To show the sincerity of this action, the country must pay reparations to the countries whose nationals suffered in World War II at Japanese hands. Furthermore, a tangible commemoration of the day when truth emerges should take hold in Japan: a memorial to the victims of Nanking. Perhaps hard feelings in the victims themselves will remain deep-seated and difficult to penetrate, but Japanese efforts to make amends can only mean an eventual easing of tensions.

As a Chinese girl growing up in the United States, I had minimal exposure to story of Nanking other than hearing my parents brush past it occasionally and my history textbook summing it up in a barebones paragraph. Only after I encountered Iris Chang's *The Rape of Nanking* did I begin to understand the enormity of the incident – and the tragedy that still lurks beneath the layers of gloss-over that have taken hold.

Because of my heritage, I am the inheritor of the story, the suffering, and the resentment of the victims. To promote awareness of Japanese injustice and furthermore, the denial of injustice, I must dedicate a part of my future to the Rape of Nanking. As a result of my continued interest in the subject, I have decided to study history and become a professor – with a focus on China. Inevitably in my career, I will come across the painful years of WWII and the Rape of Nanking. In my everyday teachings, I will bring the spirit of the atrocity to my students – extensive looks into what happened without hiding any of the dirty laundry left out by the Japanese. Also, by writing as Iris Chang wrote, I can reach many people, calling on them to take an assertive stand for bringing closure to the Rape.

Closure can only come when Japan confesses and expresses sincere remorse for the wounds it inflicted seven decades ago. The longer the world waits, the harder it will be for the perpetrators to step back and admit their wrongs.

Mary Yan Lee
Working mother, IT consultant
San Diego, California
USA

The Denial and Its Cost

"Why would you want to get involved in something that even your parents can't remember? That happened during their toddler years?"

"What do people mean by closure? Why do crime victim families feel relieved when their loved one's remains were found?"

These are questions I constantly question myself, reading about the Nanking Massacre, and about hideous crimes on the news. When I was a little child, my parents told of the sufferings of the Chinese people during wartime, how they ended up in a strange place, thousands of miles from their birthplace. From our Chinese history teacher, we learned about historical events and facts that were translated to living terms by our relatives who are now octogenarians. The most hideous of all the stories had to be about the Japanese atrocities of civilians in Nanking: the helpless hiding of female relatives, the killing of babies and soldiers alike, those with or without weapons periled. Facts blurred, but the feeling was the same: of shame, of fear, of detest, of utter sorrow! Maturity and life experience brought more questions and confusion — the exact number of victims were disputed, whether biological warfare or human experiment happened were denied, could humans with a heart and soul sink to such levels in mistreatment of another race? The only thing that became clear and understood was the reason why females needed to hide from the soldiers, not in fear of death, but in fear of treatment much worse than death.

By the time I became a parent, the struggle to disclose this part of history became a dilemma – is it a moral right to know the truth? What IS the truth? Should I protect my children from knowing about such human degradation that happened so long ago??? For a long time, I was in denial. The less hideous truth they know, the more purity of character they will retain, may be they can hold on to innocence for a little longer......

Then, an animation series became known to my sons. The craze or fad of anime brought back the "classic" little white lion; the name was also used in Disney's Lion King animated feature. Something stirred in my own memory, zimba, the white lion, the Japanese series I saw in my childhood years, the dialogs that brought resonance of the East Asian Economic union that the Japanese Imperial Army was tasked to achieve, even to my young mind then! Then I realized that denial and indifference on my part allowed the same ideology that festered during WWII era in Japan to return. Except now, the "message" is delivered to our younger generation, in forms of text book exclusion of that part of history, and in the form of whitewash of the Japanese invasion of China as liberation of the poor Chinese population from the corrupt Qing regime. My denial probably will lead to my sons getting educated in lies and half truths. It was then that I decided: the denial has got to end. As I grew out of my own denial, research led me to the discovery of a bigger denial. Because the Chinese Nationalist government was preoccupied with internal political conflict, it did not pursue any war compensation from the surrendered Japanese government. In fact, incalculable crimes against humanity were almost written off, due to this preoccupation and the desire to appear merciful or as a gesture of grandeur.

The result of this larger denial, on the part of both the then Chinese government and a large part of the current conservative wing of the Japanese government, is not as they wished: that these hideous crimes will be forgotten; that time will mitigate the hatred; that people will just survive and subsist and let bygones be bygones. Now that the living victims are few and rapidly diminishing, a new wave of revival has actually started. The efforts made in erasing that part of history from text books and history books only reinforced the deep-seated emotions in a lot of these victims and their loved ones. There has never been any closure, no one had laid the traumatized and mistreated, the murdered and violated ones to rest. Those of us with a heavy conscience and those of us awakened from our own denial and detachment are now aggravated by the current Japanese government's constant denial of the hideous acts of their predecessors. With their enormous economic strength, we are seeing a resurgence of that age-old theory of the East Asian Economic zone. Except this time, the strength is not in military might; the bullying comes in the form of their loud economic dominance and international presence achieved, no less, by the initial denial of the Allied governments involved in being merciful to the nation that surrendered after the effects of two atomic bomb attacks. I admire the courage of those conscientious Japanese voices, who realized that, by denying there were any wrong doings, the true Japanese spirit is being diminished and despised. The great heroism and chivalry inherited from their ancestors are not being espoused, but betrayed, by this open denial.

Nariaki Nakayama's recent denouncement of the Rape of Nanking, in this 70th anniversary of the atrocities, shows the world how morally corrupt his group of supporters have become. If killing even 20,000 people, as they claimed, is not against international law, then we are condoning a resurgence of a heartless, evil, bandit of a country to be an international power. There will be chaos and lawlessness in the world.

How much longer can we mire in our own denial and remain indifferent? All of Iris Chang's effort in research and essence of her life poured into her book, "*The Rape of Nanking*", would have been in vain. Her contribution to the collective consciousness and morality of mankind will be obscured if we stay indifferent and not participate in active protest of these recent outrageous lies.

Every person with a conscience will need to declare moral "war" on this outrageous claim made by Nariaki Nakayama and Toru Toida, as well as the group headed by them which declared that there was no massacre in Nanking. His fellow countryman with conscience needs to vote them off their office to reclaim Japan. If denying history disables Japan, then the good conscience of the Japanese nation and its people need to re-enable Japan by voting the liars out of office. The international community cannot condone their actions by staying indifferent anymore. We did not inherit this world from our parents; we are borrowing it from our children! How can we not do our utmost to preserve the integrity of the international culture? The consequence of denial on our part is to condone the bullying of the weak, the absence of conscience and goodwill. The consequence of denial on the part of Japan is going to lead them down the road of another bout of moral failure. As the fall of the Roman Empire proved that military might does not guarantee longevity, the resurgence of militarism or economic bullying will similarly lead to the road of doom for the country of the sun.

The Japanese nation is at a fork of the road. One road is to admit its past atrocious deeds and offer proper compensation to the victims, alive and deceased, and move on to assume their hard-earned international economic prosperity. The other road will lead them down the abyss of denial and international abandonment. As history proves to us, if we do not learn from past mistakes, we are bound to make the same mistakes again and again. The only closure for Japan as a country is to move on with conscience and apologize to the victims and their families.

Seventy years used to be a life time, and still is for a lot of people. How much longer can human race wait to get the facts of the Nanking Massacre straightened out in history books? How much longer can the Japanese government deny the truth to the world and to their own people? How much longer can this wool pulled over the world's eyes be forever cleared and the victims get their just memorial for losing their precious lives to such atrocities?

The ongoing denial did not just cost the victims their justice, it also robbed future generations that truth — as George Santayana famously warned that those who fail to learn the lessons of history are doomed to repeat it. As long as the Japanese government continues the denial of the truth, there will be no end to peaceful coexistence of the Asian countries. The world will see a resurgence of militarism, disguised in the form of economic and political blustery. We urgently need to continue the work of young Iris Chang who gave the utmost to arouse the public consciousness. We will not withstand anymore denials of the truth.

Lei Liu
High School Senior
Guangzhou, Guangdong
People's Republic of China

Denial and its Cost

"As a Chinese high school student, I came across in the newspaper the interview of the parents of Iris Chang and noticed this Essay Contest and felt obliged to participate. Iris Chang, a Chinese American, has died for the confirmation and public awareness of the history of the Nanking Massacre, while so few people in China itself have bothered with this issue. I was sad and ashamed, and that's the way every Chinese with even the minimum sense of conscience should have felt. That's why I'm writing this, maybe not fluent in language, but indeed honest in heart."

— Forewords

"Manfred Gentz, co-founder of the foundation of the German economy, speaks during a ceremony of the foundation 'Memory, Responsibility, Future' in Berlin, Germany, on Tuesday, June 12, 2007. The German fund set up to compensate victims of the Nazis' forced labor program formally ended payments Monday, it said, after distributing more than 4.37 billion Euro (US $5.84 billion) to 1.67 million victims."

"Japanese Prime Minister Shinzo Abe's denial of military's coercing foreign women into sexual servitude during World War II has drawn official protests from China, Taiwan, South Korea and Philippines, some other countries from which sex slaves were taken; Abe's comments were partly in response to non-binding resolution in the US Congress that would call on Japan to acknowledge and apologize for its mistreatment of sex slaves; Abe sparked furor when he said he would preserve 1993 government statement but denied it central admission of military's role, saying there had been no 'coercion'; Japanese historians have shown that military was involved in coercing or deceiving up to 200,000 young women throughout Japan's Asian colonies."

The two pieces of news above show just how differently the Japanese and German governments react to war victim issues. Such news could be found easily on newspapers. It's no longer a fresh topic to compare Germany with Japan on historical issues. Different ideas could be heard around this issue, some saying Japan is not as guilty as Germany in WWII because Japan had not conducted such tragedy like the Holocaust, some saying Japan is even more reprehensible as Japan has shown hardly any honesty to her invasion history. Regardless of the contradicting ideas, truth remains what it is. Japan has invaded China, and Japan should not deny. Why does the Japanese government always want to deny the war? It is a question which constantly stays on my mind. To apologize isn't hard at all, and Germany has set a good example. Denial, on the contrary, only serves to generate more animosity. Why does the Japanese Government dismiss such a simple idea? In this passage, I try to discover the reason, in my point of view, for the denial and the cost of it.

Japan and China were once close friends in history. However, in the 20th century, Japan became the biggest threat to China, conducted series of invasions which resulted in a breach between the two nations. Living in China all my life, I grew up hearing numerous stories and watching countless films of how the brave Chinese folks fought against the Japanese invasions. The fact that Japan invaded us is held as common historical knowledge, which is just undeniable. The name "Japanese Devils" (Ri Ben Gui Zi, when spoken in Chinese), as the Japanese military in WWII are referred to by the Chinese people, blurted out with hatred, could often be heard out of my relative's mouths. And they are not the only ones because almost all the people I knew in China would use these disrespectful words to describe the Japanese invaders. The older generation seems to hate Japan on a much higher level than I. My mother, who teaches political science in

South China Normal University in Guangzhou, never liked the Japanese. She said she hated the Japanese for two reasons. First, many of her relatives have suffered from the war, such as her grandparents, who, at that time, had to flee and hide away whenever the Japanese soldiers came to their village to search for women and food and take with them all the villager's properties. The second reason is interesting and is also held by many Chinese: From a moral hierarchy, Japan, as a pupil, shouldn't have invaded her teacher. We regard ourselves as a teacher because, just like the import of the western culture in the 19th century, Japan began a full-scale cultural import from, then the most powerful empire in the World, the Tang Dynasty of China (about 600 to 900 AD). In Chinese culture, it's a severely condemned act when the pupil does harm to his or her teacher. There's even a Chinese saying of "even if he is your teacher for one day, you should regard him as your father for the rest of your life." So, the national dislike of the Chinese people towards the Japanese is tremendous. Much of this is due to the Sino-Japanese war from 1931 to 1945.

Foreigners might find it hard to understand why we have such a nationwide rancor against Japan. However, when the massive damage that the Sino-Japanese War had on China is taken into account, it would not be a surprise or would even be obvious why we feel that way. At the time when Japan was beginning its full-scale invasion, China had already suffered from domestic tyrant and international intervention for almost a century. The Treaty of Nanking, The Treaty of Beijing…all being evidence of the heart-breaking undergo of a once thriving empire. Japan came as the last invader and as absolutely the most cruel. Before 1937, regional conflicts had never stopped and China had lost every time. Massacres were made by the Japanese troops in Lvshunkou (Port Arthur), killing 10,000 unarmed Chinese in 1905. On July 7,1937, the war broke out, and Nanking, then the capital of China, was captured within months. After Nanking was in Japan's hands, one of the darkest pages of human history began: within a month, 300,000 people, both common folks and surrendered soldiers, were slaughtered in the most cruel ways. There was even a killing contest held by the Japanese officials, the winner being an officer who killed 105 people in the contest. This event is something that all Chinese folks should remember for now and forever. To this day, reflections on the Massacre 70 years ago still bring many honorable Chinese into tears and feelings of insult. After the eight year war, the whole China was no more than a land of ruins and corpses after the retreat of Japanese troops. The wound, both physically and spiritually, was so deep and the pain of the Chinese people was so great, that we swore we would never forgive Japan. The war completely destroyed the Sino-Japanese bilateral relationship, planting seeds of resentment between the two nations that were once long time friends.

70 years have gone since the outbreak of the war, and the age of peace and development comes. As the pace of globalization accelerates, China and Japan have no choice but to make up the broken friendship again in order for both to achieve a better future mutually. However, Japan has not yet apologized for its war crimes, which has a negative impact on the further cooperation of both countries. The fastening of the economical and cultural bound hasn't affected the political hospitality. As long as the Japanese don't apologize, there will never be a friendly and peaceful environment for the further cooperation of the two countries. As the time goes by, the cost of the war crime denial expands as more and more Chinese people are growing increasingly impatient at the dishonesty of the Japanese government. Dozens of protests broke out throughout big cities in China, and many anti-Japanese boycotts were organized. The denial of the Japanese government fueled the rage of the Chinese in the depth of our hearts, which finally led to the lowest point ever in Sino-Japanese relationship in 2006. All of these have shown that the Chinese people could wait no more. We are stronger now, and we dare to ask for a compensation we deserve. An honest apology, simple enough, would erase all the past unhappiness. But how has the Japanese government reacted? They did nothing. The new prime minister chooses to carry on the denial. I simply couldn't understand why it could be so hard for someone to simply say "sorry". But that's just the way the Japanese government is doing.

I think the main reason why Japan refuses to face her invasion history lies in the national characteristic of Japan. The Japanese people have a great sense of honor in their blood. The spirit of the Samurai is a perfect example. They would even fight for their emperor to death, and they wouldn't ever surrender or apologize. In WWII, the spirit of Samurai was inherited by the Japanese troops. They lost the war, but they didn't think it was their fault. They thought they lost because the enemies were too strong. They waited for another chance to rise and beat all the enemies again, never think of apologizing. To save its face, Japan tries to deny the mistakes it has made, but that only serves to worsen its reputation. Moreover, no one could guarantee that Japan would not conduct another war act if Japan remained silent on apologizing. In one word, denial of the war might well be a hidden crisis for world peace.

As a high school student and one of the 1990's generations of China, a generation with a relatively open mind and less ideological bounds, I personally don't care much whether the Japanese government would give us an apology. I always have a feeling that truth is something that couldn't ever be denied. Furthermore, in a world of competence, the winner wins it all and the loser stands small. If, one day, China becomes as powerful as the United States, the Japanese government would make an apology sooner than we ask them to. On the other hand, a stiff apology would be nothing but a second insult to China. We need something out of pure heart and soul-searching. Japan would probably never apologize sincerely unless China has really become stronger than Japan, so China should continue her pace in developing the country's strength, instead of insisting on receiving a superficial apology. The world is becoming more pragmatic, our neighbor is like our second life, and we should all face the future and be tolerant to the past.

Facing the future, however, doesn't equal to letting go of the past. One of the ultimate goals of the re-rise of China is to gain back the self-confidence we lost during our long suffering history, ever since the Opium war of 1839. An apology is what we deserve and what Japan should give. Again, I would say that a simple and honest "sorry" would be good for both of us. If Japan continues the denial, they would surely pay heavier prices than they thought.

I myself have already seen lots of bad consequences the denial has brought to Japan. I have been to Germany on an exchange program for a year. There were students from all over the world participating in this intercultural program and I got the chance to make friends with people from almost every country in the world. Despite the uneasiness at the beginning, I made friends with many Japanese exchange students of my age. It was the first time for me to make friends with Japanese students. To my surprise, they seemed quite peace-loving and friendly. As all the Asian cultures have something in common, we were able to understand each other quite well. I got to know a girl called Misa from Tokyo who was the friendliest one among all the Japanese students. I talked with her for a great deal, in almost every aspect of our lives. Quite strangely, however, we all unconsciously avoided historical topics, as if afraid of offending one another. I didn't ask her if she knew about the Nanking Massacre. She probably couldn't have known it because the Japanese government has been trying to deny the truth of their invasion history. What's worse, she wouldn't believe me. She would probably think I was trying to vilify Japan for some political reason. On the contrary with the embarrassment I got with Misa, I discovered that the German students didn't show the slightest hint of uneasiness when the topic of conversation was switched to history. They would simply laugh and say, yeah, yer're right, we did a lot of horrible things in the WWII, we apologize. Due to their openness, the German students were much more popular among international teens than the Japanese, especially among other Asian students.

This shows us what a right attitude towards history could do: forgiveness from others and the inner peace in heart. The more honest you are to others, the more forgiveness you receive, and the more forgiveness you receive, the more respect you receive. The Japanese students are not receiving enough respect; even though they'd done nothing wrong themselves. At the same time, Japanese people are suffering from the mistrust from other Asian neighbors. A large part of these is due to the denial of war history of the Japanese government.

It's not fair for the Japanese teens. Japan is a good country in many aspects, and I sincerely hope both folks could be true friends so that there'd be no more war. There is an old Chinese saying: "Every one makes mistakes; as long as we apologize, friends will we always be." If the Japanese government continues to deny the history and make such unfriendliness to continue, it would be mortal to our friendship, which, if it ever came true, would be the heaviest cost of the denial.

To end my essay, I would like to quote another piece of news I just came across on the Internet. The production team of the film Nanking, which had been shown worldwide since last November, had decided to promote the film in Japan. They had been trying to employ Japanese translators with high salary to translate the film into Japanese. However, they did not find any Japanese who was interested. The film crew had asked some Japanese-Americans to help. Many agreed, even promising they would work without pay. But as soon as they saw the film, they all felt too frightened and uneasy to watch and all refused to help make the Japanese version of the film, with some even saying that they were afraid of being killed by their countrymen. The cold and solid truth was probably too hard to accept. However, when the day finally come when the truth of the invasion history as well as the truth of the Nanking Massacre is officially admitted by the Japanese government, would it then be even harder for the Japanese to accept what their fathers has done? Wouldn't they be punished by their conscience that had been buried by lies for so long?

---

1. News. www.breitbart.com "German Nazi Labor Compensation"
2. http://news.163.com/07/0627/17/3I0S1TLJ0001121M.html

Virginia Lohrmann
Undergraduate Student
Miami University
St. Peters, MO, USA

Historical Neglect

Many schools cover the holocaust as having a purely European dimension. The average American adult, like my mother and father, has never heard of Nanking, Nanjing as it is called today, or the massacre that occurred there in December 1937. Nor has the average American heard of the Tokyo trials, Nuremburg's complement. It was not until my junior year in high school that the Rape of Nanking was mentioned, and then it was only in reference to Iris Chang's book. My United States history instructor called the book "a must read".

Many scholars refer to the Nanking Massacre as the Rape of Nanking because of the atrocious nature of the crimes committed by the Japanese. It goes beyond mass murder. An entire city's population was victimized in one way or another: arson, looting, people used for bayonet practice, killings for sport, mass graves, mangled bodies, gang rapes, molestation, fetuses ripped from wombs. The list goes on and on. In fact, the Rape of Nanking is not a lone incident but perpetuated to lesser degrees through out Asia as Japan sought an empire.

It is impossible to pin point one reason why the Japanese government has been able to evade responsibility for their war crimes. A great deal has to do with how the war ended. The allies had originally planned to accept nothing less then unconditional surrenders from the Axis powers, and on every other front of the war, there were unconditional surrenders. In Japan, however, the United States gave the emperor immunity. One reason motivating the United States to give in to some concessions was guilt of the use of the atomic bombs. This guilt persists today especially with the knowledge we now have of the bombs fall out: radiation. The Soviet Union had also agreed to enter the war as the European war ended, and the United States feared that with their involvement communism would spread in Asia.

The Cold War accelerated as the 1940s came to an end. The United States needed both Germany and Japan as allies against the Soviets as the war took on greater bi-polarity. After Japanese forces left China, Civil War erupted between the forces of Chang Kai-shek and Mao Zedong. China, even though it was one of the largest and most influential countries in Asia was unable to protest or ask for retribution. When China became a Communist country in 1949, this only strengthened the alliance between Japan and the United States. China became more isolated from the Western world as they faced off in an ideological battle. "…the custodian of the curtain of silence was politics. The People's Republic of China, The Republic of China, and even the United States had all contributed to the historical neglect of this event for reasons deeply rooted in the cold war".[1]

Undoubtedly, the imperial family knew of the massacre and was intimately involved. At the emperor's command, his uncle, General Prince Asaka, replaced Senior General Iwane Matsui as commander of the forces occupying Nanking. The prince was the highest commanding officer in the city during the massacre and in Nanking for the entire duration. Looking at burial records alone, the minimum number of casualties' amounts to 369,366. Hirohito was not only the emperor, but was also Japan's commander - in - chief. Part of his responsibilities included surveying all aspects of the military. Prince Kaya, the emperor's cousin, visited Nanking and reported to the emperor late in January of 1938. Hirohito's brother, Prince Mikasa also reported what he saw after an official visit. In neither instance did the emperor make any attempt to put an end to the massacre. On the contrary, in February he received the generals who were directly associated with the massacre at his summer villa and praised them for their accomplishments. He believed that savagery in Nanking would instill fear in the Chinese and lead to their eventual subjugation. It is evident that the emperor knew the full extent of the massacre.[2]

Starting half a year after the Nuremberg Trials, the Tokyo Trials began in May 1945 and lasted until November 1948. Even though the

Tokyo trials lasted longer than the Nuremburg trials, only twenty-eight of the eighty Class A war criminals in custody were tried by the international tribunal in Tokyo. There were only seven sentenced to death. The majority of the remaining sixty-two Class A war criminals were never brought to trial, but released. No one from the imperial family was tried.[3] According to Wu Tianwei, the late Chinese-American Historian and professor at the Southern Illinois University, "Emperor Hirohito must be held responsible for the deaths of 3 Million Japanese, 35 Million Chinese, 109,656 Americans, and many million Asians; his guilt was apparently greater than that of Hitler."[4]

The difference between Germany's repentance and Japan's denial is in the fabric of these two trials. The war crimes, the crimes against humanity, prosecuted at Nuremberg and Tokyo were no different, yet, in Tokyo, the Japanese escaped from the collective guilt the German people continue to apologize for today.[5] While both the Fuehrer and the Emperor could be said to have a cult following, this following differs in extent and pervasiveness. Since Japan's Middle Ages, the emperor has been considered divine. Hitler's following, however, took on a cult-like dimension and included only a small minority of the population. The entire German Reich would not have seen the greatest honor as dying in the name of, or for, the Fuhrer. The spiritual nature of the emperor is part of the reason the Japanese have not come to terms with what they have done and taken responsibility for their actions. In order to come to terms with their past, the Japanese must accept their emperor's culpability for these atrocities.

Part of the driving force for the remembrance of the Jewish Holocaust is the Jewish community and survivors. They are determined that the world will never forget the genocide committed against them. Ironically, throughout Asia, the victims feel a greater sense of shame and stigma than their victimizers. This is especially clear in the case of those who were kidnapped and served the Japanese as Comfort Women. Many Asian cultures perceive a woman's honor to be her greatest asset. Some societies believe it would have been more honorable for Comfort Women to commit suicide after they were violated rather than survive. In Nanking, rape victims often found themselves pregnant from the assault. Many women committed either suicide or infanticide.[6] Many victims felt ashamed and many survivors still feel ashamed of what the Japanese had done to them. Many others did not survive to tell their stories. What makes it even harder for the victims throughout Asia to cope is that the aggressors were not punished as those in Europe. "Unlike their Nazi counterparts, who have mostly perished in prisons and before execution squads or, if alive, are spending their remaining days as fugitives from the law, many of the Japanese war criminals are still alive, living in peace and comfort, protected by the Japanese government."[7] The continual denial and failure to apologize by the Japanese is what Iris Chang refers to as a 'second rape'.

Crimes, perversions beyond imagination, were committed: a holocaust, but, to date, there has been no official, sincere apology. Those who committed these crimes are not held responsible, nor are they living with the stigma of their actions. After the war, they have gone on to lead prosperous and respectable lives. Until 1972 and the reemergence of a stronger conservative political force, Japan did not openly deny the massacre. During this post-war period, many soldiers' confessions and diaries not only confirmed the massacre, but also provided detailed accounts of what they had done. But, even today, 70 years later, those who committed these crimes express little remorse. In 1972, the Japanese administration, scholars, and the public began to revise history textbooks to distort the truth, dispute the number killed, and deny the massacre occurred. Massaki Tanaka not only denies the massacre occurred, but also claims that the Chinese government is to blame for the Sino-Japanese War in his 1984 book Fabrication of Nanking Massacre. In the 1990s, during an interview for Playboy Magazine, Shintaro Ishihara, a member of the Diet and a popular writer said, "it is a story made up by the Chinese…it is a lie" when addressing the Nanking Massacre.[8] The Japanese, attempting to diminish the severity of their crimes throughout Asia and, in some cases, erase them completely, have greatly injured their relationship with their neighbors.

In order to mend its relations with their Asian neighbors, Japan must apologize, not once, but repeatedly and sincerely, until they regain the trust of each of their neighbors. Japan must be the one to extend the olive branch and ask for forgiveness. Emperor Hirohito's family needs to take responsibility for their own complicity, and Japan's prime minister(s) need to apologize personally. Japan also needs to be willing to open their archives and allow the world to examine its government documents from this period not only to bear witness, but also to be part of the historical record. Japanese students must also be informed of the nature of the campaign in the Pacific during the 1930s and 1940s so that they can ensure something like the Nanking Massacre does not happen again; the public must feel a sense of collective guilt. It must become imbedded in the public's conscience so that years later the Japanese feel remorse for their militant past.

These actions can only alleviate some of the strain on Japan's diplomatic relations. Another gesture that would help mend Japan's relationships would be to offer compensation to victims of the Nanking Massacre as well as the rest of Asia. Japan's diplomacy will be tainted until they have a prime minister who will fall on their knees before the site of the Nanking massacre. Willy Brandt, West German chancellor from 1969 to 1974 and architect of Ostpolitik, fell on his knees before the site of the Warsaw Ghetto in an official visit to Poland. His efforts for reconciliation with the Soviet bloc are part of the reason he received the Noble Peace Prize in 1971.[9] Rapprochement can only begin at this point.

The Rape of Nanking, through personal accounts, pictures, and human remains, shows an aspect of human suffering that is horrifying. In the same picture, one person will be grimacing in pain or shame while another is smiling and laughing. In some sordid twist of fate, the juxtaposition of these two emotions is sick beyond the imagination and speaks louder then words. However, despite all of the evidence, this atrocity, the Rape of Nanking, has fallen through the cracks of humanities' conscience. Many people today have never heard of the Nanking Massacre; some say it never happened. It has not even been fifty years and people have already committed the same sordid crimes against other human beings such as East Bengal 1971, 1972 Burundi,

Cambodia 1975-1979, Kurdistan 1987-1988, Bosnia-Herzogovia 1992-1995, Rwanda 1994, 1999 Kosovo, and, today, Darfur. People have learned very little from the Rape of Nanking. These crimes against humanity, like genocide, have been defined and categorized, but this does not prevent them from happening again. With each new case of genocide, Nanking seems to slip further out of the public's conscience until it is almost possible for some Japanese politicians to erase it entirely.

The world is a dangerous place, not because of those who do evil, but because of those who look on and do nothing.

Albert Einstein.

It is too late to stop the rapes, save the thousands of men used for bayonet practice, the 100th man killed for sport, or the baby dangling on the soldiers bayonet 70 years ago. By lifting up the voices of the victims still struggling to be heard throughout the world, something can be done today. The Rape of Nanking must be considered to have the same weight as the European Holocaust; where we promise never to forget these atrocities and, perhaps, prevent future crimes against humanity. By stoking the public's awareness and reviving the memory of Nanking, history's lessons will be instilled in future generations. I will be one more voice whose potential to inform others is limitless, one more ripple in the pond.

Through remembering not only the Nanking Massacre, but also the Holocaust as well as all of the other cases of genocide that have followed, the world can vow never to let anything like this happen again. However, we have already vowed not to let these crimes happen and today they continue to persist, and maybe the lack of public awareness of Nanking is in part to blame. By keeping the victim's stories alive and part of the history that is passed down to future generations, the battle to save those in danger now will be kept in the forefront. We must work harder at preventing genocide before it is too late, and we need to advocate for the present victims. The only way to bring this chapter of history to a close is to instill and promote public awareness so that Nanking is as recognizable as the Holocaust. Perhaps one day there will be museums and textbooks where the Holocaust and the Nanking Massacre are placed side by side and remembered. The key is to never forget.

Evil (ignorance) is like a shadow. It has no real substance of its own; it is simply a lack of light. You cannot cause a shadow to disappear by trying to fight it, stamp it, by railing against it, or any other form of emotional or physical resistance. In order to cause a shadow to disappear, you shine light on it.

Shakti Gawain

1.Chang, Iris. *The Rape of Nanking: The Forgotten Holocaust of World War II.* 1st ed. New York: Basic Books, 1997. p11.

2.Young, Shi ed. *The Rape of Nanking: An Undeniable History in Photographs.* 2nd ed. Chicago: Innovative Publishing, p276-288.

3.New Jersey Hong Kong Network. *"Basic Facts on the Nanjing Massacre and the Tokyo War Crimes Trial".* p7-9. June 11, 2007.
http://www.cnd.org/njmassacre.jn.html

4.Tianwei, Wu. "The Failure of the Tokyo Trial". p7. June 11, 2007.
http://centurychina.com/wiihist/japdeny/tokyo_trial.html

5.Tianwei, Wu. "The Failure of the Tokyo Trial". p1-2. June 11, 2007.
http://centurychina.com/wiihist/japdeny/tokyo_trial.html

6.Chang, Iris. *The Rape of Nanking: The Forgotten Holocaust of World War II.* 1st ed. New York: Basic Books, 1997. p89-90

7.Chang, Iris. *The Rape of Nanking: The Forgotten Holocaust of World War II.* 1st ed. New York: Basic Books, 1997. P55.

8.New Jersey Hong Kong Network. "Basic Facts on the Nanjing Massacre and the Tokyo War Crimes Trial". p6-7. June 11, 2007. http://www.cnd.org/njmassacre.jn.html

9.From Nobel Lectures, Peace 1971-1980, Editor-in-Charge Tore Frangsmyr, Editor Irwin Abrams, World Scientific Publishing Co., Singapore, 1997.This CV was first published in the book series Les Prix Nobel. It was later edited and republished in Noble Lectures.
http://nobleprize.org/cgi-bin/print?from=/noble_prizes/peace/laureates/1971/brandt-cv.html

Jenny Zheng
College Undergraduate
Göteborg, Sweden

Growing up in Sweden, I was taught about the Second World War from an early age. The Jewish Holocaust was given special attention. The Swedish Government even published a booklet addressing the issue on the 50th anniversary marking the end of the war. By the end of secondary school, most students would be familiar with the atrocities committed by the Nazis in Europe.

Although I have been aware of the Nanking Massacre for a very long time, my knowledge of the event comes with my heritage. My parents knew about it, because they grew up in China, with parents who had witnessed the Japanese occupation. Some of my Chinese friends knew about it for the same reason. I found it shocking however, when I realised that some of my acquaintances with Chinese origin didn't even know about the Japanese occupation of our country, not to mention what happened in Nanking, seventy years back.

I believe this is the result of ignorance on many different levels. First of all, from my experiences in the Swedish educational system, the schools have not focused on the Japanese war crimes to the same extent as they have focused on the Nazis in Europe. Most of the time, Pearl Harbour, and the Hiroshima and Nagasaki bombings are the only historical events, with Japanese involvement, that are given significant attentions. Although I agree that those events also are of great importance, the mentioning of merely two occurrences does not give a complete picture of the war in Asia and its horrors.

Secondly, the Japanese authorities have not shown signs of willingness to preserve the darker side of their country's past. Shinzo Abe, Japan's current prime minister (like his predecessor Koizumi) is known to have visited the Yasukuni shrine, where convicted Class A war criminals, amongst others are honoured. Abe has also promoted the use of a so called 'Reformed History Textbook' which refers to the Nanking Massacre as the 'Nanking Incident'.[1] The history book also portrays the Japanese as the liberators of Asia, during the Second World War.[2]

Thirdly, I believe many Chinese parents don't like talking about heavy issues with their children, which also affects the preservation and understanding of history. From experience, I believe that many parents want their children to look to the future instead, with hopes of improvement, which is why they try to avoid the past. It is therefore important to stress the fact that the past won't disappear only because we want to forget the less glorious fractions of it. It is more likely to be repeated if we refuse to know it, since knowing the past is also a means of changing the future.

Furthermore, the element of shame is inevitable both for the persons who were tortured and killed in the Rape of Nanking and their descendants. In her book, Iris Chang describes very disturbing events, which are unpleasant enough to read about. Stepping forward as a victim to testify against the criminal, even seventy years after the crime took place undoubtedly requires a lot of courage. It is also understandable why many women who were kidnapped and forced to become 'Comfort Women' to this day are unwilling to share their stories. Many of the victims who are still alive and potential suppliers of more valuable information may not be prepared to talk due to the shame they feel, which is understandable, yet their silence is a great benefit to those who deny the fact that the Rape of Nanking ever took place.

The denial shown by the Japanese government has damaged its foreign relations with its neighbouring Asian Countries not for one but several generations. In 2005, massive protests were sparked in China and Korea after the possibility of Japan becoming a permanent member of the UN Security Council was announced. The news on Swedish television at the time showed large crowds of mainly young people in Shanghai, who had gathered to show their anger towards a country, ready to move on with a new international role, without bringing closure to its past.

In Europe, Germany is no longer seen as an enemy by the nations occupied by Hitler during World War II. This is not the case with Japan in Asia, and the reason is that Japan has not dealt with its past in a proper way to gain respect from the rest of the Asian countries. In order to gain respect, the first thing to be done is to take back all the attempts to revise history and stop forging the past.

To this day, seventy years after the Rape of Nanking, closure still seems distant. While Japan continues to deny its war crimes, the rest of the world is not doing enough to promote justice. In the West, when China is mentioned, its 'undemocratic' system is criticized most of the time. In Sweden, people believe that democracy is the solution to everything, while all injustice to humanity is due to a lack of democracy. Therefore, China itself is the cause of all its problems. This is probably why nearly nothing is mentioned about the wrongs done to a people who are constantly criticized, for the political system of their country. They do not see us as individuals, but as representatives of a political system, whether or not we are politically active, no matter what age we are. At the same time, the media image of Japan in the West is mostly very positive. Japan is comparable with Western Europe and the United States in many ways. It is industrialized and is known to have a political system, which appeals to the Western powers. When the protests against the promotion of the revised Japanese history book started in China, Swedish television only gave a brief summary of the situation. In comparison, Swedish media have frequently dedicated theme nights to the Jewish Holocaust and the war in Europe.

Those who caused and are still causing the damage have not paid enough, while the cost of denial, such as the death of Iris Chang, is yet another burden to be carried by the victims of the crime. Although I believe there is a substantial amount of work ahead for those who wish to promote awareness of the massacre, I see hope for change. Iris Chang has left the world with valuable inspiration, but the effort of one person alone will never be enough to change the world. For a change, people all over the world will need to unite in a joint effort to bring awareness to the generations to come, to save them from any further costs of ignorance and denial.

1.Japanese Society for History Textbook Reform, Wikipedia, *The Free Encyclopedia*, 18 June 2007
http://en.wikipedia.org/wiki/Japanese_Society_for_History_Textbook_Reform
2.Japan's New History Textbook, Chapters 4-5 (2005 version), Fusosha, Tokyo 2005
http://www.tsukurukai.com/05_rekisi_text/rekishi_English/English.pdf

Iris Chang (right) and her mother, Ying-Ying Chang, attending the memorial service for the victims of Nanking Massacre and photo exhibition, co-sponsored by California Bay area Chinese American communities and the Memorial Hall for the Victims of Nanjing Massacre in Nanjing, China, on December 13, 2001 at The Cathedral of Sant Mary of the Assumption, San Francisco.

Reflections on the Nanking Massacre After 70 Years of Denial
In Memory of Our Daughter Iris Chang

By Ying-Ying Chang

My husband and I were born in China during the Japanese invasion and occupation. Our parents endured those eight difficult years of the Sino-Japanese war from 1937 to 1945, experiencing the horror and tragic events of that war. Their stories were passed down to us as we were growing up, much as we would later pass our stories down to our children, including our daughter Iris Chang.

I was born in 1940 in Chungking, the wartime capital of China, during the intense battles of the Sino-Japanese war. The hardest year for China was 1937: Nanking, China's capital, fell to the invading Japanese army, and in subsequent years, Japanese forces occupied the major cities and many parts of China. The Chinese government retreated to Chungking, which was bombed day and night. In fact, I would not exist if my mother had not been fortunate enough to survive the bombs dropped on the hospital where she was waiting to give birth to me.

Three years earlier, my parents and my older sister had barely escaped from Nanking one month before the fall of the city to the advancing Japanese troops. My parents traveled hundreds of miles after fleeing from Nanking, enduring the horrible Japanese air raids until they finally arrived in Chungking. They could never forget the gruesome scenes of human destruction by Japanese air bombardment. Those shocking and frightening stories of the carnage and devastation, which my parents told their children repeatedly at the dinner table, became deeply embedded in my memory.

After the Sino-Japanese war, China was immediately plunged into civil war. Again, my parents took five of their children as they traveled thousands of miles attempting to escape the war. First, they went to Guiyang, my father's hometown in the southwestern region of China, and then to Guangzhou in the southeast. Finally, we settled in Taiwan in 1949. I attended eight elementary schools during my six years of primary school education. The lives of my parents and my husband's parents — their entire generation seemed to have been shaped by war and the terrible memories of war.

Witnessing the cruelty of those two wars and the dark side of politics, both my husband's and my parents understandably encouraged all their children to study the sciences in making their career choices. Fortunately, in 1962, my husband and I were awarded scholarships from Harvard University and had the opportunity to be educated in this country. In 1967, we received our Ph.D.s in physics and biochemistry, respectively, from Harvard.

After graduation, we did our postdoctoral work at Princeton, New Jersey, where our daughter Iris Chang was born in 1968. We subsequently moved to Urbana, Illinois to take faculty positions at the University of Illinois, settling down in that peaceful Midwestern town in the American heartland. In our intimate dinner table conversations, we described to our children our parents' war experiences and our family history. Those stories of our families confronting the tragedies of war invariably influenced both of our children. Iris, however, was the one who showed intense curiosity about and interest in our family background and her roots. We never anticipated then that those stories at the dinner table would be the impetus for her to write the book, ***The Rape of Nanking, the Forgotten Holocaust of World War II***, which would become an international bestseller and a reawakening of conscience. While she was writing the book, we helped her in every possible way we could because the "forgotten Holocaust in Asia" was, to our parents' generation, a story of life and death and of the struggle of a country for survival. From the conception of the book to the time it was published, the research, writing and revising became the central issue of Iris's life and of our own lives as well.

While writing her book, Iris often discussed with us the historical evidence and personal documents she discovered in her exhaustive research. Those materials gave us a chance to learn more about that part of Chinese history. Although we had heard extensively about the atrocities that the Japanese Imperial Army had committed in Nanking in 1937-1938 and elsewhere in China during that period, we were unaware of some of the important and compelling details. For example, we had never heard of the Nanking Safety Zone, which was established in Nanking during the genocidal massacre by several Westerners who remained there in spite of the difficulties and dangers of life in a war zone. Until Iris's research, we had no idea of the heroic deeds of those brave Europeans and Americans who risked their own lives to protect thousands of Chinese refugees who were trying to escape the mass killings, the rape, torture and systematic brutality of the massacre.

When Iris went to the Divinity School Library of Yale University to do research on the book, she was amazed to find a great number of primary sources on the massacre. There were numerous letters, diaries, reports and other documents written by American missionaries, scholars, and others who were present in Nanking at the time the massacre was taking place. Yet, for more than half a century, she could not find a single book in English that dealt specifically with that historical event: one of the most brutal and massive crimes against humanity of the twentieth century. One day, Iris was so moved that she broke down and cried after reading the diary of American missionary and educator Minnie Vautrin, who was born in Secor, Illinois, and who, like Iris, had graduated from the University of Illinois at Urbana. Iris told us that the diary of Minnie Vautrin vividly and sadly recorded the rapes and the killings and the other acts of brutality she witnessed when she was the acting head of Ginling Women's College in Nanking. Because of her admirable courage, humanity and tenacity, she saved thousands of Chinese women and children from rape and other crimes by Japanese soldiers in the Safety Zone. However, after Minnie Vautrin returned to U. S. she took her own life out of physical exhaustion and mental suffering.

In the summer of 1995, Iris went to Nanking and interviewed several victims and survivors of the Nanking Massacre, getting firsthand accounts of their individual stories. Many historical events of the massacre were recorded in the diaries, letters and reports Iris found in the archives, and the accuracy of those events was confirmed by the survivors' statements.

In 1996, Iris was able to locate the granddaughter of John Rabe, a German businessman and the leader of the Safety Zone in Nanking in 1937. Rabe was also a member of the Nazi Party. Iris was astounded to discover that Rabe's granddaughter possessed a diary and several documents and reports of her grandfather. The diary of John Rabe, which has since been translated into English and Chinese and a number of other languages, contained records of the atrocities the Japanese Imperial Army committed during the fall of Nanking in 1937-1938. Historians throughout the world have recognized the value of the diary, which was acclaimed as the first detailed account and the most credible personal testimony of the Nanking Massacre.

In her book *The Rape of Nanking*, Iris told the story from three different perspectives: the Japanese soldiers who committed the crimes; the Chinese civilians who were victimized; and the Europeans and Americans who created a safety zone and saved thousands of Chinese, many of them non-combatants, including women and children. But the book does more than just describe an orgy of violence; it reveals another shocking fact of the atrocities: the "cover-up." We did not realize it until Iris revealed in her book "how the Japanese, emboldened by the silence of Americans and Chinese, tried to erase the entire massacre from public consciousness, thereby depriving its victims of their proper place in history."

The primary force that kept out of the public consciousness of the Rape of Nanking and other atrocities the Japanese committed in Asia is political expediency. Right after World War II ended, the U. S., faced with the threat of Communism in the Soviet Union and China, rebuilt post-war Japan, the former enemy, to counteract the increasing power of the Soviet and Chinese Communists. After the Communist revolution in China, both the People's Republic of China and the Republic of China in Taiwan competed for Japanese trade and political recognition. Both governments chose not to press Japan to acknowledge its war crimes and to pay reparations to the victims; consequently, for over half a century the world forgot the Nanking Massacre and other Japanese atrocities committed during the war. In Japan, the ultra-conservative right wing groups tried to whitewash and deny the history of Japanese war crimes. The rightists deliberately obstructed important historical information about World War II by censoring text books and controlling the media. Those ultra-nationalist groups used intimidation to silence former soldiers from publicly confessing their crimes or expressing their remorse, and the rightists assaulted verbally—and sometimes physically—scholars, journalists and historians who wrote about Japan's crimes against humanity.

This is in stark contrast to what post-war Germany has done to atone for the heinous crimes the Third Reich perpetrated during the World War II, including the Holocaust. Germany not only paid billion dollars in compensation and reparations to the Holocaust victims, but also passed legislation mandating teaching the history of the Jewish Holocaust in the school system. The German people and the German government acknowledged the Nazis' genocidal acts and other war crimes, then made a sincere apology to the Holocaust victims and compensated them.

Seventy years have passed and the Japanese government still has neither made a sincere official apology, nor offered compensation to the victims of the Asian Holocaust. For seven decades, the memories of Nanking have haunted Japan as well as China. The recent denials by the Japanese government of its wartime atrocities stirred up angry protests in China and other Asian countries and brought condemnation by the international media. Former Japanese Prime Minister Junichiro Koizumi also ignored the repeated protests from China and various other Asian countries victimized by Japan and continued to visit Yasukuni Shrine, where 14 class A war criminals of World War II were enshrined. There is no doubt that the visits to the Shrine hurt and insulted the people of the victimized countries, particularly China and Korea, and that those visits also contributed to the strained relations between China and Japan the past several years.

In 2005, when the Japanese government certified a revisionist history textbook which sanitized Japan's role in the Sino-Japanese war and the Rape of Nanking, the news sparked a series of riots across China. That same year, the textbook controversy also helped to mobilize millions of people throughout China and other Asian countries to organize a signature campaign, urging the United Nations not to make Japan a member of the Security Council. The resulting loss of a coveted seat on the U.N. Security Council is a significant part of the price Japan must pay for the stubborn denial of those crimes against humanity that Iris helped to bring back from obscurity.

In the spring of 2007, the newly elected Japanese Prime Minister Abe Shinzo stated several times that the wartime sex slaves, euphemistically described as "comfort women," were not forcibly recruited or coerced by the Japanese government. Overwhelming evidence from World War II archives and the individual testimonies of sex slave survivors from Korea, China and a number of victimized Asian countries directly contradict Abe's self-serving public relations statement, which angered people in Asia and throughout the world and generated much criticism from the public media. Many observers also believe his statements facilitated the passage of House Resolution 121 in the U. S. Congress— a resolution which calls on Japan to apologize for forcing thousands of women into sexual servitude to the Japanese soldiers before and during World War II. The passage of H. R.121 also contributed, many observers believe, to the political demise of Prime Minister Abe.

The Nanking Massacre is just one of many atrocities the Japanese military forces committed during the Sino-Japanese war, which lasted 14 years –from the invasion of Manchuria in 1931 to the end of the war in 1945. In addition to the Rape of Nanking and the sexual enslavement of thousands of Asian women, the Japanese military used chemical and biological weapons that killed hundreds of thousands of Chinese people during the war. The actual death count is still rising as more evidence is unearthed, and may never be known. The horror, brutality and magnitude of the war crimes by Japanese forces cannot be easily erased from the memories of the Chinese people and the other victims throughout Asia.

In Iris's book, she quotes George Santayana's warning: "Those who cannot remember the past are condemned to repeat it." Indeed, if Japan as a nation cannot come to terms with its past, the continuing denial will undermine Japan's trust and credibility not only among Asian countries but also the entire world. Ultimately, the ones that Japan's denials and distortions of history will hurt the most are the Japanese people.

Kenzaburo Oe, Japanese novelist and Nobel Prize Laureate in Literature said, "Japan must apologize for its aggression and offer compensation. This is the basic condition, and most Japanese with a good conscience have been for it. But a coalition of conservative parties, bureaucrats and business leaders opposes." I sincerely hope the silent majority of Japanese people will have the courage to come forward and do what they know is right. I also hope their collective conscience will awaken the Japanese political leaders, so that Japan and the rest of Asia will embark on a path of true reconciliation, which is the only way that leads to a just and lasting peace in the Asian Pacific region.

It's unfortunate that Iris is no longer with us today. My husband and I have decided to devote our remaining years to continuing the unfinished work she left behind. We established the Iris Chang Memorial Fund to continue carrying the torch of her commitment to justice, peace and human rights. In her interview with Robert Birnbaum in 2003, she said: "It is important for me to write about issues that have universal significance. One of them that has resonated with me all my life has been the theme of injustice....for some reason, I seem to be bothered whenever I see acts of injustice and assaults on other people's civil liberties." Iris was passionately dedicated to struggling against social injustice and human rights violations all over the globe.

To pay tribute to her, we have made the mission of the Iris Chang Memorial Fund to educate the public about the importance of remembering history, to raise the awareness of the dark, painful history of World War II in Asia, and to support the education and research of the younger generations in the U. S. with regard to the history of war in Asia. For Iris believed that only from truth in history can we secure justice, safeguard humanity from repeating mistakes of the past, and bringing about genuine reconciliation and lasting peace among all people.

It's hard to imagine anything sadder than a mother losing a gifted, beautiful and humane daughter. I can never think of Iris without a sadness that threatens to overwhelm me, but I take pride in her life and work. Whenever I think of her, she is simply our beloved daughter. She is hard working and gets things done. She is vivid and talkative. She not only can write but can speak eloquently. She is a person you will never feel bored around. To the contrary to some common notion that she was always serious, in reality, she was quite happy. She is always very curious and has a touch of innocence, a trait she never lost with the years. In short, she was complex, yet a very simple person.

In June 1998, in the acceptance speech she delivered on the occasion of receiving Max Beberman Award from her high school in Urbana, Illinois, she said to the high school graduates, "Please believe in THE POWER OF ONE. One person can make an enormous difference in the world. One person — actually, one idea— can start a war, or end one, or subvert an entire power structure. One discovery can cure a disease or spawn new technology to benefit or annihilate the human race. You as ONE individual can change millions of lives. Think big. Do not limit your vision and do not ever compromise your dreams or ideals...."

She was my daughter but also my friend and my mentor. Her struggle for justice and peace is now mine.

I wrote this article with Maya Angelou's words in mind, "History, despite its wrenching pain, cannot be unlived, but if faced with courage, need not be lived again."

(The article was published in *Harvard Asia Pacific Review*, Spring 2008, Vol. 9, No.2, p.75-78 and reprint with permission.)

Representatives from U. S. and Canada visiting U.S. Congressman Michael Honda in his office in Washington D. C. before the passage of H. Res. 121 in U. S. House on July 31, 2007. Seated:The Honorable Mike Honda. Back (from left): David Tsang, Cathy Tsang, Barry Chang, Daisy Chu, Flora Chong, Joseph Wong and Stan Tsai.

Photo courtesy of Flora Chong

Global Alliance celebrated the passage of H. Res. 121 in U. S. House of Representatives on July 31, 2007 at a press conference in Cupertino, California. The resolution called for the Japanese government to offer a formal national apology to its wartime military sex slaves.

Photo courtesy of Ignatius Ding

213

Global Alliance, led by Peter Li and Ignatius Ding, organized a high school teacher China study tour in the summer of 2007. The group visited Sino-US-Russian Airmen Martyrs Memorial in Nanjing. The study tour was designed for high school teachers to visit various sites where war crimes were committed by Japanese military during its invasion from 1931 to 1945. Iris Chang Memorial Fund was one of the supporters for the study tour. Photo courtesy of Ignatius Ding

The high school teachers visited German John Rabe's house in Nanjing, now a museum, in commemoration of his courageous effort to protect and save 250,000 Chinese refugees in the international Safety Zone.

The high school teachers visited a Hebei massacre site in Northern China, now a memorial museum. The Japanese troops massacred the villagers in Meihuazhen, with only few children left to bear witness.

The high school teachers visited Germ Warfare Exhibition Hall in Yiwu, Zhejiang. Between 1931 and 1945, Japanese deployed deadly biological weapons in the war zones in direct violation of the 1925 Geneva Protocol.

The high school teachers visited a memorial site in Shijiazhuang, in Northern China, where Japanese military conscripted civilians into slavery and sent to work in Japan. The forced labors were treated in inhumane conditions and the death rate in labor camps located in Japan was more than 51%.

Stanford University students sponsored a special panel discussion, "Nanking, 1937-2007", in commemoration the 70th anniversary of the Nanking Massacre, on November 1, 2007. The moderator, San Francisco Superior Court Judge Julie Tang addressed the audience.

Photo courtesy of Kou-Hou Chang

Stanford University special panel discussion on Nanking Massacre on November 1, 2007. The panelist (from right): Peter Stanek, Elena Danielson, Ying-Ying Chang, Shau-Jin Chang, Violet Feng and Daro Inouye.

217

Members of RNRC visited Iris Chang's grave in November 2007, the 3rd anniversary of her demise. From left, Julie Tang, Ying-Ying Chang, Shau -Jin Chang, Peter Stanek, Jean Bee Chan and Eugene Wei.

Harvard University students sponsored a panel discussion, "Hidden Horrors of WWII in Asia, 70 years after the Nanking Massacre" on November 8, 2007. The panelist (from left): Daniel Barenblatt, author of *A Plague Upon Humanity*, Shau-Jin Chang, Ying-Ying Chang and Agnes Ahn.

The documentary film "Nanking" was previewed in Boston on November 9, 2007 in commemoration of the 70th anniversary of Nanking Massacre. Ted Leonsis(also shown in insert), the producer of the film, was answering questions from the audience after the screening. More than 800 people attended the event.

Photo courtesy of Chin-Wen Lee and Chu-Tze Chou

The documentary film "Nanking" was previewed in Boston on November 9, 2007. The event was organized by Boston WWII Asian History Society. From left: Albert Yang, Wen-Jun Qiao, Raymond Eng, Sarinna Chiang (principle organizer), Ying-Ying Chang, Ted Leonsis and Shau-Jin Chang.

Photo courtesy of Chin-Wen Lee

Four survivors of Japan's military sexual slavery system from Holland, the Philippines, Korea and China (front row, 2nd, 4th, 5th and 6th from left) were invited to testify at the Canadian Parliament by Canada ALPHA in November 2007.

Photo courtesy of Canada ALPHA

Canadian movie "Iris Chang—The Rape of Nanking" was previewed on November 11, 2007 in Toronto. On stage introduction (from left), Yo Yo Sham (singer for the theme song), Olivia Cheng (portrayed Iris), Shau-Jin Chang, Ying-Ying Chang, Joseph Wong, Flora Chong, Anne Pick (co-producer), Helen Lu and Bill Spahic (director).

The world premiere of the movie "Iris Chang—The Rape of Nanking" in Toronto Bloor Theater on November 12, 2007. A long line of people was waiting in front of the movie theater.

Dennis Avery (center), the major supporter of the movie "Iris Chang—The Rape of Nanking", was at the entrance of Bloor Theater for the world premiere of the movie. Without the generous contribution of Dennis and Sally Avery and the Avery-Tsui Foundation, the making of the movie would not have been possible.

The world premiere of the movie "Iris Chang—The Rape of Nanking" in Toronto Bloor Theater on November 12, 2007. On stage introduction of the crew (from left): Russell Gienapp (photography), Paul Adlaf (sound), Joseph Wong, Yo Yo Sham, Flora Chong, Michael Betcheman (writer), Oliva Cheng, Anne Pick, Ying-Ying Chang, Shau-Jin Chang and Bill Spahic.

The Vancouver premiere of the movie "Iris Chang—The Rape of Nanking" in Vancouver Ridge Theater on November 15, 2007. (Photo courtesy of Vancouver ALPHA)

Book signing after the screening of the movie "Iris Chang—The Rape of Nanking" in Vancouver on November 15, 2007. From left: Olivia Cheng, Ying-Ying Chang, Shau-Jin Chang, Thekla Lit (President of BC ALPHA) and Jenny Kwan (the first Chinese Canadian in the Member of the Legislative Assembly of the British Columbia).

Live TV interview by Vancouver mandarin Channel M talk show host Guo Ding after the premiere of the movie "Iris Chang—The Rape of Nanking" on November 17, 2007 in Vancouver. From left: Guo Ding, Shau-Jin Chang, Ying-Ying Chang and Thekla Lit.

Book signing of *Iris Chang and the Forgotten Holocaust,* a publication of best essays from Iris Chang Memorial Essay Contest 2006, at screening of the film "Nanking" in Walker Art Museum, Minneapolis, MN on November 28, 2007. Far left: Kaimay Terry, President of ALPHA, MN Chapter.

Mr. Yoshikuni Kaneda, the First Prize winner of 2007 Iris Chang Memorial Essay Contest, was honored on December 8, 2007 before the preview of the movie "Iris Chang—The Rape of Nanking" at San Francisco City College. From left: Peter Stanek, Yoshikuni Kaneda, Shau-Jin Chang, Ying-Ying Chang and Peter Li.

Photo courtesy of Kou-Hou Chang

Nanjing Ji (memorial service for Nanking Massacre victims) on December 8, 2007 in commemoration of the 70th anniversary of the Nanking Massacre in San Francisco.

Photo courtesy of Kou-Hou Chang

Nanjing Ji in San Francisco on December 8, 2007. One minute silence in memory of the victims of Nanking Massacre.

Nanjing Ji on Dec. 8, 2007 in San Francisco. Judge Julie Tang (left), RNRC community liaison Jak-Min Yee (center), and Judge Lillian Sing (right) in the memorial service.

Photo courtesy of Ignatius Ding

The opening of a new Peace Park and a new exhibition hall of the renovated Memorial Hall for the Victims of Nanking Massacre in Nanjing on December 13, 2007, the 70th anniversary of the Nanking Massacre.

The survivors of Nanking Massacre Qin Jie (first from left), Chang Zhi Qiang (second from left) and Xia Shu Qin (fourth from left) attended the preview of the movie "Iris Chang—The Rape of Nanking" in Nanjing on December 15, 2007. They appeared in the movie telling their personal stories of horror during the Nanking Massacre 70 years ago.

In commemoration of the 70th anniversary of the Nanking Massacre, several artists in US organized a Nanking Massacre Memorial Painting Exhibition which was held on December 15-24, 2007 in Santa Clara, California. Shown on the left was one of the paintings in the exhibition done by the Bay area artist, Lingshan, entitled "Life's Scars, Comfort Women 3". (Photo courtesy of Lingshan)

227

Volunteers gathered in Cinian-Zheng Durin's (second from right) house on January 5th, 2008 in preparation of the film "Nanking" post cards for distribution and for publicizing the film theatrical release in Bay Area of California.

Photo courtesy of Kou-Hou Chang

Global Alliance promoted the film "Nanking" in a press conference in Cupertino, California on January 14, 2008.

Photo courtesy of Ignatius Ding

On the occasion of Chinese New Year celebration on February 15, 2008, Global Alliance, ICMF and the Bay Area Chinese American community honored the producer, Ted Leonsis and the co-directors, Bill Guttentag and Dan Sturman, for their contributions in making the film "Nanking". From left, Ignatius Ding, Bill Guttentag, Ying-Ying Chang, Shau-Jin Chang and Peter Li.   Photo courtesy of Daniel Zhou

St. Louis Alliance for Preserving the Truth of Sino-Japanese War organized a preview of the movie "Iris Chang—The Rape of Nanking" in University of Missouri--St. Louis on March 7, 2008. Mr. Sherwin Liou, the President (first from left), and Mrs. Liou (first from right) were with supporters and volunteers at the screening.

Photo courtesy of St. Louis Chinese Journal

San Diego Association for Preserving Historical Accuracy of Foreign Invasions in China (APHAFIC) organized a preview of the movie "Iris Chang—The Rape of Nanking" on May 18, 2008. Iris Chang's parents Shau-Jin and Ying-Ying Chang (center) were invited for the Q & A session after the screening and spoke at the annual meeting of APHAFIC. Also shown in the photo are Nancy Lo (front row, second from left), President of APHAFIC; Jack Meng (back row, second from right), Vice President of APHAFIC. Photo courtesy of Ping Ma

The 2008 high school teachers China study tour, led by Peter Li and Peter Stanek, visited Nanjing University Institute for History of Nanjing Massacre. The China study tour was organized by Global Alliance and supported by several affiliated organizations.

Iris Chang Memorial Essay Contest 2007
Awards

First Prize: Yoshikuni Kaneda
Second Prize: Kevin Ng
Third Prize: Philip D. Iglauer

Iris Chang Youth Award

Jenny Chen
Glenn McLaurin
Daniel J. Pearlstein
Tianshu Zhang

Writers of Essays of Honor

Shayaan Zaraq Bari	Minjie Chen
Adrienne Y. L. Chuck	Victor Fic
Joe Goodwill	Carol Leung
Wei Li	Robert T. Marcell
Delroy Oberg	Thomas Park
Michael D. Sepesy	Lillis Taylor
Jerry Jun-Yen Wang	Mary E. Whitsell

Writers of Essays of Distinction:

Melissa K. Benson	Jenny M. Beverage
Michele Black	Nora S. Burnham
Daniel Davis	Adam Donais
Edward C. DuBois	Zahid H. Javali
Liyun Jin	Charles Johnson
Jessica Kuo	Iris Lee
Jeffrey Lee	Mary Yan Lee
Matthew Lee	Javier Little
Jiayu Liu	Lei Liu
Sharlene Liu	Virginia Lohrmann
Ting Lu	Efrain Morales
Sriparna Saha	Katelynn E. Sander
John Sherman	Felix Zhang
Jenny Yue Zheng	Sheng Zhou
Yi Hui Zhou	Doreen Xu

世界抗日戰爭史實維護聯合會

Global Alliance for Preserving the History of WW II in Asia
http://www.global-alliance.net/

Iris Chang Memorial Fund
P. O. Box 641324, San Jose, CA 95164-1324, USA
http://www.irischangmemorialfund.net

☐ **Diamond Level Sponsor $10,000**

☐ **Platinum Level Sponsor $5,000**

☐ **Gold Level Sponsor $2,500**

☐ **Silver Level Sponsor $1,000**

☐ **Other Donation** _____

Sponsor's / Donor's Name_____

Address: _____

Phone number: _____ E-mail: _____

Please make checks payable to **Global Alliance/Iris Chang Memorial Fund** (Refer to 94-3378611, the tax-id for the Global Alliance - a 501 (c)(3) not-for-profit educational organization, for your tax deductible donations.) and mail to:

**GA/Iris Chang Memorial Fund
P. O. Box 641324
San Jose, CA 95164-1324
U. S. A.**

**Your contributions will be greatly appreciated. Thank You!!!
Contact S. J. Chang, Co-manager of the Fund at
ICMF@irischangmemorialfund.net**